Poetry and Public Language

Poetry
and Public Language

edited by

Tony Lopez & Anthony Caleshu

Shearsman Books

Published in the United Kingdom in 2007 by
Shearsman Books Ltd
58 Velwell Road,
Exeter EX4 4LD

This volume was funded in part by The University of Plymouth.

ISBN-13   978-1-905700-64-6

Contents

Acknowledgements

This collection of essays has its basis in the conference Poetry and Public Language held 30 March to 1 April 2007. The conference was a collaborative venture sponsored by The University of Plymouth and Dartington College of Arts and promoted in association with Peninsula Arts. The refereeing committee comprised Tony Lopez and Anthony Caleshu for Plymouth and John Hall and Mark Leahy, both of Dartington College of Arts. Conference events were organised on the Plymouth campus and on the Dartington estate and included a performance by Lyn Hejinian and Barrett Watten at Dartington College of Arts promoted by Dartington Arts. Complementing the conference, John Hall organised Public Minutes, a poetry reading by conference delegates and Mark Leahy curated Public Pages, a specially devised Peninsula Arts exhibition of Text Art and Visual Poetry that was shown at the Cube 3 Gallery, Portland Square, University of Plymouth in March and April 2007 and continues to be available in digital form at www.dartington. ac.uk/publicpages/index.asp.

While we thank all who attended the conference, and indeed contributed to this book, we'll single out Lyn Hejinian and Barrett Watten. In planning the conference, the first thing we did was invite these two major figures in the movement known as Language Writing, which is perhaps by now the most influential and best documented manifestation of the avant-garde in late twentieth-century English-language poetry. A distinctive feature of the Language movement was its cooperative enabling social networks of public events and publications with magazines, book series, talks, performance events, programmes of readings and the deliberate painstaking and constructive contribution to the reception of the work made by several overlapping writing communities. *The L=A=N=G=U=A=G=E Book*, edited by Bruce Andrews and Charles Bernstein (Carbondale and Edwardsville: Southern Illinois UP, 1984), gives some indication of the extent of that work. No authors of that movement have done more to encourage and promote the work of their peers than Hejinian and Watten with the editorial management of Tuumba Press, *This* Magazine and Press, and their joint editorship of *Poetics Journal*.

A conference requires considerable institutional investment and we gratefully acknowledge funding from The University of Plymouth, Faculty of Arts Research Committee, and Dartington College of Arts. A special mention for their encouragement and strategic support goes to Harry Bennett, Andrew Brewerton, David Coslett, Mike Hope and Jeremy Diggle. Our administration team of Susan Matheron, Anne Jervoise and Sarah Measures did a wonderful job and generous help on the spot came from David Caddy, Sarah Hopkins, Lucy Newton, Emily Critchley and Larry Lynch. A last and most dedicated word of thanks to Tony Frazer of Shearsman Books who, as well as being our publisher, supported the conference throughout with his stylish bookstall.

Preface

In Barry MacSweeney's poem *Jury Vet*, elements of a sado-masochistic fashion show are combined with a scandalous English Official Secrets Act trial of 1978. The coercive power of the secretive modern military state and the pressures on identity of commodity fetishism are not criticized but revelled in by MacSweeney. William Rowe is our guide in this slippery and seductive terrain.

In Allen Fisher's hybrid essay-poem 'Confidence in Lack', a correlation is established between Keats' negative capability and the uncertainty principle in quantum mechanics, demonstrating the creative power of believing/not believing Plato and performing indirect poetic measurement via distant entangled particles. He uses this quantum method to propose (subject to funding) an intrinsic reflector from the ground up.

On 13 January 1972 in Derry/Londonderry, British soldiers shot 26 civil rights protestors. 13 were killed outright and another died four months later from his wounds. Many witnesses testified that all those injured were unarmed and five of the wounded were shot in the back. The first official tribunal of this incident exonerated the soldiers, including those in command. Andrew Browne's essay investigates Thomas Kinsella's poetic response to British government propaganda during the era known as 'the troubles'.

How does it alter our understanding of a poem to discover that it is written in gay code? How can we integrate conflicting and contested readings with our experience and our knowledge of poetic truth? Ian Davidson looks again at moving poems by Frank O'Hara.

'Could we have those trees cleared out of the way?' Lyn Hejinian responds to an early abstract Barrett Watten poem 'Mode Z', that uses negative dialectics in a non-depiction of landscape and identity. It is not Zukofsky, nor Oppen, nor Wordsworth: it is certainly not Eliot. The poem engages and deranges our expectations of poetry and the reading shows how that process is built out of historical consciousness even though the poem remains a kinetic meaning-engine turning in virtual space.

In Barrett Watten's 'The Expanded Object of the Poetic Field; or, What is a Poet/Critic?', he identifies one misleading or redundant version of the poem as the universalized object of New Critical 'close reading' and contrasts it with a contemporary poetic writing that undermines modernist expectations of autonomous high-art authorship. He demonstrates a hybrid poetics of the assembly line and thus recuperates the genre-breaking works of Gertrude Stein and William Carlos Williams, either ignored or widely misunderstood by recent critics.

This collection of essays brings together 26 papers presented at *Poetry and Public Language: A Conference on Contemporary Poetry*. We have done our best to encourage an inclusive debate among a variety of viewpoints and different approaches to contemporary poetics. Most essays here explore the writings of recent and contemporary English or American poets who engage with avant-garde poetics, as conceived differently in different social and political circumstances, including poems by Charles Olson, J.H. Prynne, Frank O'Hara, Allen Fisher, Barry MacSweeney, Peter Reading, Tony Lopez, Tom Raworth, Robert Duncan, Rae Armantrout, Basil Bunting, and our conference keynote speakers: Lyn Hejinian and Barrett Watten. Other essays by Robin Peel on Emily Dickinson, Brendan Cooper on Robert Lowell and Allen Ginsberg, and Christopher Orchard on Geoffrey Hill, explore how writers of different times and traditions have appropriated public language and contested political and aesthetic meanings. Both Philip Terry on the Oulipo Workshop of Potential Literature and Scott Thurston on the poetics of Watten, Bruce Andrews and Ira Lightman, seek productive opportunities to renew contemporary writing practice. Still further, select essays concentrate on the social experience of poetry and poetics, such as the development of the British and Irish Poets E-List described by Kit Fryatt, and the London Poetry Wars of the 1970s investigated by Robert Sheppard.

A number of essays address just what is meant by 'public language', and this line of enquiry fosters an interesting dynamic, whereby a particular methodology and mode of construction is investigated. As the essays make clear, public language may inhere in the stylized rhetorics and slick coinages of our consumer society, in the instrumental power of political and bureaucratic jargons, in the language of specialist or professional expert knowledges such as science, engineering and technology, in the media-driven newspeak of television, radio and web, or even in echoes of recognizable literary works, whether well-known and loved allusions or hackneyed old hat. The list could go on, of course: it represents a poetry interested in sourcing material from outside the fabric of the immediate self. Where authors of the early twentieth century dealt in an allusive intertextuality, often compressed in a mythic frame, more recent authors seem fascinated to explore the possibilities of sampling wider non-literary sources and popular or even debased culture. This signals a practice which increasingly makes use of collage: fragmenting narrative lines, transfiguring rhetoric, shifting voices and registers. Where one poet might appropriate a 'swirling mix of unintimate vocabulary' (as Peter Middleton explores in Hejinian's recent book *The Fatalist*), another might focus their poem on a particular strain of language usage (as in Michael Kindellan's sense of Olson's use of Captain John Smith's 17th century book *Advertisements*).

These essays make clear that such a modus operandi has particular motives, and often we find such poetry being explored for its political concerns, as the critics Robert Hampson, Carrie Etter, Richard Kerridge, Hélène Aji, Matthew Chambers, Piers Hugill, and Catherine Martin find in the works of their chosen poets. That said, the more personal facets and concerns of a poetry which employs 'public language' are also emphasized, as in essays by Andrea Brady on early Raworth, Will Montgomery on Armantrout, and Susan Nurmi-Schomers and Kathy-Ann Tan on Hejinian.

Over and over, we find a useful tension between the public and the private spheres, which correlates with the tension between specialized and restricted language-sets and the more general language or 'ordinary language' that seeks to encompass the whole range of human knowledge and experience. There is by now a long-established serious doubt as to whether such a unified knowledge is possible and yet it is not clear how poetry is possible unless such an imaginative synthesis is available. The turn to 'public language'—as subject, as axis to understanding, as screen between the individual and the world—is explored, for better or worse, as a turn towards social experience.

Plymouth, 2007   Tony Lopez and Anthony Caleshu

Poetry

and

Public Language

Barrett Watten: Poetry and Historiography

Hélène Aji

In his preface to *Il formaggio e i vermi*, historian Carlo Ginzburg argues the importance of witnessing in the writing of history.[1] As he takes up Bertolt Brecht's proletarian reader's question ('Who built Thebes of the Seven Gates?'), he also lays emphasis on the unsaid and unsayable underlying each and every historian's narrative: how does one deal with the resistance to investigation and objective account which stems not only from ideological choices and the historiographer's decisions but is also the direct consequence of irretrievable or suppressed sources? If one is to integrate the uncertainty and ignorance, which the very idea of so many anonymous agents and witnesses of history generates, the foundations of historiography are shaken under the 'weight' of a question that has no answer. And this scientific question has ramifications beyond the revaluation of historical discourse: reaching out to our daily survival in history. This is why Primo Levi poignantly reflects on the status of Anne Frank in the public's perception and (impossible) understanding of the Holocaust: 'Anne Frank moves us more than the millions of victims that suffered like her but whose image has remained in the dark. And maybe it should be so: if we were to share the sufferings of each and all of these victims, we could not live any more.'[2] Both approaches try to actualize the tension between necessary inscriptions of the past and willing as well as unwilling omissions and recombinations.

From *Progress/Under Erasure*, to *Bad History*, Barrett Watten consistently constructs a common field of action for poetry and history, leading one to think about the writing of the poem in terms of historiography: a contextual, political and ethical form of discourse which cannot do without a serious examination of its methods and its aims. A reading of these texts allows us to propose approaches to Watten's writings as they articulate the issues of witnessing and anonymity. These issues can be seen as recurring preoccupations in Watten's work, for instance, as one reads his criticism of Gertrude Stein's *The Making of Americans* as an 'epic of subjectivation' (*Modernism/Modernity* 95): countering the formalist reading which Stein herself promoted—according to which the text would be the unfolding of iterated attempts at beginning to highlight the stylistic feat of Stein's own patterns of repetition—, Watten opts for an interpretation in which the text works out 'a poetics of identity as a construction' (*Modernism/Modernity* 96). In his reading of the Oedipal episode (a son wins over his desire to kill his father, thus re-enacting the similar act of self-control that prevented his father from killing his own father), Watten underlines the process through which personal experience, especially when traumatic, can be integrated into collective experience through the double narrativizations performed by trauma narrative and by historical narrative:

> Such "heroic" repetition makes a narrative of collective destiny out of a retrospectively fantasized, founding trauma. Stein's anecdote proposes itself as a skeleton key to the authorizing myth of patriarchy, presenting, in miniature the repetition compulsion of its fantasized first principles.
>
> (*Modernism/Modernity* 97)

However, this reading, as Watten demonstrates, does not account for the 'complicated matrix' (*Modernism/Modernity* 99), which is constituted through the discarding of the linear simplicity of lineage in favour of an envisioning of the subject's construction in terms of social and familial networks. This abandonment of linearity for the ramifications of the network is not just a change in our view of the individual's construction, proposed by Stein at the onset of *The Making of Americans*, it also corresponds to a more general evolution in the ways history can be thought about. Chronology and its teleological implications as projections of history are cast aside along with linearity, whereas the notion of a network entails the possibility of a plurality of actualizations of history through the plurality of narratives that recount its events in the terms of their present making: in 'the present continuous,' to take up Stein's words. In Watten's own *Bad History*, the unfolding of the text refuses to follow chronological linearity as the dates at the bottom of the pages move from 1991 back to 1990, then on to 1993 and 1994.

What such an evaluation of history produces, when expanding out of the formal and willfully abstracted realms of the literary and 'bleeding into history' (Watten *Lust for Life* 61), can be seen as a radical negativity, which Watten underlines in his analysis of Foucault's treatment of Jacques Rivière's confession as it 'reaches the final instant in which the work locates its truth in the world at the limit of its unaccountability' (*Lust for Life* 62). When this negativity is simply understood as the negation of all positivity—i.e. of all historical positives—, it inexorably leads to an aporetic moment in which pervasive doubt affects all discourses. The very notion of truth is to be cancelled in the proliferations of the signs of subjectivities at work autonomously, simultaneously and possibly contradictorily. In his essay on the work of Kathy Acker, Watten offers an alternative, which is also an entry-point into his own poetry: the aim is not so much, to return to Foucault and Rivière, to question the truthfulness of certain discourses but to become aware of the interaction between the methods of documentation and the construction of discourse. There are lacunae that must not be forcefully filled in; their very presence, in all its negativity, guarantees the continuation of discourse:

> As long as such gaps between the discursive elements remain open, we are in the domain of construction and may avoid the false positives of history; this is how genealogy keeps the inaccessible moment of event open through a play of negativity that at the same time constitutes discourse and judgment. (Watten *Lust for Life* 63)

But, to pursue this in Watten's acknowledgment,

> It is legitimate to question here the nature of this avoidance: if we refuse all positivity (of personal identity or event), on what possible basis can we make a judgment or write a narrative? (*Lust for Life* 63)

Taking up the example of Acker's novels, Watten works out the notion of discourses that would not propose unified narratives informed by the dominant ethical positives but allow for the 'possibility that resulting identity is a disrupted construction' (*Lust for Life* 70): 'it is not simply that identity is an other; identity is an impossible historical event of coincidence and undoing' (*Lust for Life* 71).

The 'bad event' which happens to the 'I' of *Bad History* possesses the same quality of a 'disturbance of identity occasioned by a historical event':

> A bad event happened to me, but its having occurred became
> even more complicated in my thinking about it. Even if this
> event had happened only to me, it was only recently made
> available for retrospection; it had to be proved as taking place
> in every other event. (Watten *Bad History* 5)

And what the text performs has a lot in common with what Watten sees
as Acker's obstinate writing of the event:

> In the event, identity is dissociated and revealed; Acker
> continues to write the event. More precisely, Acker continues
> to look at writing as the dissolution of an event within
> a structure that can heal it. Her continued desire for the
> dissolution of identity—of literary coherence, a stable canon
> of works, of a consistent address—begins here, with the
> trauma of an event in which identity could only be seen as an
> interruption of history. (Watten *Lust for Life* 73)

The 'I' of the first section of *Bad History*, a section numbered one in
Roman figures, thus also entitled 'I', tries to return to the primary
traumatic event but it is not just its identity that is dissolved: the event is
also missing. Thus, to give one possible reading, history has turned 'bad,'
because it has become conceivable that it could be subtracted altogether
from attention, that it could become detached from the actuality of
events. Thus writing history could not be negated only through the
questioning of its accountability to events, but by the very possibility of
an absence of events. The traumatic event would then be, provocatively,
the recognition of this subtraction of event, of this irretrievable loss.
This is what Watten implies as he elaborates immediately after the
passage I just quoted: 'after the war' triggers the question 'which war,'
and many losses of the event get inscribed into the poem.

In both the study of Stein and the commentary on Acker, Watten
elaborates from his core preoccupations with the individual psyche in its
construction by and of historical events. The passage from the personal
to the collective is achieved through a movement of extension and
expansion, which makes the issues of poetics and those of historiography
coincide. One must write on, not only despite the questions and the

aporias, but also because of them, in repeated attempts to defeat them first by recognizing them, then, in a Wittgensteinian manner, by working to push back the limits they have set. One of the consequences of this coincidence between the objectives of poetry according to Watten and historiography is the question he asks as he analyzes the presuppositions of Sherman Paul's mode of criticism in *The Lost America of Love*: 'what if crisis is outward and historical, as well as a negotiation of self with the object?' (Watten *Genre* 296). Characteristically, Watten uses a question to counter what he sees as a one-way reading of poetry as the actualization of intention, and as a critical investigation that limits itself to the elucidation of this intention through the production of mimetic texts. And characteristically the question is formulated not as an alternative ('either...or...') but as a coincidence: 'as well as.'

Intention exists, and Watten will not deny it; and sometimes it is apparent, it appears, as Jackson Mac Low ironically recognizes when he gives the title 'Intention Disappears' to a poem intended for John Cage's birthday, but, objects Watten, 'seeing poetry as an unfolding of intention within the larger matrix of tradition predicts the turn to language to be taken up by poets in the next generation' (Watten *Genre* 285). Above all, it leads to a self-defeating investigation of events that cannot be documented: intention if it ever crystallizes is shifting; in the analysis of Paul's quest for intention, it comes to stand for the event that undeniably happened, since, to quote from *Bad History*, 'it has been proved as taking place in every other event,' but can only be assessed indirectly, through the mediation of its traces. The event becomes the dark matter of history, and of the poem, a necessary assumption, and an untouchable reality. In Watten's work, to 'frame' 'bad history,' one must take the risk of a 'return to a poetics grounded in history, rather than a myth-based or language-centred "regularity in dispersion," as the prime mover for any discursive formation of "literature" that underwrites our claims to literary value. This is precisely the genealogy of "bad history" in the New Americans' poetics of love' (*Genre* 313). Symptomatically, the rejection of a type of criticism that does not attempt to recontextualize the poem but rather imitates its form—the disconnectedness of some texts in Watten's examples, or the narrative quality of others as in

Paul's *So to Speak: Re-reading David Antin*—calls forth the title of Barrett Watten's own book, *Bad History*.

One way of seeing it would be the interpretation by Philip Metres as he focuses on the First Gulf War part of *Bad History*, then extends his analysis to the whole volume, underscoring the oscillation between complicity and oppositionality in the poem:

> *Bad History*, therefore, is an epic of worried subjectivity, attempting to resist even while knowing its own complicities and limits—all the while refusing to bracket the moment at which the text is being produced. (Metres 19)

According to Metres, the text is shaped by Watten's evaluation of oppositional art in the 1990s: it does not respond to the context of events, but only to the events; it seeks approval from its supporters but does attempts to convince others; it does not question identity politics, and consequently fails to question itself.[3]

> So even as *Bad History* refuses the traditional subjective position of the nationalist epic poet, it is also inflected by the successes and failures of oppositional art from the period; rather than simply relying on a self-protective oppositionality, it becomes a subjective history swinging between complicity and resistance. (Metres 21)

However, rather than 'swinging between complicity and resistance,' which is but another version of the alternative, it seems to me that what is at stake in *Bad History* is an iterated practice of the 'as well as,' as in 'complicit as well as resistant,' a situation much more complex than the Manichean 'either...or...,' as it leaves the text ajar, letting us catch a glimpse of its layering, of its interferences and simultaneities.

Poetics here coincides with historiography as both tell us about the possible coexistence of several histories not as a result of counterfeiting but as a play of hypotheses in a situation of radical uncertainty. The example of the 'secret' meaning, which he gives to Manuel Brito in an interview, is not so much about secrecy, a fiction which Watten's use of inverted commas underlines, as about the juxtaposition of two different interpretations of the same set of facts (Watten in Brito 182). Two or more: Watten's poems raise the same issues as Jacques Derrida did about the writing of ethnology in 'Structure, Sign and Play in the Discourse of the Human Sciences' (90); moving beyond duality, they achieve in various contexts instances of the Derridean de-centring, combining the realization that there is no centre with the ethical urge to be witness to and leave testimony of this quandary. In Watten's words, 'Such is the night in the mountains' should be read, at the end, as a both familiar and unearthly 'suchness' (Watten *in* Brito 194).

Hélène Aji is Professor of American and Modernist Literature at Université du Maine, France.

Notes

[1] Ginzburg, xi: 'In passato si potevano accusare gli storici di voler conscere soltanto le "gesta dei re". Oggi, certo, non è piú cosí. Sempre piú essi si volgono verso ciò che i loro predecessori avevano taciuton scartato o semplicemente ignorato. "Chi costruí Tebe alle sette porte?" chiedeva già il "lettore operaio" di Brecht. Le fonti non ci dicono niente di quegli anonimi muratori: ma la domanda conserva tutto il suo peso.'

[2] My translation from the French text quoted in Galesloot 8.

[3] On this, see Metres 20–21.

Works cited

Brito, Manuel. *A Suite of Poetic Voices: Interviews with Contemporary American Poets.* Santa Brigida: Kadle Books, 1992.

Derrida, Jacques. 'Structure, Sign and Play in the Discourse of the Human Sciences.' David Lodge and Nigel Wood, eds. *Modern Criticism and Theory.* Harlow: Longman, 2000. 88–103.

Galesloot, Hansje. *Maison d'Anne Frank.* Amsterdam: Anne Frank's House and Museum, 2001.

Ginzburg, Carlo. *Il formaggio e i vermi.* Turin: Einaudi, 1999; *The Cheese and the Worms: The Cosmos of a Sixteenth-Century Miller.* Trans. John and Anne Tedeschi. New York: Penguin Books, 1982.

Mac Low, Jackson. 'Intention Disappears.' Manuscript. Jackson Mac Low Papers, Mandeville Special Collections, Geisel Library, University of California San Diego: MSS 180 Box 49 Folder 15.

Metres, Philip. 'Barrett Watten's *Bad History*: A Counter-Epic of the Gulf War.' *Postmodern Culture* XIII 3 (2003). http://www3.iath.virginia.edu/pmc/ Accessed through Project Muse, 10 Jan. 2007.

Paul, Sherman. *So to Speak: Rereading David Antin*. London: Binnacle Press, 1982.

Paul, Sherman. *The Lost America of Love: Rereading Robert Creeley, Edward Dorn, and Robert Duncan*. Baton Rouge: Louisiana State UP, 1981.

Stein, Gertrude. *The Making of Americans*. Normal: The Dalkey Archive, 1995.

Watten, Barrett. 'An Epic of Subjectivation: *The Making of Americans*.' *Modernism/Modernity* V 2 (1998) 95–121.

Watten, Barrett. 'Foucault Reads Acker and Rewrites the History of the Novel.' Amy Scholder, Carla Harryman, Avital Ronell, eds. *Lust for Life: On the Writings of Kathy Acker*. New York: Verso, 2006. 58–77.

Watten, Barrett. 'The Lost America of Love: A Genealogy.' *Genre* XXXIII 3–4 (Fall-Winter 2000) 279–317.

Watten, Barrett. *Bad History*. Berkeley: Atelos, 1998.

Watten, Barrett. *Progress / Under Erasure* [1985, 1991]. Los Angeles: Green Integer, 2005.

Tom Raworth: Poetry and Public Pleasure

ANDREA BRADY

It is a very good sign when the harmonious bores are at a loss about how they should react to this continuous self-parody, when they fluctuate endlessly between belief and disbelief until they get dizzy and take what is meant as a joke seriously and what is meant seriously as a joke.[1]

Several critics have offered accounts of the temporal experience of reading the poetry of Tom Raworth. Keith Tuma writes of the reader's obligation 'to confront the constructedness of the text, entertained and regularly defeated by the temporality of reading'; he adds that the poetry 'self-consciously sets the fixity of the printed word... against the temporality of reading.'[2] Raworth's frequent arbitrations of the text's artifice—his use of graphic interventions, commentary on earlier word choices, and revisions of proceeding lines—remind his readers that the poem is a machine built in the past. The poem is anterior to, but dependent on, the reading which constructs it. Peter Middleton sees the reader's participation as rather more risky: the poem's 'punning torture is also a readerly projection, a violence brought to the poem by the reader.'[3] Maybe our attempts to impose pattern and cohesion on the poem's randomness are 'projections' of a subjective cohesion from which Raworth's poetry is attempting to dissuade us, 'a violence' of criticism against the subject barred by language. If so, reading Raworth begins in contingency, and develops our capacity to take pleasure from our own contingency as readers. By contingent, I mean not simply the dependence of the concept of the self on self-critical forms of linguistic articulation, but the self-as-possible: as a concept appertaining to the understanding, held in potential alongside the persistence of the actual, the objective.

So Tom Raworth's readers evolve in experiences of artifice and transition, past and present. This, too, might suffice as a contingent beginning: we may better understand the humour of these texts if we read them while stoned, we may be able to replicate their speed if we speak them through cocaine and amphetamines. How can we say how these different speeds feel? What does the experience of this quick aesthetics of comedy, repetition, discontinuity and oblivion do to the reader?

In this essay, I want to consider the relationship between speed, form, and pleasure through some readings of Raworth's early work. I'm drawing on Raworth's books of the 1960s to the mid-1980s, in particular those short burlesques written before the long form had taken hold. I want to investigate what makes these 'public' works, in particular, how they communicate pleasure from writer to reader; I want to describe a pleasure that arises in reading them which is not just the smug pleasure of a clever close reading, and to question the philosophical status of that pleasure. But I may not get what I want. For although pleasure is a vital part of our aesthetic experience, its elaboration by theory has never seemed really adequate. In comparison, the attribution of meanings to difficult poetry seems easy enough, even if it perplexed Raworth's own father, in a letter Raworth incorporates into his *Letters from Yaddo*. Thomas Alfred Raworth wrote that

> There seems to have been a poetry explosion, and the resulting poeticised particles are too small for me to handle mentally with any satisfaction. Sometimes I seem to hover on the edge of a meaning to these minutiae of sensibility, but finally it eludes me. Perhaps it is a private world that I am not supposed to enter. A pity, because beauty does not lose by being shared.[4]

Raworth senior was a highly literate reader who had at least some access to his son's 'private world.' He takes for granted that beauty should be 'shared,' made public, but that these poems are only the exhalations of a beauty, which happens somewhere else. This reading must relinquish its attempt to describe the experience of 'hovering' on the edge of meaning, collecting particles, and give in to a conservative discourse of aesthetics, of beauty, to take the sting out of its failure to comprehend. (I begin to suspect that aestheticians talk in order to displace the inarticulable anxiety of experience, and that poets are their opposites.)

But we do know what Ron Silliman means when he describes Raworth's work of the 'late eighties and early nineties,' as poetry in which 'Raworth is far more apt to deploy a language that is public in its origin, the discourse of journalism and administration.'[5] It is after the transition (roughly contemporary with the beginnings of Thatcher's premiership in 1979) to the long poem and to expressly political discourse when, for Silliman, Raworth begins to deploy 'public' language. In identifying a transition from humour, brevity and homely or mysterious free-association in the early work to a 'public' discourse brewed out of the iotas of an identifiable historical and political context, Silliman sets a problematic limit to the notion of the 'public.' There are formal consistencies between the earlier, short lyrics, swimming in the blank of the page, and the later book-length poems with their headlong propulsion. As Keith Tuma points out, apparently transitional poems in books like *The Mask* (1976) use the asterisk to 'shift perspective or redirect narrative frameworks or observations'; in sequences such as *Ace* (1974) the pauses are gone, accelerating 'such shifts by running lines up against one another and manipulating the interstices *between* them.'[6] Readers have been taught by the disjunctions of the early work to navigate radical discontinuities in fields of reference, but the formal continuities of the long sequences also test our ability to hold the poems' apparently limitless relational capacities in our heads. In place of the shock or laughter which the sudden pratfalls of the earlier poetry might elicit, the later poems can induce vertigo, a dissociation between the activity of reading and the activity of generating meanings, in which the reader recoils not just from her strange position but also from her desire actually to throw herself over that edge, into an abyssal language whose depth (to quote Raworth quoting Coolidge) is 'as deep as the distance between (for instance) a noun (in the mind, in the dictionary) and its object somewhere in the universe.'[7] This capacity to unsettle the reader is not a simple tactic, however much it is familiar as an avant-garde technique. And its effect, in my experience, is not unpleasant: neither is it strictly contemplative. I'll try to open up that distinction, between the pleasant and the contemplative, over the course of this essay.

Just We Two

we know where we are by shape
in your idea of village
(keep away — i'm writing

> you look down at your hand
> holding a red pen writing red
> we know where we are by shape[8]

In an interview with Barry Alpert in 1972, Raworth describes line breaks as 'the only way to keep the speed going,' to get 'somebody from the top to the bottom without losing them off the side of the page.'[9] Raworth's lineation retains the reader within the competing fields of space and attention. It does not merely preserve momentum: it also regenerates syntax. The next line renews or undermines what has come before. Such movement emphasises the subjectivity of reading: each pass at the poem will create alternative relations between words or parts of poem. The transmission of meaning from clause to clause is unreliable, and depends on the activities of the reading to generate its temporary energy. But is this true of the short poems? It is easier to build and retain connections between their disparate lines, for example, between the intimacy of shape in a village and a body, between the importance of shape to 'we too' and to the writing process itself. The poem feels like a snapshot, a finite instant in time whose significance can be left to unfold in the afterglow of the event. Part of its pleasure may be the excitement of intruding on 'we too,' a simultaneously intimate and inclusive number, and the delight in sharing the knowledge of 'where we are' in the poem's form—as we find our place in a familiarised aesthetic and personal environment, so we must also adapt the poem's estranged formal wisdom into a recognisable and perhaps more banal truth about cohabitation. It is those estrangements, the unfamiliar relations created in the shift from line to line, also distinguish the pleasure of this poem from more conventional lyric of direct address. Now let's consider:

Taxonomy

> the albatross drawer
> this is the drawer where we keep the albatrosses   (CP 97)

We could read meanings into this poem, from the symbolism of the albatross in Coleridge's *Rime of the Ancient Mariner*, to a critique of linguistic categorisations which might consign living things to the status of museum specimens. We could contextualise the joke poem within avant-garde experimentation, scent an American 'fresh air' flowing through it, fumigating the stale smell of high modernist *anomie*. We could recognise in the albatross Baudelaire's 'prince de nuées,' the prince of clouds who haunts the storm and scoffs at the bowman, or even the old Monty Python sketch. But Raworth tells us that the albatross can be kept in the drawer—we don't have to reckon with all this. Such critical analysis would kill the joke, ground the ungainly flight of the poem on the critical deck, to ugliness and scorn. And the poem *is* mostly a joke, a deflation of expectations through *slowness* (take the trouble to say 'albatrosses') and repetition: what else could the albatross drawer be but a drawer for the albatrosses? Why must you always ruin things by analyzing them? But… the comedy suggests the possibility of a relation between the poem and ourselves, which the poem—in its quick gratification and expiration—perhaps doesn't fully deliver. And humour is unpredictable: you might not think it's funny, or, you might not think so twice. The absurdity of the poem's status as an object of contemplation arises from its deliberate limitation: it almost seems not to care enough about the reader's reaction to try to be funny. Why should this poem be, and be public?

Poems like 'Taxonomy' which satirise poetic dignity also 'enact their own lack of legitimacy and their unease about the uses to which they may be put,' Middleton argues.[10] As Raworth writes in *Logbook* (CP 87), 'The word I choose so precisely becomes next day the key word in an advertising campaign to sell a brand of stockings, because the word means *what comes to mind first*. As the renaissance painter should have sensed his picture on the packet around those same stockings with SIZE NINE printed across the detail which took him three days to paint. Because the stockings have always been there, and we are all USEFUL.' There is no time to stop and lament how commodification turns the mark of poetic singularity into a jingle. These poems are not useless in the way that Kant wants art to be useless, preserved 'in the albatross drawer' out of exchange. The excesses of the gratuitous text (among which, the desire for privacy is the most gratuitous) are locked in a relationship of legitimation and discontent with the utility of things. Their utility as a form of resistance is that they make themselves available to an anticipated recuperation, but they are ready to contaminate those discourses which recuperate them (including critical discourse such as this one) with their occasional, blunt stupidity.

Som

> i've also got some stars and moons
> put a moon down by my nose
> a special cloak... right
> it's got lots of stars and moons   (CP 142)

Raworth describes the creative mind as operating 'along the cracks as a cohesive force.'[11] By the rapidity of its transitions between found, assembled or invented text, his poetry sutures together the wounds in culture. Its inconsistency of reference is a kind of coherence, which we are forced critically to generate in the process of reading even as we are taught to distrust it. Raworth's early work teaches us to experience the line, the primary unit of composition, as repeated stops and starts. For example: 'time stopped / life going on' (141). Our survival depends on our willingness to concede to the line break: time stopped, CUT, life [is] going on? Or, if we refuse it, 'time stopped life [from] going on.' It is the transition from word to word, from instant to instant, which gives meaning, and the poet must concede the paradox of his situation, building permanence out of the transience of syntax. As he writes in *Logbook*, 'The last message to come through on the old transmitter was ELECTRICITY WILL STOP... and we have no way of knowing if the last word was message or punctuation' (CP 87). Electricity *will*: it is the future, it transforms; or, it will stop, forcing us to rely on alternative energies. Termination is the condition of the writing's survival. I can't go on I'll go on: 'the fuse / must not go out'; 'yours / till the energy / gaps again,' Raworth writes in *Ace*, 'i glow / and flicker' (CP 201). The flickering rhythm of the heart is the death drive's mambo: 'from nothing bangs again the heart each time.' With every rest, the heart's beat must heave itself shuddering back into life.

Your Number Is Up

colour t.v.
works in a drawer
colour t.v.   (CP 73)

There is no assurance that a poetry of susceptibility will carry
on either. In that interview with Alpert, Raworth explained that 'I
can't write a long poem because I don't have the connections to make
between whatever the bursts of energy are.'[12] The poem 'Stag Skull
Mounted' was typical of these early compositions, in that it came 'really
like a wave. I felt I wanted for a while to chart whenever the "poetic
impulse," whatever that is, hit me. Like there are times when nothing
is there except a buzz, some sort of ozone or something, or some sense
of what I feel is a poem.' 'Stag Skull Mounted' is fashioned 'from the
jerks of thought and vision' (CP 76). Each poem in this short sequence
is constituted by noting the time and date of its composition. It is the
moment, rather than the word annotated out of that moment, which
seems important: '12.256 am. June 1st. 1970': 'looking at my watch' (CP
78); 10.26 pm. June 5th. 1970: the poem is merely, 'word.' Half an hour
later, at 10.59, there is: [nothing]. These poems not only reveal their
temporal constructedness: that seems to be all they are. While the skill
of improvisation has always been central to Raworth's poetry (he told
Charles Bernstein that 'I admit to no plan': 'years ago I thought I was
writing a thing called "a poem"—way back in the 1960s. ...But now it's
just like, head off into the unknown'), these poems seem to be fully
generated from the passage of time alone. He wrote that 'my favourite
poem / is / still / is' (CP 74). That verb's generality seems founded
in its utility in describing the *present*, and the ideal poem is only 'is.'
Is this part of the reason that Raworth's poetry can seem so difficult
to critique? Roland Barthes describes criticism as 'always historical or
prospective: the constatory present, the *presentation* of bliss, is forbidden
it; its preferred material is thus culture, which is everything in us except
our present.'[13] We could say that criticism, and the writer's desire to
be its object, is a form of the reality principle, dependent on delayed
gratification, 'the postponement of satisfaction' and the 'temporary

toleration of unpleasure.'[14] Raworth's 'preferred material' is the present, the temporal home of the pleasure principle: 'i can not prove a second ago / to my own satisfaction' (CP 105).

Since the *Philebus* (34a–36c), we have been taught to regard pleasure as the anamnesis of more archaic satisfactions which return the self to a state of equilibrium. For Plato, pleasure and pain are movements between states; Kant describes them as intermittent successions, because health 'always consists only of erratic sequences of pleasant feelings (constantly interspersed with pain)';[15] Freud suggests that they are movements of tension and psychic energy. So, pleasure and pain are experienced as wholly present, temporary transitions in the shift toward *askesis*: both past and future are present to them only as the region of their oblivion. They are identified with life itself, with liveliness, the organic. Unlike other emotions which are constituted by their reference to missing concepts, such as hope, fear, anger, or trust, pleasure is difficult to describe because description depends on displacement from the present of meaning and activity in which pleasure is experienced. These difficulties—and I'm not convinced I've offered an accurate account of them—introduce an aporia into aesthetic experience, which actually constitutes aesthetics as a discipline. Starting from Kant's development of a disinterested, non-conceptual, universal and yet subjective aesthetics, in which pleasure can only be elevated to a law of judgement through its universal communicability, writing about art has always relied on the *in*communicability of subjective pleasure as a way of delimiting the field of aesthetic inquiry, while insisting that pleasure is the ineliminable category in which the response to the artwork is contained.

My simple perception of pleasure is that it (in its complex interactions) is what differentiates me as an individual from others. While communities can be built around common identifications of values (which are, perhaps, built on common experiences of pleasure), within those communities my own elaboration of pleasure depicts my experiences as mine. So how can the pleasure of a poem be described, without supplanting the critical justification of pleasure for the experience of pleasure? If I wish publicly to assert that reading Tom

Raworth's poetry gives me pleasure, it is easy to say *why*, but not *how*. As Barthes argues (34), because critical labour 'would end explaining the chosen texts,' 'no "thesis" on the pleasure of the text is possible; barely an inspection (an introspection) that falls short.' Avoiding the social or political particularities of pleasure, Barthes recommends that the critic become a voyeur of reported pleasures, perversely observing 'clandestinely the pleasure of others' (17). Such voyeurism figures as a subject of Raworth's own writing. In the poem 'Music Box' he observes that 'through one of our windows today / these people are dancing in another country' (CP 142). He's probably watching TV. The people he sees look distant: 'in another country.' Their happiness may well be staged: 'they just wear them for this dance / look very happy while they're dancing,' but are they? Is it a set-up? And what about the reader of this poem? She is triply removed from their happiness, which is conveyed through a physical performance (which might also be labour; it's certainly art), to a camera, through a TV screen, into Raworth's living room, onto the page, and out into the field of her experience. The site of pleasure is no longer their pleasure, which has been transferred along a chain of representations: it is the pleasure of reading, a pleasure in which the dancers do not participate. And anyway Tom, what's so great about watching other people watch TV?

What this poem, and 'Taxonomy,' raise, is the problematic necessity of participation in the production of aesthetic pleasure. Pierre Bourdieu has confronted the anxiety about participation in Kant's rejection of the 'impure taste' of 'the tongue, the palate and the throat.' That anxiety arises in the face of the art object's attempted seduction of the consumer, its invitation 'to regress to the most primitive and elementary forms of pleasure.'[16] In other words, the defence of a purely intellectual contemplation allows the consumer to distance himself from the artwork, and to refuse to participate in its sensual delights. Its invitation to participate can produce disgust, a 'singular sensation' for Kant, in which 'the object is represented as obtruding itself for our enjoyment, while we strive against it with all our might.'[17] According to Bourdieu's reading, such an object 'annihilates the distancing power of representation, the essentially human power of suspending immediate, animal attachment to the sensible and refusing submission to the pure affect, to simple aesthesis' (498). A different kind of pleasure —the pleasure of sublimation and of distance—replaces the 'animal attachment to the sensible,' which Kant elevates to the universal condition of aesthetic appreciation itself. 'Thus, the "purest" form of the aesthete's pleasure, [...] aesthesis purified, sublimated and denied, may, paradoxically, consist in an asceticism, *askesis*, a trained, sustained tension, which is the very opposite of primary, primitive aesthesis' (490). This kind of pure aesthesis as asceticism may be recognisable to readers of contemporary avant-gardist poetry, but it is also a learned reading behaviour which is not easy to overcome simply through the anarchic rhythms of comedy. Bourdieu challenges the supposition that aesthetic asceticism distinguishes its practitioners as ethically superior, or more: it is 'an indisputable measure of the capacity for sublimation which defines the truly human man' (491). By separating off the rational (as a category for Plato in which true pleasures may also be contained) from the hedonistic, Kantian aesthetics also universalise as a condition of cognition the separations of class, and distinguish the humanity of the hegemonic class who is the subject of 'pure taste' from the animality of the working class who cannot resist the affective draw of the artwork.

Although he critiques Kant's aesthetics which 'debase' art to 'a pleasant or useful plaything,'[18] Adorno also expresses anxieties in the face of seduction by the pleasurable which reflect his commitment to modernist art's resistance to unfreedom through form. Adorno defends pleasure in *Aesthetic Theory*: 'if the last traces of pleasure were extirpated, the question of what artworks are for would be an embarrassment' (13). However, the pleasures which interest him are not entailed in an 'animalistic' relation to art which attempts to 'dominate' the object 'by physically devouring it' (11). He approves the 'emancipation of art from cuisine or pornography' by idealist aesthetics, and notes that 'Kant was the first to achieve the insight, never since forgotten, that aesthetic comportment is free from immediate desire; he snatched art away from that avaricious philistinism that always wants to touch it and taste it' (10). This fear of an infantile relation to art, driven by the desire to ingest the object (or the anxiety that the object will ingest me), produces a critical aesthetics in which the immediacy of the artwork is always figured negatively.

These concerns, abstruse as they may be, bear directly on this discussion of Raworth's poetry. I have argued, in line with many other critics, that this poetry demands participation. The reader must work to establish continuities, to unlock patterns of association in the longer work; in the short poems, the dumb jokes, whimsy, domestic imagery or graphic interventions in the page space, also work to deflate the dignity and permanence commonly associated with verse and to seduce the reader through the pleasures of comedy. In this way, they encourage the reader to develop a sense of the contingency of the moment and of the experiences ciphered in the verse, and to develop an intuitive (in Raworth's use of the term, not Kant's) rather than an intellectual set of responses to poetry's acts of signification. Like many late modernist artworks, Raworth's poems offer an alternative to the cannibalistic immediacy which Adorno imputes to the seductive artwork and the philistine. Rather, they involve the reader in a critical, self-aware participation in the development of form. The form, the poetry's tenuous cohesion, holds in tension the antagonisms of the empirical (our freedom or unfreedom) while also offering a means toward their negation.

> **Everything 'Under' the Sun**
>
> a likely button of yes
> immobilised
>
> all 'over' the world
> some radios are off and some are on
>
> eat what you want
> learn your own lessons
>
> if you want
> don't let the revolution hold you back   (CP 141)

These poems generate their energy in a recklessly present instant, the instant of composition or of reading, discouraging analysis, memorization or reflection ('pure taste'). They disable memory, building the reader's skill for resistance not through the transmission of information (which is banalized) but through a *techne* of links. In this way, they reject the monopoly of the ruling class on the legitimation of pleasure, and submit the learned critic to the 'violence' of a *real* and creative participation. Not the false participation of a linguistic assembly that already has the rules and answers worked out for us: enter PIN, transfer funds from critical account to poetic process, withdraw. But an unsafe participation: the pleasure of going downhill, far too fast.

Andrea Brady is Lecturer in English at Queen Mary, University of London. Poems by Tom Raworth are reprinted here by permission of Carcanet Press Ltd.

Notes

[1] Friedrich Schlegel. from the *Lyceum [Critical] Fragments* 108, cited in 'On Incomprehensibility' (1800), in *Classic and Romantic German Aesthetics*, ed. J. M. Bernstein, Cambridge Texts in the History of Philosophy (Cambridge: Cambridge UP, 2003).

[2] Keith Tuma. *Fishing by Obstinate Isles: Modern and Postmodern British Poetry and American Readers* (Evanston, IL: Northwestern UP, 1998) 69, 234–5.

[3] Peter Middleton. 'Silent Critique: Tom Raworth's Early Books of Poetry,' *Removed for Further Study: The Poetry of Tom Raworth*, ed. Nate Dorward, The Gig 13–14 (May 2003): 7–30.

[4] Tom Raworth. 'Letters from Yaddo,' *Visible Shivers* (Oakland, CA: O Books, 1987), n.p.

[5] Ron Silliman. 'Politics and Speed,' *Removed for Further Study* 233–241 (236).

[6] Keith Tuma. 'Collaborating with "Dark Senses",' *Removed for Further Study* 207–216 (210).

[7] Tom Raworth. 'Notebook (1971),' *Removed for Further Study* 89–101 (95).

[8] Tom Raworth. *Collected Poems* (Manchester: Carcanet Press, 2003), 143. All further references will be abbreviated 'CP' and included in the text.

[9] Barry Alpert. 'Tom Raworth: An Interview,' *Vort* 1 (1972): 29–46 (42).

[10] Middleton. *Removed for Further Study* 27.

[11] 'Notebook,' *Removed for Further Study* 170.

[12] Alpert 33.

[13] Roland Barthes. *The Pleasure of the Text*, trans. Richard Miller (Oxford: Basil Blackwell, 1990), 22.

[14] Sigmund Freud. *Beyond the Pleasure Principle*, in *The Standard Edition of the Complete Psychological Works*, trans. James Strachey, vol. XVIII (London: Hogarth, 1955), 10.

[15] Immanuel Kant. *Anthropology from a Pragmatic Point of View*, trans. Victor Lyle Dowdell, Rev. ed. Hans H. Rudnick (Carbondale and Edwardsville, IL: Southern Illinois UP, 1978), Book II, §60, p. 132.

[16] Pierre Bourdieu. *Distinction: A Social Critique of the Judgement of Taste* (London: Routledge, 1984), 486.

[17] Immanuel Kant. *Critique of Judgement*, trans. J. H. Bernard (New York and London: Hafner, 1951), §48 p. 155.

[18] Theodor W. Adorno. *Aesthetic Theory*, Ed. Gretel Adorno and Rolf Tiedemann, trans. and ed. by Robert Hullot-Kentor (London: Athlone, 1997) 12.

A Poetic and Public Critique:
Thomas Kinsella's Response to the Widgery Tribunal

Andrew J. Browne

Eight days after the publication of Lord Widgery's 'Report of the Tribunal appointed to inquire into the events on Sunday, 30 January 1972, which led to loss of life in connection with the procession in Londonderry on that day', Thomas Kinsella responded with *Butcher's Dozen*. The shooting dead of thirteen unarmed civilians on Bloody Sunday shocked Irish people both north and south but the British Government's Tribunal of Inquiry, conducted by Widgery, added insult to injury. As Gerald Dawe remarks, Widgery seemed to turn 'reality inside-out [...] making the unarmed marchers into a guerrilla force and the paratroopers into a restrained and disciplined army'.[1]

In his poem, Kinsella contrasts the legal findings of the Tribunal with the voices of the dead marchers in such a way as to allow them to stand as witnesses before his fictional court. The words of the Tribunal combine with the voices of the dead, often ironically, allowing the inanity and hypocrisy of the report to be shown. Kinsella compares the seeming cover-up evident in the Widgery Report with the public indignation by contrasting the language of the Tribunal with what occurred on the day. The poem is composed as one long poem but works in two parts with the first mirroring the language of the Tribunal while the second uses the socio-political issues of Northern Ireland for its semantic base.

Kinsella's narrator is stunned to hear an 'answering sigh' as the ghosts of the thirteen dead protestors materialise before him. The first ghost describes himself as a 'hooligan' applying terminology that Widgery uses to describe the protestors (Widgery 6. References from this text will hereafter be cited using parenthetical references using a W followed by page number).[2] This term comes from the Army's operations order which uses the heading 'Hooliganism' when describing the 'scoop-up operation' which was the attempt at arresting the protestors that resulted in the deadly confrontation (W, 8).

Kinsella's ghosts describe themselves as 'blighters' using a British vernacular which turns the language of Widgery and the paratroopers back on itself by placing it into the mouths of the dead men as they state their innocence. Widgery also quotes the Brigade Log where the protestors are referred to as 'yobbos' which fits in with the usage of vernacular terminology (W, 11). The dead men show the irony of the report as it fails to see the truth through its limited and prejudiced witnesses and indeed, through its own terms of reference.

One of the most striking allusions to the Report is Kinsella's usage of the ghost of Gerald Donaghy. Kinsella has the ghost announce itself:

> A Bomber I. I travelled light
> – Four pounds of nails and gelignite
> About my person, hid so well
> They seemed to vanish where I fell.
> When the bullets stopped my breath
> A doctor sought the cause of death.
> He upped my shirt, undid my fly,
> Twice he moved my limbs awry,
> And noticed nothing. By and by
> A soldier, with his sharper eye,
> Beheld the four elusive rockets
> Stuffed in my coat and trouser pockets.
>
> (Kinsella, 2001, 133–34. References from this text will
> hereafter be cited using parenthetical references using
> CP followed by page number).[3]

The narrative chronology of this account is taken directly from Widgery's Report and the poem recalls the events in the same order. Kinsella shows that the irony lies within the Report's manipulation and wilful ignorance of the evidence by presenting the Report's own evidence but in the context that Widgery ignores. Kinsella is appalled that an attempted cover-up is overlooked and even whitewashed out of significance. The fact that a medical doctor examines the body, twice, and does not find the bombs is noticed by Widgery but he finds this to be 'a relatively unimportant detail of the events of the afternoon' (W, 31) which appears as an appalling oversight or deliberate ignorance of what the nationalist community was saying happened that afternoon.

Kinsella continues his exploration of the language of the Tribunal through the mouths of the dead protestors:

We three met close when we were dead.
Into an armoured car they piled us
Where our mingled blood defiled us,
Certain, if not dead before,
To suffocate upon the floor.
Careful bullets in the back
Stopped our terrorist attack,
And so three dangerous lives are done
– Judged, condemned and shamed in one. (CP, 134)

The ghost speaks in an ironic tone mocking the wording and assumptions of the Tribunal. The piling of the bodies into the back of the armoured personal carriers (APC) by the paratroopers is shown as one more indignity already piled upon the dead and dying men but also alludes to the crucial question as to where the lead traces found on the dead men came from. Widgery insinuates that the men were either firing or near weapons being fired yet also casually puts forward and passes over the fact that the residue could be from the APC. The three men Kinsella refers to are probably John Pius Young, William Noel Nash and Michael McDaid upon which Widgery comments:

> [based upon] the soldiers' evidence about civilians firing from the barricade a very strong suspicion is raised that one or more of Young, Nash and McDaid was using a firearm. No weapon was found but there was sufficient opportunity for this to be removed by others (W, 28).

Kinsella reacts to a court of justice using vague terms such as 'strong suspicion' and assumptions based upon insufficient evidence such as a gun that no witnesses saw except the paratroopers.

Kinsella's spectres get inside the language of the Tribunal and mock its pretensions to truth by contrasting the words to the actions. Kinsella's reading of the Report and his own poetic tribunal show that Widgery's fault was not a lack of evidence but a deliberate and wilful misreading of the available evidence. It is this awareness that drove Kinsella to establish his own truth by exposing the internal contradictions of Lord Widgery's Report.

The earlier part of the poem deals directly with the wording and evidence of the Widgery Report while the later part deals more openly with the societal and historical reasons behind the situation that led to the massacre, and thus uses the terminology involved with those issues to create meaning within the poem. The direct response of *Butcher's Dozen* represents something of an oddity within Kinsella's usually more oblique poetry but also fits into his interrogation of the impact of Ireland on the individual's psyche. As an immediate reaction we can see within it an analysis of various aspects of Irish society that Kinsella is interested in; of not only what the northern problems mean for a southern citizen but also the general question of Ireland and its effect on the individual. It is towards these issues that the latter part of the poem aims. By line 82 we find one of the spectres engaging with the wider issue of the north:

> Stir in, with oaths of loyalty,
> Sectarian supremacy,
> And heat, to make a proper botch,
> In a bouillon of bitter Scotch.
> Last, the choice ingredient: you.
> Now to crown your Irish stew,
> Boil it over, make a mess.
> A most imperial success! (CP, 134–35)

Kinsella summarises the historical growth of Ulster and compares it to a boiling cauldron containing the Ulster Scot inheritance alongside the suppressed nationalist minority heated up into the political chaos that was Northern Ireland in the 1970s. Significantly, Kinsella recognises that '[t]he choice ingredient' is 'you' and that this muddle, although a recipe from British imperial history with sectarian violence firing it to a boil, is reliant upon the individual's reaction to the social, political and historical reality of Northern Ireland and his or her decision to engage with and continue its vicious cycle.

Kinsella is connecting with these issues in the poem as they are being represented in his contemporary society. The continuing violence helps to define the south's relationship to the north as one of a repression of that relationship in the face of continuing strife. Another recurring concern during the time of the Report's release is the upcoming vote for entry into the European Economic Community. As Ireland modernises and moves out of the economically depressive post-war years and into the later twentieth century, a chance to escape the economic hardship that symbolised its early years is emerging. A desire for security and economic prosperity contributed to the ongoing revisionism[4] in Irish historiography. A similar drive also added to repression of the relationship of southern people towards their nationalist neighbours in the north. The majority of southern Ireland was willing to put the past colonial rule as well as the ongoing strife in the north behind them or out of their mind in order to get on with the process of modernisation. The narrator's voice interjects into the poem at line 101 to explain the relationship of the southern government and its voices of revisionist ideology to the northern problem:

> It seemed the moment to explain
> That sympathetic politicians
> Say our violent traditions,
> Backwards looks and bitterness
> Keep us in this dire distress.
> We must forget, and look ahead,
> Nurse the living, not the dead. (CP, 135)

Kinsella's 1979 commentary on *Fifteen Dead* also highlights this concern with the revisionist nature of the Irish government: 'Politicians in responsible positions urged what amounted to a Violence Eradication Scheme, as though violence were a contagious disease curable by the elimination of infected bodies [refusing] to consider the eradication of the causes of violence'.[5] The refusal of the southern government to face the causes behind the northern Troubles, which lie just as much in the creation of their state as the other, amounts, for Kinsella, to wilful ignorance and culpability.

The poem goes on to consider nationalist violence and questions the refusal to recognise its legitimacy. Kinsella sees that the violent nationalist response is delivered on terms that the occupier has established:

> You condescend to hear us speak
> Only when we slap your cheek.
> And yet we lack the last technique:
> We wrap for order with a gun,
> The issues simplify to one
> – Then your Democracy insists
> You mustn't talk with terrorists. (CP, 135)

The irony here is that the colonised must use the language of the coloniser (itself a form of violence) in order to be heard but when the colonised don the language and actions of that violence they are ostracised as terrorists.

Kinsella then critiques the remnants of colonial rule in the sectarian hatred of the Orange Order:

> Sashed and bowler-hatted, glum
> Apprentices of fife and drum,
> High and dry, abandoned guards
> Of dismal streets and empty yards,
> Drilled at the codeword "True Religion"
> To strut and mutter like a pigeon
> "Not An Inch – Up The Queen";
> Who use their walls like a latrine
> For scribbled magic [.] (CP, 136)

Kinsella is most vitriolic here and probably also at danger of falling into the traps of his own sectarian approach to the Unionist community, but he is noticing that the imagery of sectarian hatred and fear is available to the Unionist power brokers.

Amazingly, considering the tone of the poem to this point, it ends with a modest hint of hope. Kinsella shows that the solution to the northern problem lies within and without the state. From without, England can recognise its culpability '[a]nd brood at home on her disgrace / – Everything to its own place.' (CP, 137). And from within, Ireland's mixed cultural heritage can be recognised:

> We all are what we are, and that
> Is mongrel pure. What nation's not

Where any stranger hung his hat
And seized a lover where she sat? (CP, 137)

Kinsella comes to the conclusion that Ireland is not the polarities of identity that Unionism and Nationalism kill for but rather a mixture of peoples whose only future is to put the divisions behind them, along with the British occupying army, and mingle as one. At the time this may have appeared as a naive answer to the northern problem in its immediacy, but as of today no other solution seems possible.

Much of the immediate reaction to Bloody Sunday in the south of Ireland was the same anger as Kinsella's but as IRA atrocities appeared to match and outmanoeuvre those of the British paratroopers, and as Irish revisionist history attempted to distance the south from the northern Troubles, [6] Kinsella's response fell out of favour. One of Kinsella's most strident critics was Edna Longley of Queen's University Belfast. Longley stated that *Butcher's Dozen* 'constitutes a more dubious arousal of the heroic passions of the past'.[7] For this critic, who has consistently called for a division between poetry and politics, Kinsella's poem is part of the problem with northern affairs and it represents the rhetoric behind the violence it disparages.

What the criticism levelled at Kinsella for his political affiliations fails to take into account is that he has constantly interrogated nationalist discourse. Thus, as early as his first collection in 1956, Kinsella sought answers to the usage of Irish mythology for nationalist ends. In the poem 'Test Case', for example, Kinsella notices that the 'heroic agenda' is 'readier than flags rippling in the sun' (CP, 2).

Shortly after the Bloody Sunday massacre and before the beginning of his tribunal, Widgery was informed by the British Prime Minister Edward Heath that 'it had to be remembered that we were in Northern Ireland, fighting not just a military war but a propaganda war'.[8] Recently released information like this has helped validate Kinsella's ironic and angry approach to this document. The Saville Inquiry seems to be confirming Kinsella's anger and reaction, and although the Widgery Tribunal itself may never be officially sanctioned the results of its Report are now rightfully seen as erroneous. Kinsella's indignation now seems, thirty-five years later, to be justified. *Butcher's Dozen* stands on its own in Kinsella's oeuvre as a significant part of his own poetic sensibility which he decodes throughout his poetic career through an examination of his personal and social background. It is also an important document that represents the anger of one man reflected through the public language of the Tribunal and the people of southern Ireland. It represents not only a poem but a public document which, in its official reception, shows not only a people's anger but also two societies' language of denial and concealment.

Andrew J. Browne is a doctoral teaching fellow at the National University of Ireland, Galway.

Notes

[1] Gerald Dawe, 'In the Violent Zone: Thomas Kinsella's *Nightwalker and Other Poems*', *Tracks* 7 (1987): 27.

[2] The Rt. Hon. Lord Widgery, 'Report of the Tribunal appointed to inquire into the events on Sunday, 30 January 1972, which led to loss of life in connection with the procession in Londonderry on that day', Her Majesty's Stationery Office, 1972, *Cain* Web Service http://cain.ulst.ac.uk/hmso/widgery.htm

[3] Thomas Kinsella, *Collected Poems* (Manchester: Carcanet Press, 2001).

[4] Revisionism in Ireland involved the attempt to rewrite Irish history outside of the monomaniacal concerns of Irish nationalism that dominated the Irish Republic's first decades.

[5] Thomas Kinsella, *Fifteen Dead* (Dublin, The Dolmen Press, 1979) 57.

[6] Kevin Whelen, 'The Revisionist Debate in Ireland', *Boundary 2* 31:1 (2004) http://web.ebscohost.com.libgate.nuigalway.ie/ehost/pdf 190–191

[7] Edna Longley, 'Searching the Darkness: Richard Murphy, Thomas Kinsella, John Montague and James Simmons', *Two Decades of Irish Writing: A Critical Survey*, ed. Douglas Dunn (Cheshire: Carcanet Press, 1975) 136.

[8] Diarmaid Ferriter, *The Transformation of Ireland 1900–2000* (London: Profile Books, 2004) 627.

'I don't want my acts determined by any authority whatever': The Public Gesture of Basil Bunting's 'The Spoils'

Matthew Chambers

'The Spoils' engages with the *fact* of World War II, and sees that war as an ethical and indeed meritorious demonstration of the limits of material accumulation and power. Bunting's 'public gesture,' in a 'poem including history,' employs certain lessons on life, death, and materiality, but as a demonstration of something practical and livable Bunting's poem intervenes in public discourse by seeing history, in Zukofsky's terms, as the 'attraction of living recorded.' It offers details of daily life, not the grand abstractions of dogma or nostalgia: the one dictates 'truth from above' and the other brackets off (and ossifies) what no longer is and possibly never was. 'The Spoils' offers its public a generative model for rethinking the world after the war.

Bunting spent much of World War II in the British Royal Air Force, serving in various capacities primarily in the Middle East. His attitude toward the war, and toward his service in an army, can be gauged in a letter he wrote to Louis Zukofsky in 1941. Bunting offers the following détourning of a tool of war in response to a question Zukofsky had posed.

> What do I "feel with a machine gun?" Well, it depends on the gun. I criticize a machine by nearly the same criteria as I do a work of art... My machine-gun is a Hotchkiss, & I feel towards it something similar in kind to what I feel for Egyptian sculpture. Anyway, its worth a lot of loving care, like a good sextant or microscope— and is in an altogether higher class as machine than a motorcar or radio. Maybe that measures just how far I am out of key with this age of gadgets. But I think Holbein or Bach or Praxiteles, as well as Alexander, would have appreciated a Hotchkiss gun: whereas a lot of our machines might merely have astonished them.
>
> (letter to Zukofsky (22/9/41))[1]

The dark humour aside, Bunting adopts a familiar attitude not only toward the weapon under discussion, but the war in general. The poem, then, is a conversation in which he attempts to filter this new experience through a sort of aesthetic rigour he has constructed over the past two decades, and thus the war is no more foreign to his sensible experience than an art object. However, the way in which he 'makes sense' neither glorifies nor exaggerates his circumstances: even as he historicizes the machine gun as 'modern,' his ahistorical musing on its appreciation by the likes of Bach or Holbein does not employ them into a particular world construction. In other words, he is neither simply aestheticizing war nor functionalizing art, but rather doing both, and in the process, blurs the formal categories to see how they can speak to one another. In this gesture we can see the beginnings of a concern that will inflect Bunting's 'general intention' in 'The Spoils'.

In his 13th March 1951 letter to Zukofsky he tentatively attempts to explain the 'argument' of the poem.

> General intention? If I could put it in prose I wouldn't take the trouble to write a poem. First movement...general no doubt, but more or less particularly characteristic of the Semitic peoples, which takes life as a journey (to Zion, to Jinnat) best performed with few impediments, and is indifferent to the furniture at the inn. (The second movement contrasts that with the people who go in for architecture and furnish as though they intended to live here forever.) The advantage of the journey idea is that death becomes a familiar, almost a friend. No Lucretian cold-comfort required.

Later in the letter he speaks of war 'not as a horror, not as an opportunity for self-congratulating glory... but simply as an activity which has pleasure of its own, an exercise of certain faculties which need exercise: in which death is neither a bugbear nor a consummation, but just happens...part of the fun.' He wants to treat war as vital to, not a disruption of and departure from, a lived life. He has experienced war first hand, and rather than viscerally rejecting or embracing its operation and effects in some traditional manner, he wants a way to argue for its necessity without symbolically inflating its occurrence.

> People group bads and goods too easily, dont admit that heavy brutality may coexist with aesthetic merits just as they

dont admit there may be merits in war, which is associated in their minds with the stupid slaughters of 1914–18 or the last battles of your Civil War to the exclusion of all virtue except endurance. But resolution and effort can be gay instead of grim, and the death and ruin have had their importance exaggerated. That is not to deny their existence nor to advocate multiplying wars. But freedom from war like freedom from poverty, can be pursued at the expense of things better worth preserving than peace and plenty, of which, I should say, the most important, and most threatened, is personal autonomy. Freewill entails sin! I dont want my acts determined by any authority whatever.

(letter to Zukofsky (19/4/51))

Bunting's argument is that war highlights 'resolution and effort' in defense of 'personal autonomy.' When we apply terms without assessing particulars first, we are imposing a false authority to organize the facts. It is thus vital that we learn from the experiences of war, and do not evaluate it through abstractions.

'The Spoils' is one of Bunting's 'sonatas', albeit (as he said) a 'spoilt' one (18).[2] It contains three movements. The first is a series of monologues by the Biblical sons of Shem: Asshur, Lud, Arpachshad, and Aram. The second is told from the point of view of a contemporary narrator looking back at the glories of the medieval Seljuk dynasty (as it mainly existed in Persia). The last section moves forward to current concerns of economy and war. The movements interact only in that the same thematic concern is treated in three distinct forms. This concern throughout how one's material circumstance (wealth, poverty) inflects the quality of one's life and how one lives. The poem opens:

> Man's life so little worth,
> do we fear to take or lose it?
> No ill companion on a journey, Death
> lays his purse on the table and opens the wine.
> (45)[3]

From the outset, death is viewed as familiar, and even benign: at the very least a participant in the ordinary. He is seen here in an intimate way, as he takes his place, without ceremony, at the table. This leads into the four sons of Shem each expressing their concern over the 'markets' and their mortality. The attitudes among the brothers range from Asshur's evasiveness ('Another shall pay the bill if I can evade it') to Lud's seeming detachment from the local failing market ('There is no clamour/ in our market, no eagerness for gain') to Arpachshad's denial of earthly needs ('apt to no servitude, commerce or special dexterity/...What's to dismay us?') (46,47). Life does not seem to be lived by material concerns in these particular tribes. As Bunting has it, what history teaches is not always economic reform; indeed, problematically or not, sometimes it teaches detachment from economy altogether to ensure a quality of life.

The form of this movement—four distinct, but interconnected voices—superficially appears similar to Pound's appropriation of historic voices in his long poem. However, Bunting distinguishes his form of the sonata from Pound's adaptation of the 'fugue.'[4] The sonata, as a musical form, employs one or more instruments in unison, as opposed to the 'contrapuntal' nature of the fugue. Bunting uses the sons of Shem to illustrate his 'general intention,' but in its multiplicity of voicings, he opens up the possibility for varieties of response: either in agreement or disagreement.

The second movement offers an extended view of the Seljuk empire, and particularly, its interest in building temples to represent the glory of Islam. Bunting assesses two different instances of these projects, and how he values one project for its organic structure over another built with 'fudged' motives leads us to his figuration of 'autonomy' as the true freedom from the material world. This figure is presented in the image of a falcon taking flight.

> Have you seen a falcon stoop
> accurate, unforseen
> and absolute, between
> wind-ripples over harvest? Dread
> of what's to be, is and has been —
> were we not better dead?
>
> His wings churn air
> to flight.

Feathers alight
with sun, he rises where
dazzle rebuts our stare,
wonder our fright. (51–2)

Two images work in conjunction here: the falcon taking flight, and Death re-entering the poem. By figuring the falcon as taking flight over 'harvest,' Bunting is symbolically representing freedom or autonomy as transcendence over material concerns. And to weigh life in values of past, present, and future, such 'dread,' is a living death ('were we not better dead?'). The trick is that the falcon so completely transcends those enmeshed in material concerns that we cannot see it, or are blinded by it ('dazzle rebuts our stare'). Through this imagery Bunting once again rejects materiality as a factor in individual freedoms, and if anything, we lose our identity (our very lives) if we willingly comply with its forces. The compression of these lines hardens their expression, and thus supplies this passage with a particular force.

The third movement of the poem is the most autobiographical of the three, and mainly ranges from Bunting's experiences patrolling the North Sea to traversing the deserts of Tripoli. In the following passage Bunting describes a trek into Tripoli during the war (it is worth quoting at length).

Broken booty but usable
along the littoral, frittering into the south.
We marvelled, careful of craters and minefields,
noting a new-painted recognisance
on a fragment of fuselage, sand drifting into dumps,
a tank's turret twisted skyward,
here and there a lorry unharmed
out of fuel or the crew scattered;
leaguered in lines numbered for enemy units,
gulped beer of their brewing,
mocked them marching unguarded to our rear;
discerned nothing indigenous, never a dwelling,
but on the shore sponges stranded and beyond the reef
unstayed masts staggering in the swell,
till we reached readymade villages clamped on cornland,

> empty, Arabs feeding vines to goats;
> at last orchards aligned, girls hawked by their mothers
> from tent to tent, Tripoli dark
> under a cone of tracers.
> Old in that war after raising many crosses
> rapped on a tomb at Leptis; no one opened.   (54)

In a desert similar to those of the first two movements, we are given a virtual list of the end products of the economy of war. The material objects in this scene have all been rendered useless. We move from 'discerned nothing indigenous' to 'Arabs feeding vines to goats' and 'girls hawked by their mothers,' which is the only life being lived outside the immediate context of the war. Perhaps, through their detachment from the war, the local people can survive the mass chaos and destruction that litters their landscape. This idea is reinforced at the end of this passage when the narrator 'raps' upon a tomb, and not receiving a response— Death has been demystified through a morbid, 'knock-knock' joke. It is the 'everydayness' of death that can be accepted if one does not hold the material dear, and instead embraces the process of their life as a life *to be lived*.

This section ends with a scene in the North Sea. Here we see the narrator meditating on where he is bound, and what purpose it will serve in his life.

> In watch below
> meditative heard elsewhere
> surf shout, pound shores seldom silent
> from which heart naked swam
> out to the dear unintelligible ocean.
> From Largo Law look down,
> moon and dry weather, look down
> on convoy marshalled, filing between mines.
> Cold northern clear sea-gardens
> between Lofoten and Spitzbergen,
> as good a grave as any, earth or water.
> What else do we live for and take part,
> we who would share the spoils?   (55–6)

This poem ends with a calm acceptance of an inevitable death. It does not matter how one dies or where one is buried ('as good a grave as any, earth or water'). Further, he ends with a question, which leaves all the paths he has trodden through this poem open. What remains important to Bunting is self-determination. There is no external authority which grants us special privilege in this life or the next, and those who seek such privilege are subject to the poem's critique. Only when we accept that what is common to all is *essential* to all, then will we truly recognize our individuality. The poem's 'public gesture' lies in its appeal for the necessity of individual autonomy. 'The Spoils' argues for a death that is as ordinary as a lived life, and a life unencumbered by materials, which curtail the autonomy Bunting felt was so dear to us all.

Matthew Chambers is a PhD student at the State University of New York at Buffalo. Poems by Basil Bunting are quoted by permission of the Estate of Basil Bunting; letters from Bunting to Louis Zukofsky are quoted with permission from the Estate of Basil Bunting, and the Harry Ransom Center, University of Texas, Austin. The author wishes to thank John Halliday for the permissions, and Peter Quartermain for his generous insight.

Notes
[1] It is important to note that Bunting concludes by saying he considers none of this while the gun is in use.

> As to firing the Hotchkiss, that only happens 'in action'—we musn't waste ammunition—so that there are more urgent things in mind than appreciate the gun's accuracy & reliability, or one's own skill. I'm not aware of having hit any plane or person yet, so I can't say what that feels like.
> (letter to Zukofsky (9/22/41))

The distinction between 'function' and 'aesthetics' still pertains in the *act* of war, it is only in his leisure time that he can afford to frame the war as he wishes.

[2] 'Basil Bunting Talks About Briggflatts' (*Agenda* 16:1)

[3] Bunting, Basil. *The Complete Poems*. New York: New Directions, 2000.

[4] *Basil Bunting On Poetry*. Ed. Peter Makin. Oxford: Oxford UP, 1999. These competing monologues are specifically not functioning as would the clamour of a 'fugue.' Bunting, in a late lecture on Pound, addresses the limits he sees of such a form in poetry:

Pound, however, and Zukofsky after him, was fascinated by the close texture of the fugue and by its somewhat spurious air of logicality. They wanted to know whether the design of the fugue could be transferred to poetry. A short but incomplete answer is that it can't. A fugue is essentially contrapuntal, several voices imitating each other, yet free of each other, all talking simultaneously, whereas poetry is written for one voice at a time or, at most, for voices in unison. (135)

Public Poets of the Cold War: Robert Lowell, Allen Ginsberg, and the 'Two Camps' of American poetry

BRENDAN COOPER

In discussions of American poetry since World War II, critics have recurrently perceived the canon as a form of duel between two antagonistic factions. For instance, in his anthology of 'innovators and outsiders' in American poetry since 1950, Eliot Weinberger writes that '[f]or decades American poetry has been divided into two camps, not quite Republicans and Democrats, but more like the ruling and opposition parties in some particularly messy parliamentary system [...] The ruling party has always maintained a policy of exclusion: only certain forms, certain subjects and ways of dealing with them have been deemed permissible at any given moment. For the opposition, poetry is a place where one can, one should, talk about everything, and where the diversity of content determines the variety of forms' (xi–xii). Weinberger presents the 'opposition' here as liberating rebels against the restrictive forces of mainstream formalism and traditionalism; and yet, his advocation of such emancipatory inclusiveness simultaneously involves the imposition of a restrictive canonical formula. Weinberger's depiction of the American poetic canon as a duel between two warring 'camps' brings about its own exclusivity, since it indiscriminately denies the relevance of any so-called 'mainstream' poets to the kinds of liberating perspective he seeks to praise.

In his afterword to the same anthology, Weinberger elaborates on this same idea, by discussing the dominance of the New Criticism in the American academies of the 1940s, and its legacy in poetry of the mid-century. The influence of the New Critical project of a 'return to traditional prosody and rhyme' brought about a 'second generation' of New Critical poets—'Howard Nemerov, Randall Jarrell, Robert Lowell, Elizabeth Bishop, Delmore Schwartz, Richard Wilbur, Anthony Hecht, John Berryman, among many others'—who, Weinberger claims, all comparably developed their shared grounding in New Critical theory into a reprehensibly self-indulgent postwar confessional style. Weinberger's disdain for such poetry could not be made much more obvious: these writers are merely 'overgrown disturbed child prodig[ies]' whose methodology consists of dropping a phrase like 'pubic hair' into a sonnet, or of detailing the trauma of their personal lives within the stultifying framework of resolutely traditional 'well-turned phrases.' It is against this postwar 'Establishment' that the truly significant poets of the era—Weinberger's 'new avant-garde, the century's second great flowering'—chose to react (396–7).

It has become fairly standard to view American poetry since the Second World War in terms of this division between mainstream and avant-garde. I wish here to challenge the way in which this prevalent conception of the canon encourages an under-acknowledgement of the various overlappings and points of comparative possibility that exist between canonically segregated American poets. In particular, I wish to show that such comparative possibilities exist even between the two poets most overtly and famously representative of the 'establishment' and 'countercultural' subdivisions of postwar American poetry—Robert Lowell and Allen Ginsberg. Ginsberg is not usually discussed alongside Lowell except as a kind of polar opposite, a countercultural figure whose 1950s fame matched Lowell's and whose anti-establishment Beat attitude represented a direct challenge to the New Critical formalism and conservativism of which Lowell was, supposedly, an unrivalled exemplar. Marjorie Perloff, for instance, depicts these two figures as quite diametrically opposed: Ginsberg as rebel, 'gay, Jewish, Beat, politically radical'; and Lowell as the archetypal establishment icon, labelled 'outstanding poet of his generation' so widely that by the 1960s the era was being dubbed 'the Age of Lowell' (81–2).

Such an oppositional perspective does not admit the fact that the careers of these two figures intersected in various ways. Far from existing in entirely different worlds, Lowell and Ginsberg engaged in correspondence in the late 1950s (Hamilton, *Letters*, 342–5). In 1961, Ginsberg and several of his friends visited Lowell to supply him with psilocybin, a psychedelic drug (Miles 281–2). Towards the end of Lowell's life, he gave a poetry reading with Ginsberg, in which the latter stepped forward to defend Lowell against a heckler from the crowd—the Beat poet, Gregory Corso (Hamilton, *A Biography*, 459–60). The implication of these points of connection is that the segregation of Lowell and Ginsberg into incompatible establishment and countercultural subdivisions of postwar American poetry is not fully supported by the available facts about their lives. In his poem 'Television Was a Baby Crawling Toward That Deathchamber', Ginsberg proclaims 'I give thee happy tidings Robert Lowell and Jeanette MacDonald' (CP 272), a citation of iconic figures from the worlds of literature and film respectively that suggests Ginsberg to be interested in a more direct dialogue with Lowell than many of the critics who have written on these two poets.

One means by which such comparative possibilities can be elucidated is through attention to their shared commitment to the idea of poetry as a form of public language. Recognition of the connective threads between Lowell and Ginsberg's political engagement with their common cultural context of Cold War America reveals their work to be more profitably comparable than established codifications of the canon are able to accommodate. In 'Inauguration Day: January 1953', for instance, Lowell's depiction of a New York cityscape, with its oppressive mechanical subway 'vaults' and the 'green girders' of the dilapidated El, encapsulates the sense of latent anxiety that permeated American culture in the early 1950s (CP 117). The motifs of snow and ice, in this poem, suggest a static sociopolitical and spiritual lifelessness, but also the instability that is intrinsic to each of these substances—an instability that hints at the turbulence underlying Cold War American political life. This backdrop of snow and ice, furthermore, implies the movement of American culture not into a hellish inferno but a lifeless winter devoid of spiritual energy. The phonetic resemblance between 'ice' and 'Ike' associates the new president with this phenomenon of spiritual deadness. Yet the fear of 'nuclear apocalypse' is also strongly felt in this poem—where the 'lack-land atoms, split apart' clearly alludes to the cultural effects of the atomic bomb, and recalls *Time* magazine's assertion that the bomb heralded 'a new age in which all thoughts and things were split' (Henriksen 85).

Lowell's poem is thus alert to the new anxieties of the nuclear age in which advanced scientific understanding of 'stars' and 'atoms' has led to unprecedented qualities of cultural instability. But the 'fixed stars' also relate to Lowell's dialogue with American Civil War history here, since they connote the stars of the American flag and hence infer

America's Civil War past in which the Southern and Northern states were 'split apart.' Grant and Eisenhower are implicitly compared as past and present presidents who were also both military leaders, 'God[s] of our armies,' a phrase intimating their usurpation of the power traditionally assigned to a transcendent deity. Cold Harbor, at which Grant needlessly sacrificed hundreds of his own soldiers, 'resonates for Lowell because it prefigures the calculated slaughter that would typify the Second World War' (Thurston 91). Indeed, the name 'Cold Harbor' may have particularly appealed to Lowell through its simultaneous echo of both the Cold War and another traumatic moment in America's recent military history, Pearl Harbour. The poet's cry to Grant's statue of 'Horseman, your sword is in the groove!' both echoes Yeats's self-epitaph in 'Under Ben Bulben' and also parodically connotes the apocalyptic horsemen of the book of Revelation—in particular, the rider of the Red Horse, to whom 'it was granted to take peace from the Earth, and that man would slay one another; and a great sword was given to him' (Revelation 6:4). The statue of Grant hence embodies the contemporary extinction of apocalyptic Christian prophecy. In place of a horseman of the apocalypse, the poem provides a lifeless horseman of bronze, his sword impotently fixed in its groove. As a figure from America's Civil War past that Lowell uses to condemn contemporary America, Grant is a '[c]yclonic zero of the word,' in which image the 'word' signifies not a transcendent divine Word but merely a zero, a nothingness. The eschatological framework of Christianity is absent from this contemporary American urban landscape in which stands only this monument to a dead military '[g]od.'

This incorporation of religion into a political critique of contemporary American culture constitutes a significant thread of comparative possibility between Lowell's work and that of Ginsberg. The opening to 'Howl' combines an indictment of sociopolitical oppression in the modern American city with spiritual visions that incorporate a variety of Western and Eastern religious sources:

> I saw the best minds of my generation destroyed by madness,
>   starving hysterical naked,
> dragging themselves through the negro streets at dawn looking for
>   an angry fix,

angelheaded hipsters burning for the ancient heavenly connection
    to the starry dynamo in the machinery of night,
who poverty and tatters and hollow-eyed and high sat up smoking
    in the supernatural darkness of cold-water flats floating across
    the tops of cities contemplating jazz,
who bared their brains to Heaven under the El and saw
    Mohammedan angels staggering on the tenement roofs
    illuminated,
who passed through universities with radiant cool eyes
    hallucinating Arkansas and Blake-light tragedy among the
    scholars of war [...]   (CP 126)

Ginsberg introduces his 'best minds' here as visionaries forced into madness, starvation and hysteria on the New York streets by the oppressive sociopolitical climate of contemporary America. His political diatribe directs itself towards the institutions of America: the 'universities' are presented as forums for bellicose 'scholars of war' that are unable to harbour the individuality and spiritual illumination of his 'best minds'. The spirituality of Ginsberg's vision and the energy of his political protest are hence intertwined. The images of the 'starry dynamo' and 'machinery of night' convey the encroachment of the modern technopolis onto the natural landscape; and the 'ancient heavenly connection' sought by the 'angelheaded hipsters' is given a connotation very distinct from any traditional, Judaeo-Christian enlightenment in the light of the slang meaning of 'connection' as 'drug-dealer'. The traditionally incompatible experiences of spiritual vision and hallucinogenic drug-vision are thus provocatively conflated, in a direct rejection of the asceticism and restrictive morality of traditional religious doctrines. Ginsberg's opening, then, populated variously by 'Mohammedan angels,' 'Blake-light tragedy' and the 'supernatural darkness of cold-water flats,' clearly represents a religious perspective provocatively and deliberately distinct from the major currents of religious sentiment in 1950s America.

    Ginsberg's figures 'bared their brains to Heaven under the El,' whilst in Lowell's 'Inauguration Day,' the poet hears 'the El's green girders charge on Third' ... predominant conceptions of the American poetic canon demand that these depictions of the 1950s New York cityscape can have little in common. Certainly, Ginsberg's free-flowing lines bear little formal resemblance to Lowell's densely packed, iambic tetrameter sonnet. Yet each of these poems intertwines the language of religion with the language of political critique in order comparably to condemn the social and political mechanics of the Cold War American city. Lowell presents a New York scene in which the decay of the El metonymically embodies the decay of contemporary America, and the replacement of old 'natural' orders—such as Christianity—with the artificial ephemerality of the urban space. The '[c]yclonic zero of the word' he identifies in Grant, and by association in Eisenhower, represents a recognition of this absence of absolute spiritual order, and its replacement with the oppressive authority of the American government. Ginsberg similarly depicts a decaying contemporary urban scene that is dominated by restrictive bodies of authority. The 'starry dynamo in the machinery of night' described by Ginsberg is comparable to Lowell's 'fixed stars, all just alike/ as lack-land atoms,' in that each image conveys the infiltration of technological artificiality into modern urban life, as well as hinting respectively—via 'dynamo' and 'lack-land atoms'—at the frighteningly destructive possibilities of twentieth-century technological progress. Thomas Edwards observes that in Lowell's 'Inauguration Day,' 'not people but machines drum and charge in this poem, and the horseman is evidently not a man but a statue, succinct evidence of what ceremony does to life' (217). This idea of a pernicious replacement of the human with the mechanical is very much in line with the Beat attitude and provides some important common ground between these two poems. In a 1963 interview Lowell suggested that '[t]he terrible danger now is of the great impersonal bureaucratic machinery rolling over everything and flattening out humanity'—a statement so reminiscent of the Beat position that it prompted Lowell's interviewer, Al Alvarez, to suggest that the Beats were presently 'cashing in' on precisely this cultural development (83). The danger Lowell identifies, of a 'bureaucratic machinery' destructively imposing itself on contemporary society, strikingly echoes the nightmarish vision of cultural authority Ginsberg depicts in Part II of 'Howl': 'Moloch whose mind is pure machinery! Moloch whose blood is running money! Moloch whose fingers are ten armies!' (CP 131).

'Howl' and 'Inauguration Day' are, therefore, not as radically opposed as they might at first seem: as political critiques of contemporary America that use the dilapidated landscape of New York as a vehicle for the confrontation of modern spiritual and sociopolitical malaise, these two poems are far more comparable than discussions of Lowell and Ginsberg tend to acknowledge. It is in their responses to the contemporary urban scene that they differ. While Lowell is content to perceive American culture as a 'mausoleum' devoid of spiritual promise, Ginsberg takes the inadequacy of this culture as a cue for the articulation of a personalistic, rebellious religious vision. Throughout 'Howl,' Ginsberg finds spirituality in the very material world he experiences: the city streets are home to 'orange crates of theology' and 'the drunken taxicabs of Absolute Reality,' while sex yields 'a vision of ultimate cunt and come eluding the last gyzym of consciousness' (CP 128–9). His oppressed and rebellious 'best minds,' at odds with the restrictive attitudes of American society both politically and sexually, access spiritual experiences that incorporate provocative reconfigurations of the language of traditional religious doctrine. In contrast to Lowell's downcast perception of a contemporary world drained of the possibilities of absolute order, Ginsberg constructs an anti-traditional religiosity via which he counters the dogmatic restrictiveness of traditional religious doctrines.

Ginsberg's spiritual politics are hence, while evidently distinct from Lowell's, nevertheless comparable in a manner that casts questions over the continuing perception of these two figures at opposing poles of postwar American poetry. One might with justification suggest that accurate understanding of their work has been obscured via its persistent misrepresentation in another form of 'public' space—that of criticism. The recurrent critical tendency to sideline direct comparative analysis of these two poets' work in favour of convenient labels through which they can comfortably be located in the canon has hindered recognition of the moments at which their poetries might, if not converge, then at least articulate comparable, shared responses to the social and political climate in which they both wrote. An elucidation of such threads of comparative possibility between the political engagements of Lowell and Ginsberg hence not only facilitates a re-evaluation of their poetry; it also more broadly demands a reassessment of established codifications of the post-World War II American poetic canon.

Brendan Cooper has recently completed a PhD at the University of Cambridge.

Works Cited

Alvarez, Al. 'Robert Lowell in Conversation' in *Robert Lowell: Interviews and Memoirs* ed. Jeffrey Meyers. Ann Arbor: University of Michigan Press, 1988. 74–83.

Edwards, Thomas R. *Imagination and Power: A Study of Poetry on Public Themes.* London: Chatto and Windus, 1971.

Ginsberg, Allen. *Collected Poems 1947–1980.* Harmondsworth: Viking, 1985.

Hamilton, Ian. *Robert Lowell: a Biography.* London: Faber and Faber, 1983.

Hamilton, Saskia, ed. *The Letters of Robert Lowell.* London: Faber and Faber, 2005.

Henriksen, Margot A. *Dr Strangelove's America: Society and Culture in the Atomic Age.* Berkeley, CA: University of California Press, 1997.

Lowell, Robert. *Collected Poems.* Ed. Frank Bidart and David Gewanter. London: Faber and Faber, 2003.

Miles, Barry. *Ginsberg: A Biography.* London: Viking, 1990.

Perloff, Marjorie. 'The Return of Robert Lowell.' *Parnassus: Poetry in Review* 27.1–2 (2003): 76–102.

Thurston, Michael. 'Robert Lowell's Monumental Vision: History, Poetic Form, and the Cultural Work of Postwar Lyric.' *American Literary History* 12.1–2 (Spring-Summer 2000): 79–112.

Weinberger, Eliot, ed. *American Poetry Since 1950: Innovators and Outsiders.* New York: Marsilio, 1993.

All in the Poems

IAN DAVIDSON

Reading Frank O'Hara's *Collected Poems* I become interested in the way certain words seemed to appear with an unusual frequency in the early work. One example, 'blue', both a noun and an adjective and, less commonly, a verb, seems to have a variety of functions. In 'Poem' (13–14), 'the moon turns blue' in a poem in which 'we love at night' and 'birds sing out of sight'. A blue moon, the second full moon in a month, is an infrequent occurrence, approximately every two and a half years. To moon is to wander listlessly; and when a 'moon turns blue' then that wandering turns to depression. Yet to moon is also to 'expose' yourself, normally in the night sky, and to bathe your skin in moonlight. And if a moon turns blue in the way a blue film is blue then exposure leads to sexual behaviour. Yet the moon turning blue is, according to the poem, a consequence of the way 'The birds push apples through / grass'. It's unclear whether the apples come up through the grass or whether they're rolled in the grass like footballs yet later in the poem I find 'the apples and birds / move us like soft words' and 'couple' in the next line seems a reference to physical coming together as well as the couplets from which the poem is constructed. The birds also 'sing out of sight'. I get confused about the bird, look it up in the dictionaries and find a noun and a verb. I remember that 'bird' is a slightly derogatory term for a young woman, and that 'bird' is a spell in prison and that performers are 'given the bird'. I'm not sure this helps. I find out that bird is a term for a homosexual prostitute, and 'birdie' an effeminate man, and then realise that apples are fruit, and fruit is a retro term for a homosexual and that Eve ate the apple in the Garden of Eden and therefore gained knowledge of good and evil. The poem unravels rapidly, but seems to go off in a number of directions at once, in a way that is at variance with the close written rhyming couplets. It is, in total, a gentle poem, quite beautiful in its lack of insistence after the slightly clunky opening couplet with its arrhythmic echo of 'jump' and 'thump'. But of course I've not got close to why 'China' or 'Chinese' appears in the poem. Is China the most distant and exotic land he can imagine, and he is suggesting it as a place where physical activity can be open, in comparison with where 'we, in secret, play'? Yet if it is symbolic it is not only in the sense that it creates another world, in which connections transcend the apparent time and place of the poem, its present. The plurality of possible meanings in birds and apples (although China is the world's primary producer of apples) simultaneously distance the poem from its present and keep it grounded in the present. The suggestion of a coded language develops a sense of privacy and intimacy that seems at odds with the declaration of the opening line and its evocation of distant places.

This combination of relationship between a coded language and a personal intimacy occurs in other poems. In 'Memorial Day 1950' (17) the child wears 'tight blue pants' and tells his parents that they should 'love only the stones, the sea, and heroic figures'. A few lines on he 'wasn't surprised when the older people entered / my cheap hotel room and broke my guitar and my can / of blue paint'. I'm reminded of Wallace Stevens poem 'Man with a Blue Guitar', and that for Stevens blue is a symbol of the aesthetic imagination. This incursion into a private space by the 'older people' becomes an incursion into the purity of the potential aesthetic imagination. Blue is also symbolic of heaven and of purity—the Virgin Mary wears blue clothes in Christian iconography. The blue room reappears in 'Gli Amanti' (The Lovers), where the sexual potential of 'buttocks between the billowing drapes' is reduced to 'pearls dropped loudly to the floor' (126–7).

In 'A Letter to Bunny' (22–3) with its suggestion of the intimacy of a love letter he says 'I still fear to mention the blue / flowers. They scared me most and I / prolong other talk. There were fields of / them all around the place, all blue, all innocent'. Later in the poem he separates 'blue' from 'flower' when he asks '… is blue what they mean by / "shun posterity" and "the price of fame" and "fear of death"?'. Yet the next section, by referring to the epistolary form of the poem as a letter to Bunny Laing, seems to questions the idea that a poem can consistently transfer meaning outside the particular person to whom it is addressed: 'When anyone reads this but you it begins / to be lost. My voice is sucked into a thousand / ears and I don't know whether I'm weakened.' The poem, the lines suggest, can only be fully understood by the recipient. O'Hara might be 'away', as he says in the poem, and reduced to using the asynchronous medium of writing rather than the embodied immediacy of speech, but for Laing he is also 'here', in the writing. The final confession in the poem that he 'ran to you in the summer / night and upset us both' is followed by the reflection that 'even if the / rose has been ruined for all of us by religion / we don't accept these blue flowers'. The rose is, in Christian iconography, the symbol of hope, love and beauty. The rosary, and O'Hara's catholic background would have made the rosary an important part of his upbringing, was originally made of rosehips, hence its name.

In the poem 'A pleasant thought from Whitehead' (23) the narrator says 'I am feeling / assertive. I slip a few / poems into the pelican's / bill and he is off! out / the window into the blue!'. Blue is where the poems go to. In 'February' (53) the poem's narrator says 'I thought freshly and tried / to change the colour of my / habit.' Later in the poem however 'My old hurts / kept attacking me at odd / moments, after too many / songs, on public conveyances, / in the blue light of bars.' In 'Panic Fear' (59) he is lost in the woods and 'The sky may be blue, but not / so blue as it ought to be' and by the end of the poem 'the leaves are like teeth'. In 'Jane Bathing' (89), following a description of a swimming trip with (presumably) Jane Freilicher, 'Blue wraps itself about the pill we are spitting out anyhow'.

Many things in O'Hara's life are, of course blue. The sense of bright beach light in many of the earlier poems suggests a blue sea, and a blue sky over the sea. The jeans he wears are blue. His eyes are blue. A dictionary search reveals another range of references to blue. The police are the boys in blue and he wore a blue uniform in the navy. Blue refers to quality, to blue stocking, to blue chip, true blue, to winning a blue in playing for the first team and blue blood. It is also a reference to vulgarity, and blue language is a synonym for swearing and a blue pencil is an instrument of censor. Blue films are pornographic, and have a 'material of a sexual nature'. Blue is also an emotion, associated with both 'blues' and 'jazz' music. There are phrases which use the word blue; you can shout until you are 'blue in the face', and surprises can come 'out of the blue' or as a 'bolt from the blue'.

There are other references to 'blue' outside the usual dictionary references. In particular, a number of dictionaries of 'gay slang', including Paul Baker's *A Dictionary of Polari and Gay Slang* and various websites define blue as 'Gay, referring mostly to males'. The idea that O'Hara's poetry contains words that are used in a homosexual subculture, is neither new nor surprising. Gooch refers to it in his biography of O'Hara, and so does Hazel Smith in her book *Hyperscapes in the Poetry of Frank O'Hara*. Alice Parker in her study of O'Hara's work, *The Exploration of the Secret Smile: The Language of Art and Homosexuality in Frank O'Hara's Poetry*, published in 1989, refers to the way in which:

> The homosexual sub-culture also informed much of the subject matter celebrated in O'Hara's poetry. The ... deliberate use of that subject matter and of the language practice of the gay world [note the singular – practice] ... is of vital importance to any understanding of his poetic (Parker 1989: 8)

Yet, intriguingly, Parker does little of the close reading from across the range of O'Hara's work that is required in demonstrating its particular importance to the individual poems, although she frequently refers to gay slang as a kind of 'sedimented meaning'. Other commentators from the 80's, Bruce Boone for example (Boone 1979), are more interested in identifying a 'gay' praxis between life and writing, and prefer to work in more theoretical and generalised ways to demonstrate how O'Hara's work is part of 'gay' literature. What seems to get lost in these different approaches are the ways in which O'Hara's use of particular words spans European concepts of poetic language in Symbolism and Surrealism and more media driven postmodern linguistic surfaces. This does not simply mean that words in the poem can have different meanings, or that they are ambivalent, but that there are a number of concepts of language at play, and the idea of *how* it might mean.

The use of a code, and its suggestion that consistent meanings can be transferred between time and place so long as the reader has the code book (in this case a dictionary of gay slang) or, more pertinently for O'Hara, insider knowledge of the New York gay scene, is one possible language usage among others. I went back to the poem 'Today' (15), partly because it is a poem that has received attention from a number of critics. Malcolm Phillips in his essay 'Frank O'Hara Today' from

2004 (Phillips 2004: 37–46) describes it as being about the relationship between ephemera (kangaroos, sequins, pearls) and the recent horrors of wars (beacheads, biers). Marjorie Perloff in *Poet Amongst Painters* describes it as a 'short surrealist poem that is merely clever' (Perloff 1998: 43).) Gregory Bredbeck in his 1993 essay 'B/O — Barthes's Text / O'Hara's Trick', in which he develops an interest in 'the promise of a 'homosexual semiotics' (Bredbeck 1993: 268) similarly bypasses the individual words and their meaning and says that 'The "content" is mostly in terms of tone, an imitation of the breathy exclamatory conversations associated not with poetry but with gay bars' (Bredbeck 1993: 277). In his autobiography of O'Hara, Brad Gooch describes the poem as exhibiting a 'pragmatic American feeling for the solidity of objects' (Gooch 1993: 146). Lowney in his 1991 paper on O'Hara talks of 'Today' as a response to Williams' 'No Idea but in Things' and that the poem 'foregrounds the ephemerality of the everyday' rather than merely defamiliarising it. William Watkin in his online blog (Watkin 2007) refers to the way 'the homily of the ending ruins the poem' and how the 'final idea of meaning coming from their rock-like stability is disappointing'.

Yet O'Hara does assert at the end of the poem 'They do have meaning' (O'Hara 1979: 110). And the words in the poem do have other meanings. Kangaroos and aspirin are both WW2 or 1950s slang which refer to prostitution. Sequins simply reinforce the notion of the poem as a theatrical camp performance, while pearls, jujubes, rocks, beachhead and harmonicas are all slang references to genitalia or oral sex. The interjections in the poem; 'You really are beautiful' now becomes addressed to a lover and 'the stuff they've always talked about still makes a poem a surprise' can now be read as surprise and pleasure in his sexual encounters.

One reading, and particularly one that can only be understood by those with particular experiences, does not deny the possibilities of others. The idea that the references to gay sexuality could co-exist with more political references to war is supported by the poem 'October', apparently written two years later, and in which he combines a recollection of 'war headlines / and personal hatreds' (CP: 109–10).

The end of the poem similarly combines these two themes and while 'a truce / with Iran or Korea seems certain' the poem's narrator is being 'beaten to death / by a thug in a back bedroom'. (Although Gooch in his autobiography does link this poem to a specific event in O'Hara's life). The end of 'Today', 'They do have meaning', becomes wonderfully ambivalent, keeping the idea of the lists as ephemera, and as references to a sexual encounter, both in play, but also reinforcing the idea that all have meaning.

We therefore end up with multiple readings, unsurprising in itself, but made more complex by one reading having a consistent meaning to a very specific audience. It's almost as if O'Hara is providing two different poems, one that a knowing readership will 'get' with a smile, and one through which the dumb heteros must stumble, picking up meaning as they go, and clumsily trying to make sense out of the poem without knowing the code. An understanding of the different ways in which O'Hara uses language adds to the readings of his earlier work, but I believe it's more important in the way different uses of language can be followed through the trajectory of the *Collected Poems*. By the time of the 'End of the Far West', in O'Hara's words, 'There's nobody at the controls!' (483); the coded meanings have dropped away, leaving poems constructed out of a range of words and phrases often with direct reference to films, radio shows, and actual events or places, or apparently spoken by media characters. There are film stars such as Joel McCrea and John Garfield, the radio play *The Green Hornet*, the Bird Cage Theatre in Tombstone, 'Western' characters such as Wyatt Earp and Judge Hawkins and real events such as the World Fair. O'Hara has found his place within the 'voices'. He has developed uses of poetic language which allow him to use cosmopolitan ephemera without placing them in a symbolic framework. The interest is in the encountered phenomena and their working within poetic forms and O'Hara has moved to a more explicit application of the pluralities of situated meanings.

Ian Davidson is Lecturer in English and Creative Writing at Bangor University.

Ian Davidson

Works Cited

Baker, Paul. *Fantabulosa: A Dictionary of Polari and Gay Slang*. London: Continuum, 2004.

Boone, Bruce. 'Gay Language as Political Praxis.' *Social Text*, 1979: 59–92.

Bredbeck, Gregory W. 'B/O — Barthes's Text / O'Hara's Trick'. *PMLA*, Vol. 108, No. 2 Mar., 1993: 268–282.

Gooch, Brad. City Poet: *The Life and Times of Frank O'Hara*. New York: Knopf, 1993.

Lowney, John. 'The "Post-Anti-Esthetic" Poetics of Frank O'Hara,' *Contempory Literature*. 32:2, Summer 1991: 244–264.

O'Hara, Frank. *Collected Poems*. Berkeley: University of California Press, 1995.

Parker, Alice C. *The Exploration of the Secret Smile*. New York: Peter Lang, 1989.

Perloff, Marjorie. *Frank O'Hara, Poet among Painters*. Chicago: University of Chicago Press, 1998.

Phillips, Malcolm. 'Frank O'Hara Today.' *Edinburgh Review* 114. 2004: 37–46.

Smith, Hazel. *Hyperscapes in the Poetry of Frank O'Hara*. Liverpool: Liverpool UP, 2000.

Watkin, William. http://williamwatkin.blogspot.com/search?q=frank+o%27hara+today+meaning+ (May 31 2007)

The Public Language of Global Warming
in Peter Reading's -273.15

CARRIE ETTER

For some years now, Peter Reading has constructed his books as polyphonic sequences. That is to say, the unpaginated texts present, in place of individual poems, recurring voices as well as an array of different 'languages.' As David Kennedy describes it, these sequences 'are works of collage in which apparently pre-existing voices and documents are incorporated but not assimilated in a manner that strongly recalls the modernism of Pound, Williams and Zukofsky' (127). The blurring of generic boundaries in such a poetic enterprise, as Thomas Day remarks in his review of the volume, suggests that poets write not just for one another, but for a larger public as well (180).

In his latest volume, -273.15, or, absolute zero, the temperature at which all molecular motion stops, Reading presents science journalism as a public language, which is to say that it is marked by common social use and function. I say science *journalism* to highlight its audience: science journalism aims to reach the general public, as opposed to scientific papers, whose audience generally consists of other scientists. In terms of style, science journalism generally consists of declarative statements and supplementary exposition. To be accessible to the lay reader, its sentences are often fairly short and direct, and as it frequently addresses cause and effect, its sentences tend to be active rather than passive. One form of science journalism allows for what we might consider poetic effects in its use of rhetoric, and that is in the science editorial, which regularly appears in popular science journals as well as in daily newspapers.

Reading's use of science journalism as one of the recurring texts in -273.15 urges its public ownership, suggesting the need for the lay person to come to terms with global warming personally and take responsibility for it. That is not to say that the book holds out much hope for salvation; on the book's first page, Reading makes clear the direction he sees global warming headed with its terse statement: '(After the heatwaves: Heat Death, Entropy, / Absolute Zero...).'

Emphasising this public ownership, Reading introduces the language of science journalism to the book in the asides within an everyman's:

and didya read how a survey of all them Brit birds and butterflies shows there's some sorta population decline?, [Yes, in a series of censuses that combed about every square yard of England, Scotland and Wales over forty years, more than 20,000 volunteers managed to count each bird, native plant and butterfly they could find. They reported that the populations of all the species surveyed were in sharp decline— many extirpated completely.] and didya read how two surveys of 1,200 sumthin plants showed a decrease of 28%? [Yes, frail planet undergoing its sixth great extinction—Cambrian, Devonian, Permian, Triassic, Cretaceous, Holocene]

Here, to suggest the science journalist's voice responding to the everyman's, the bracketed sections each begin with the journalist's agreement, evoking the sense of speech rather than writing. The language becomes slightly more colloquial in the second aside, with the journalist calling Earth 'frail planet.'

The next appearance of science journalism, five pages later, now foregrounds that language, with two asides providing different functions:

thus we know that Global Warming, rather than causing gradual, centuries-spanning change, will push the climate to tip-point, fast. The ocean/atmosphere system controlling their frail planet's climate will change things radically— maybe in less than a decade. [The struggle naught availeth.] And consider the geopolitical implications. And consider the urgency of overwhelmed societies, the haves and have nots. And consider the 4% of the Arctic ice cap melted per decade since 1970, the decline of the North Atlantic's salinity reduced over the past forty years, the possible effect of this on the Great Atlantic Current, the cooling of much of Europe and the U.S. if the flow ceased, the droughts, the dust-bowls and the ashes... [You, at the back, should've sat up and fucking well paid attention]

Amid what reads as a science editorial, Reading places two asides. The first comes from Arthur Hugh Clough's poem, for which the title is the first line: 'Say Not That the Struggle Naught Availeth.' In its original context, this line exhorts the addressee to fortitude in the face of battle, yet it has since been used widely with other connotations in editorials, speeches, essays, and reviews.[1] Here, however, Reading revises the exhortation into a declaration when he deletes the first three words, 'Say Not That,' and simply declares 'The struggle naught availeth'; which is to say, it is too late for human intervention to diminish or curb global warming to any significant degree.

The second aside could represent a number of possible voices, and I read it as the poet's persona, frustrated and angry. The reader and industrial countries generally are conflated into the 'you,' the student who sits at the back of the class to avoid responsibility for learning, and in the poet's claim that the addressee 'should have fucking well paid attention' lies an accusation of neglected responsibility.

As already indicated, science journalism is just one of the many languages or voices in *-273.15*, alternating among pastiches of Christopher Smart's 'On My Cat Jeoffrey'; fragmented reports of the destructive effects of climate change, both recorded and predicted; an everyman's account of the same, as we saw in the first passage; the poet as speaker in direct address; and exchanges between the poet and Noye, as Noah was called in medieval mystery plays. This is to say, that while all the various languages and passages address climate change, the language of the science journalist is just one. This sense that the science journalist must compete among other voices to be heard is reinforced by the inclusion of fragmented reports (*Figure 1*, opposite). These passages come from an article, 'Climate Collapse,' originally published in the American newsstand magazine *Fortune* and widely reprinted.[2]

Portions of this article appear four times in the course of the book, and each time the text appears in some way distorted. The first time looks like a photocopy of the article as it appeared in print, but the copy is poor and obscured in a number of places. The second and third appearances of a passage from the article are in the same typeface as most of the book, but it begins and ends in the middle of sentences and letters are missing from many words. The last extract looks as though it has taken from the magazine appearances of the article enlarged quotations inset in the course of the piece. In all the disfigured extracts, the reader can

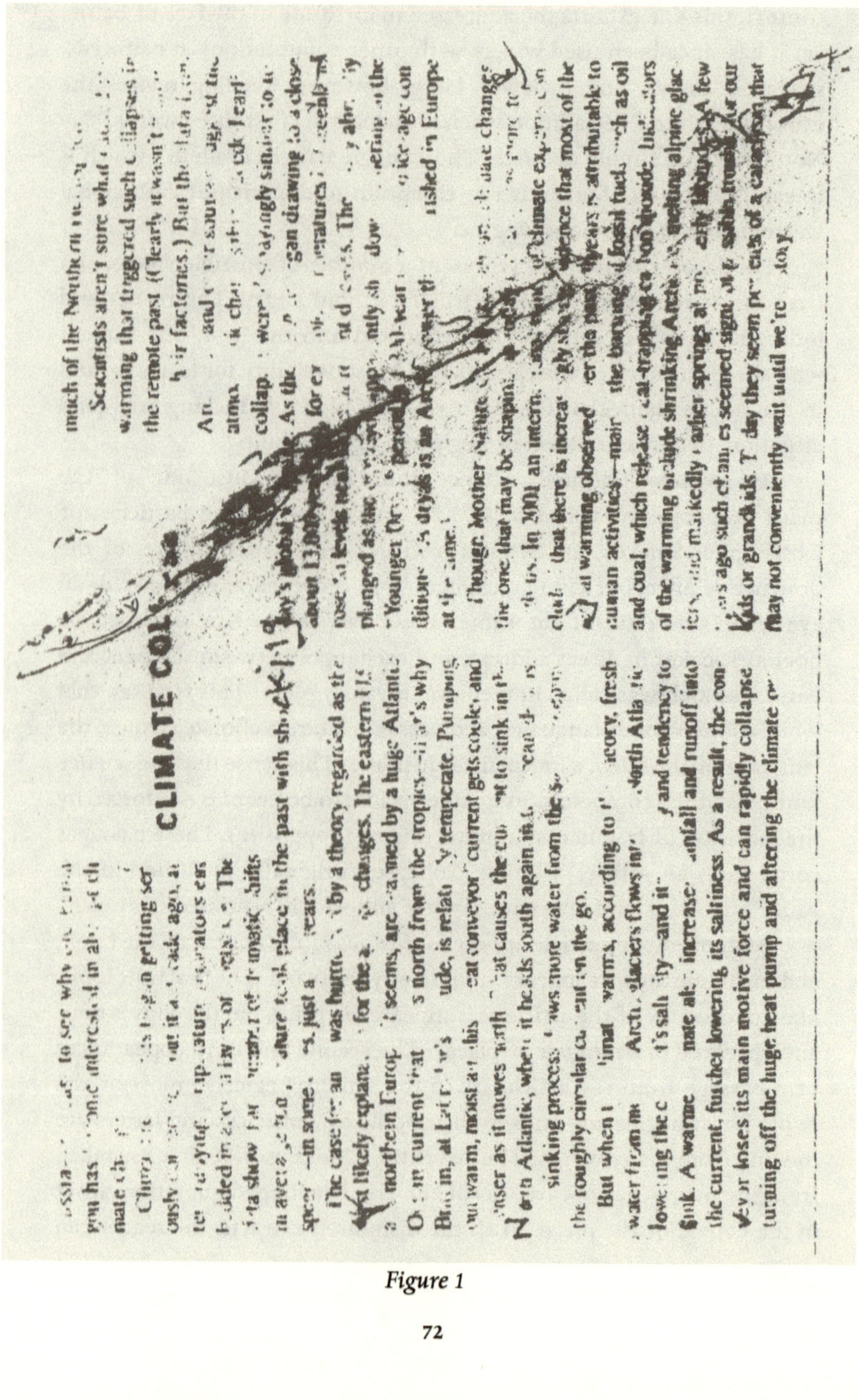

Figure 1

only make out so much of the article and only with some effort. These presentations mimic the lay reader's anticipated experience of reading articles on global warming: only so much information is apprehended or retained, and only the patient, active reader will take anything away.

The book's last found text comes from an adaptation of a European Space Agency/NASA press release that was widely used by the media, 'Hubble Sees Galaxies Galore.' As the title indicates, this piece concerns not global warming but distant galaxies. The point behind including this extract becomes clear when the aside that follows is taken into consideration. One piece of information in the Hubble extract is that the light of the stars photographed was generated more than 13 billion years ago, while the aside notes that the light from Mars takes ten minutes to reach Earth and The Big Bang occurred approximately 14 billion years ago. This time scale underscores the quickness with which humanity has triggered devastating climate change. As Kennedy writes, '[I]t is important to bear in mind that Reading's work is always concerned to measure the human, and, particularly, its late twentieth century manifestation, against the largest possible temporal perspective' (121).

And what have we gained in exchange? What have we risked the world for? Further down the same page as the Hubble extract, Reading portrays a Western speaker in the quotation: 'And *this* one is taken from the Mosque, darling; it took *ages,* though, to get there. And *these* are the Smiths—I can't remember *where* they are from.' One of the greatest contributors to the quantity of CO_2 in the atmosphere has been leisure travel, and here Reading satirizes one such traveller to imply that such travel has become a class marker in and of itself, with such travellers so intent on racking up the miles that they gain little if anything from the experience.

The last time science journalism appears in *-273.15*, poet and science journalist are one. The passage begins, 'Past midnight, and my umpteenth Zinfandel. / I type the Science Spotlight for tomorrow's / edition of the *Global Sentinel*.' The column indents and the 'Science Spotlight,' it seems, begins with a declaration of the extent of species loss and a range of examples. As the piece nears conclusion, the poet interjects, 'In my same column thirty-eight years back:' and then suggests he quotes with another indent: 'The earth is threatened by its own pollution... / Western Industrial Man is facing, *now*, not just a challenge but a climacteric...' Though the poet persona's science journalism does not lack any letters, as in the passages from 'Climate Collapse,' his message, too, has not fully reached its audience, for thirty-eight years after his and other such warnings, the planet has lost many species with far more expected to disappear. As the passage concludes, 'Those in the *front* seats should have paid attention' (emphasis added). Where in the earlier combination of science journalism and poet persona, Reading says that those at the back should have paid attention, now he looks to those at the front—those who one would have expected to respond to such a crisis have failed to respond appropriately and in time.

The last page of the book looks like a photocopy from the author's own notebook (*Figure 2*, overleaf). Lyn Hejinian, in 'The Rejection of Closure,' suggests how we might read this page:

> "Field work,' where words and lines are distributed irregularly on the page [...] are obvious examples of works in which the order of the reading is not imposed in advance. Any reading of these works is an improvisation; one moves through the work not in straight lines but in curves, swirls, and across intersections, to words that catch the eye or attract attention repeatedly' (43–44).

The work of the final page, and the work of *-273.15* as a whole, is to effect such 'curves, swirls, and... intersections' among the book's voices and languages. We may begin by reading down the page, but the final marks on it return us to the book's precarious balance. -273.15, absolute zero, is circled, then scribbled out, as though Reading initially saw 'the unequal struggle' ending there but, more hopefully, decided against it. Then Reading appears to change his mind again, writing 'stet' and making a tick beside it. As Hejinian continues, 'The implication (correct) is that the words and the ideas (thoughts, perceptions, etc.—the materials) continue beyond the work. One has simply stopped because one has run out of units or minutes, and not because a conclusion has

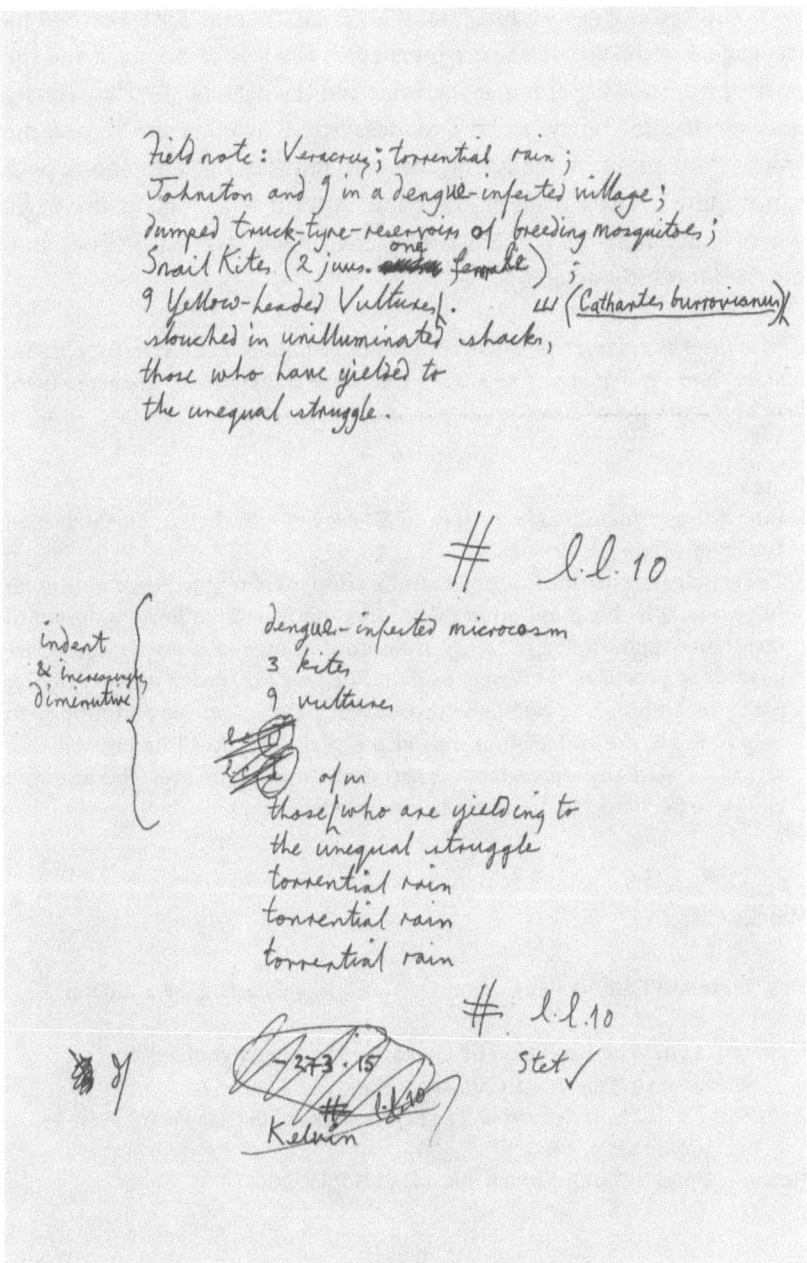

Figure 2

been reached nor 'everything' said' (47). *-273.15* may have reached its last page, but the use of science journalism as a public language and the poet's invocations to those at the front and the back of the class clearly indicate that Reading's 'words and ideas' strive to 'continue beyond the work.' Perhaps it is a publishing accident, but Reading's notebook page is not quite the last page of the book. After it is a single blank page, where more remains to be written, envisioned, argued, hoped, and, most importantly, acted on.

Carrie Etter is Lecturer in Creative Writing at Bath Spa University. The two images from Peter Reading's -273.15 (Bloodaxe Books, 2005) are reproduced here by permission of Bloodaxe Books Ltd.

Notes
[1] Interestingly including a review in *Ecology* of the book, *Environmental Impact of Mining in Canada.*
[2] The article stresses the economic ramifications of climate change, as though to persuade its business-oriented readers that it will be less expensive to invest in ameliorating it rather than continuing with environmentally hazardous practices. This may explain Reading's choice of this particular piece, its ambition to persuade those with political power and money to help improve the situation. It may also explain why Reading presents the article as virtually unreadable, expressing pessimism over the author's ability to persuade such people to change their ways.

Works Cited

Day, Thomas. 'Diluvian Discontents.' *Cambridge Quarterly* 35.2 (2006): 178–80.

Hejinian, Lyn. 'The Rejection of Closure.' *The Language of Inquiry.* Berkeley: University of California Press, 2000. 40–58.

Kennedy, David. *New Relations: The Refashioning of British Poetry 1980–94.* Bridgend: Seren, 1996.

Reading, Peter. *-273.15.* Tarset: Bloodaxe Books, 2005.

Confidence in Lack

ALLEN FISHER

It has been evident that in spite of, or in deference to, the restricted and figurative use of language, much that is public has involved catching a logic bus into an aspiration for coherence. My apprehension and understanding has been that good poetry is at great variance to these expectations, both with regard to logic and coherence, and with regard to making vocabulary available and this should lead to confidence in lack—a confidence that poetry, when it is at its most efficacious, cannot propose logic, as it is variously perpetuated in paternal and public thinking, and cannot aspire to coherence, as this is also prescribed. In particular, poetry needs to make these proposals or have these aspirations in a period following the extensive pollarding and retro-harnessing of modernism and its huge variety of materialist and fascist engines.

In February 2007, writing for *Nature*, an international weekly journal of science, a group of physicists, supported by the American army, Yale University and commerce, proposes to resolve the issue of photon number states in a superconducting circuit where they expect to distinguish between coherent and thermal fields, apparently two different orders of vocabulary, and create a photon statistics analyser which will generate non-classical states of light and perform superconductivity quantum bit-photon conditional logic, the basis of a logic bus for a quantum computer.

This paper thus celebrates a dilemma. Poetry and engagement with a public, like Science and its public, provide a significant mismatch, potentially involved with self-deception, or more often, active deceit. The premise for this mismatch derives from a range of incapacities and inabilities necessary to the frailties that underpin vulnerabilities that contribute to sensitive thinking; that contribute to the æsthetic and ethical basis for all written, poetic and scientific practice. This is a necessary dilemma in conceptual and historical terms, set against the western proposals for logic and its modernist aspiration to cohere.

Schuster et al, in February 2007, produced a description of a circuit quantum electrodynamic experiment within the permitted parameters of exactness and with confidence in lack of exactness. 'Electromagnetic signals are always composed of photons ... and the discreteness of the photon's energy is usually not evident.' (Schuster 515–518)

Schoelkopf, et al., note that, 'Cavity quantum electrodynamics (Mabuchi 1372–1377) is a test-bed for quantum optics (Walls) that allows investigation of fundamental questions about quantum measurement and decoherence, and enables applications such as squeezed light sources and quantum logic gates. Humans cannot see the processes of these applications. To achieve virtual observation, 'an atom is placed between two mirrors, forming a cavity that confines the electromagnetic field and enhances the atom-photon interaction strength... The results obtained ... also suggest a method for conditional logic.' (Schuster)

Since ancient times, thought in the west has debated the difficulties between direct perception and information derived from machines, between demonstrations of truth and informed presumption or speculation. Plato, a seminal thinker behind the demands of logical thought and truth, provides a number of significant examples. His description of how poets operate in his *Apology* immediately indicates the difficulty proposed.

Grube translates Plato's words, 'After politicians, I went to the poets, the writers of tragedies and dithyrambs and the others, intending in their case to catch myself being more ignorant than they. So I took up those poems with which they seemed to have taken most trouble and asked them what they meant, in order that I might at the same time learn something from them. I am ashamed to tell you the truth, gentlemen, but I must. Almost all the bystanders might have explained the poems better than their authors could. I soon realized that poets do not compose their poems with knowledge, but by some inborn talent and by inspiration, like seers and prophets who also say many fine things without any understanding of what they say. The poets seemed to me to have had a similar experience. At the same time I saw that, because of their poetry, they thought themselves very wise men in other respects...' (Plato, Grube 22)

Poets' confidence in lack was further criticised by Plato in Book X of *The Republic*; Cornford's translation concludes, 'that all poetry, from Homer onwards, consists in representing a semblance of its subject, whatever it may be, including any kind of human excellence, with no grasp of the reality. . . . the poet, knowing nothing more than how to represent appearances, can paint in words his picture of any craftsman so as to impress an audience which is equally ignorant and judges only the form of expression; the inherent charm of metre, rhythm, and musical setting is enough to make them think he has discoursed admirably about generalship or shoemaking or any other technical subject. Strip what the poet has to say of its poetical colouring and I think you must have seen what it comes to in plain prose.' (Plato, Cornford 323–324)

Eric Havelock, Charles Olson's source for much of the information and rhetoric of his poetics, addresses Plato's attack in his *Preface*, Plato opens by characterising the effect of poetry as a 'crippling of the mind... It is a kind of disease, for which one has to acquire an antidote. The antidote must consist of knowledge "of what things really are". In short, poetry is a species of mental poison, and is the enemy of truth.' (Havelock 4) On this notion of truth we might as well continue our deceit. 'Plato's target seems to be precisely the poetic experience as such. It is an experience we would characterise as aesthetic. To him it is a kind of psychic poison.' (Havelock 5)

Plato banished the poets 'because *their* means of discourse obstructed the development of the abstract powers it was Plato's concern to nurture.

Charles Olson means to re-establish the poets, that is, give them a public language, 'but first (Olson) must re-acquire for them certain habits of language and thought which Platonic revolution caused to become displaced.' (Stein 103)

The practice of 'syntax by apposition' is related for Olson to his understanding of the 'shift' in cosmological perspective effected by Relativity Theory and the institution of the spacetime continuum as the context for events of reality. In *The Special View of History* Olson emphasizes: 'the inclination of purpose and chance, accidence and necessity, form and chaos, as being within actual process, is the cosmological justification' (Olson) for 'concretism.'

Adorno links the failing coherence of modernism with what he identifies as the semblance of meaning. 'All modern art after impressionism, probably including even the radical manifestations of expressionism, had abjured the semblance of a continuum grounded on the unity of subjective experience, in the 'stream of lived experience.' Whatever is integrated is compressed by the subordinating authority of the whole so that the totality compels the failing coherence of the parts and thus however once again asserts the semblance of meaning.' (Adorno 155)

Even Foucault prefers to re-establish the states of coherence and writes, 'We are no longer inside truth but inside coherence of discourses, no longer inside beauty, but inside complex relations of forms. (His understanding, of what I would call a pattern of connectedness, is to discuss identity) ... integrating itself into the coherence of discourses or the indefinite network of forms, effaces, or at least renders vacuous and useless, that name, that individuality whose mark it carries for a certain time and in certain regards.' (Foucault 290–291)

Julia Kristeva offers a kind of contra-view when she writes of Hannah Arendt, 'Having ... acknowledged the disconnection between the enacted story and the narrated story, Arendt does not believe that the essential feature of narration can be found in the fabrication of a coherence within the narrative or in the art of spinning a tale,' (Kristeva 73) which she subsequently confirms, 'If we get too wrapped up in the coherence of a plot, we forget that the main goal of plot is to disclose,' (Kristeva 74) and 'It can manifest that essential logical process can only if it becomes action itself,' (Kristeva) and as Kristeva had noted earlier, 'Action, even as Arendt understands the term, cannot by itself guarantee a free and creative life. The resumption of the 'life of the mind,' on the other hand, is capable of providing such a guarantee, as Arendt provided in her later writings.' (Kristeva 42) 'Arendt's experience as an intellectual proves, quite simply, to be an examined life – a life uprooted from biology through labor, work, and, in particular, action. Yet it was also a life that harboured the superior form of human existence that is varied and incomplete thinking, provided such thinking is shared with a diverse and contradictory world.' (Kristeva 20)

Private pretence and public affirmation, particularly in terms of recommending a range of ethical activities, lead poets to a range of addresses, from engaged involvement to escape. What poetry is capable of through deliberate and detailed poetic investigation, of poetic form and the variety of vocabularies used, often leaves the best poetry incapable of matching the public demand for continuous and linear expression, ostensibly the demand for complete meanings. The subject is too large to encompass and the paper demonstrates this in its confident approach to its lack of solutions and any proposal for complete understanding.

The ideas of coherence and endings – or plot knowing – as substance for aesthetic choice are anathema to intelligent feeling and all engender a lack of confidence.

Alan Turing predicts this in his unsolvability solutions. Turing proved 'the existence of mathematical problems that cannot be solved by any systematic method. (Turing 576) 'The argument of 'Solvable and Unsolvable Problems' illustrates why it is that the need for intuition cannot always be eliminated in favour of formal rules.' (Turing 580) Turing, in the conclusion to his essay, writes, 'The results which have been described ... are mainly of a negative character, setting certain bounds to what we can hope to achieve purely by reasoning. These, and some other results of mathematical logic may be regarded as going some way towards demonstration, within mathematics itself, of the inadequacy of 'reason' unsupported by common sense.' (Turing 595)

Earlier I drew from what Bernard Williams stressed about the degree to which polite ethical thought in the societies of the West today rests on or involves self-deception or more active deceit. It depends on the private pretence, public affirmation, or purposeful suggestion of what is, for those concerned, knowably false.

Jim Baggot, out of the physics department in Seattle, pulls this into a different focus. He writes, 'as we increase the displacement of the destination of the (electromagnetic) wave further and further, the spacetime dependencies of the waves become increasingly 'misaligned': at specific points in spacetime, peak no longer lines up with peak, trough no longer lines up with trough. The result is destructive interference and a loss of coherence of the light.' (Baggot 48)

'The pragmatism and instrumentalism typical of the younger generation of theoreticians involved in [Quantum] theory's early development, such as Heisenberg, Dirac, and von Neumann, called for a coherent mathematical framework which worked. To these physicists, it did not matter too much that the deeper meaning of the theory's concepts appeared to become increasingly disconnected from the reality that the theory was trying to describe.' (Baggot 59) It thus begins to equate to poetry in public display.

The need is engendered from a raft of considerations and this paper celebrates its lack of completeness or holistic conception. The addresses are first to connectedness and entanglement (and their direct relation to æsthetics and its components in consciousness and cognition). This will be further damaged by a hint of discussion about measurement, unsolvability, errors, disconnectedness and the inevitability of decoherence. The trail leads into rudimentary understandings of quantum lack and the resulting confidence position, leads, as it does so, into the underlying topic of this paper which I first named, with a gobstopper in my mouth, truth, and second with a celebration of Keats' Negative Capability, 'when a man is capable of being in uncertainties, mysteries, doubts, without any irritable reaching after fact and reason.' (Keats) Complexed by the entanglement, the rhetoric of contradictions, in his 'Ode to Autumn'.

Two further examples from scientific literature will add to this range: Raymond Bradley et al, are an eclectic group of scientists who have measured Northern Hemisphere temperatures during the past millennium, concerned with inferences, uncertainties, and limitations. An abstract from the group noted 'expanded uncertainties prevent decisive conclusions.' (Bradley 759–762)

Elsewhere, in a follow-up to journalistic mistakes, they state 'more widespread high-resolution data are needed before more confident conclusions can be reached.' (MacKerron 627)

Gordan MacKerron reviewed *Uncertainty Underground: Yucca Mountain and the Nation's High-Level Nuclear Waste*, (MacKerron 633) 'Varying degrees of reassurance emerge from ... [a] hydrology-based set of papers, from virtually complete (with regard to hot upwelling) to much more uncertain (transport in the saturated zone) data.... There are good sections in the volume 'on the distinctions between risk (the probability of something going wrong, from which decision-making at least has a starting point) and the inevitable uncertainties over very long periods into the future, for which precise risk levels are unknown and probably unknowable.' (MacKerron)

Paying attention to confidence and its lack, Roland Omnès provides a good summary for decoherence. 'The most worrying difficulty in the interpretation of quantum mechanics is certainly the problem of macroscopic interferences, which are apparently predicted by any linear theory and practically never observed so much so that they would look absurd if we were to see them. Reflection on this problem as led to the idea of decoherence, which is certainly the most important discovery of the modern interpretation,' (Omnès 73–74) which after a stretch of examples notes, 'When a history includes a phenomenon that is specified by decoherence, there can be no consistency for a later property that would contradict this phenomenon or its consequences.' (Omnès)

One cannot logically deny it. It gives rise to an indelible record that retains its consequences, even if it is erased or dissipates. It remains present in the inward details of the wave functions, decoherence forbidding the consistency of its negation.

Any history that would try to (logically) deny it (or its later consequences) necessarily violates the consistency conditions and therefore the rules of logic.' (Omnès 83)

'Of course, authority is also displayed in the handling of theory and interpretation, but in the humanities and the sciences alike, one can have confidence in that only if one can respect the writer's dealings with everyday truths.' (Williams 22) I am again in the condition Arendt knew as 'The frailty of human affairs.' (Kristeva 45) The patterns of connectedness, that appear to have the potential to enhance coherence, are necessarily imprecise. They are a 'shift from a world structured by boundaries and enclosures to a world increasingly dominated, at every scale, by connections, networks, and flows.' (Mitchell 5)

'Connectivity has become the defining characteristic of our twenty-first-century urban condition.' (Mitchell 12) But poetry needs planned imperfection, not exactness of match, '...the ultimate network will operate by the quantum-magical means of quantum entanglement and teleportation of quantum states from one site to another.' (Mitchell

10–14) As Arendt put it, 'She did not herself want to become entangled again; she wanted to be the immutable soil which absorbs everything into itself.' (Arendt) 'As information carriers in quantum computing, photonic quantum bits have the advantage of undergoing negligible decoherence. ... One solution is to introduce an effective nonlinearity by measurements resulting in probabilistic gate operations. (Prevvedel 65)

Omnès clarifies the entanglement condition exemplified in Keat's 'Ode to Autumn' and leaves it undone when he notes, 'The entangled state is a ... superposition of two distinct physical systems. (Thus a state of two realities in a collage.) This is a very frequent situation because any composite system whose wave function is not simply a product of the wave functions of its components is entangled.' (Omnès 38) (I think of cognition and its relation to æsthetics.) John S. Bell was more concise in his 1986 paper, there are 'mathematical counterparts in the theory to real events at definite places and times in the real world (as distinct from the many purely mathematical constructions that occur in the working out of physical theories, as distinct from things which may be real but not localized, and as distinct from the 'observables' of other formulations of quantum mechanics, for which we have no use here).

As poets writing with history hitting us in the face, we may have no problems understanding Mitchell's statements that 'The digital world is logically, spatially, and temporally discontinuous,' and 'The discontinuities produced by networks results from the drive for efficiency, safety, and security.' (Mitchell 15) But 'If you want to build complex structures' presumably like poems can be, there's no point trying to minimize errors, and to correct errors automatically when they occur.' (Mitchell 69)

Bernard Williams asks, 'Can the notions of truth and truthfulness be intellectually stabilised, in such a way that what we understand about truth and our chances of arriving at it can be made to fit with our need for truthfulness?' (Williams 3) Can poetry be made to 'fit' our need for public language? In his book *Instant Confidence*, Paul McKenna proposes a reversal of Plato, 'When you know what you're talking about, you don't need to know what you're going to say.' (McKenna)

Allen Fisher is Professor of Poetry and Art at Manchester Metropolitan University. The complete version of this essay is published in Confidence in Lack, *Sutton, Surrey: Writers Forum, 2007.*

Works Cited

Adorno, Theodor. *Æsthetic Theory,* trans. by Robert Hullot-Kentor and edited by Gretel Adorno and Rolf Tiedemann, London: Athlone Press. 1997.

Arendt, Hannah. *Rahel Varnhagen: the Life of a Jewess,* ed. Liliane Weissberg, trans. Richard and Clara Winston, Baltimore and London: John Hopkins UP, 1997.

Baggot, Jim. *Beyond Measure: Modern Physics, Philosophy, and the Meaning of Quantum theory,* Oxford: Oxford UP, 2004.

Bradley, Raymond S., Malcolm K. Hughes, and Michael E. Mann. *Geophys. Res. Lett.,* 26 (1999).

Foucault, Michel. 'On the Ways of Writing History' in Michel Foucault, *The Essential Works of Foucault 1954–1984,* volume 2, *Aesthetics,* edited by James D. Faubion, trans. Robert Hurley and others, London: Allen Lane, 1998.

Frunzio, L., J. Majer, B. Johnson, M.H. Devoret, S.M. Girvin & R.J. Schoelkopf. 'Resolving photon number states in a superconducting circuit,' *Nature,* 445, (2007).

Havelock, Eric A. *Preface to Plato,* Oxford: Basil Blackwell, 1963.

Keats, John. 'Letter 9, to George and Thomas Keats, 21st December 1817', in Stanley Gardner (ed). *Letters of John Keats,* London: University of London Press, 1965.

Kristeva, Julia. *Hannah Arendt,* trans. Ross Guberman, New York: Columbia UP, 2001.

Mabuchi, H. & A.C. Doherty. 'Cavity quantum electrodynamics: Coherence in context', *Science,* 298, (2002).

MacKerron, Gordan. Review of *Uncertainty Underground: Yucca Mountain and the Nation's High-Level Nuclear Waste,* edited by Allison M. Macfarlane and Rodney C. Ewing, MIT Press, 2006, *Nature* 442, 2006.

McKenna, Paul. *Instant Confidence: The Power to Go for Anything You Want!* London: Bantam, 2006.

Mitchell, William J. *Me ++ The Cyborg Self and the Networked City,* Cambridge, Massachusetts: MIT Press, 2003.

Olson, Charles. *The Special View of History,* edited by Ann Charters, Berkeley, California: Oyez, 1970.

Omnès, Roland. *Understanding Quantum Mechanics,* New Jersey: Princeton UP, 1999.

Plato. *Apology,* edited by John M. Cooper, translated by G.M.A. Grube, Indianapolis: Hackett Publishing, 1997.

Plato. *The Republic,* translated by Francis MacDonald Cornford, Oxford: Oxford UP, 1941.

Prevvedel, Robert, Philip Walther, Felix Tiefenbacher, Pascal Böhi, Rainer Kaltenbaek, Thomas Jennewein, and Anton Zeilinger. 'High-speed linear optics quantum computing using active feed-forward', *Nature,* 445 (2007).

Schuster, D.I., A.A. Houck, J.A. Schreier, A. Wallraff, J.M. Gambetta, A. Blais, L. Frunzio, J. Majer, B. Johnson, M.H. Devoret, S.M. Girvin and R.J. Schoelkopf. 'Resolving photon number states in a superconducting circuit,' *Nature* 445 (2007).

Stein, Charles. *The Secret of the Black Chrysanthemum,* Barrytown, New York: Station Hill Press, 1987.

Turing, Alan, 'Solvable and Unsolvable Problems', *The Essential Turing: Seminal Writings in Computing, Logic, Philosophy, Artificial Intelligence, and Artificial Life,* edited by Jack Copeland, Oxford: Clarendon Press. 1954.

Walls, D.F. & Milburn, G.J., *Quantum Optics,* Berlin: Springer, 2006.

Williams, Bernard. *Truth & Truthfulness: An Essay in Genealogy,* New Jersey: Princeton UP, 2002.

'Norms and Forms':
10 Years of the British & Irish Poets e-mail list

KIT FRYATT

British and Irish Poets is an e-mail list hosted by the National Academic Mailing List Service, known as JISCmail.[1] JISCmail is an online tool to promote communication in the UK-based academic community, though its subscriber base is international. Subscribers to British and Irish Poets, like the members of any JISCmail list, receive a copy of each email posted to the list, either at the moment of posting, or in a daily digest format. It is possible to search the list archive through the JISCmail site.

The British and Irish Poets list was begun by Richard Caddel in 1996. Initially just 'British Poets', the title of the list was expanded to British and Irish Poets in 2001, though this change was not registered with JISCmail until early in 2007. To the perpetual irritation of its Irish members and managers, it picked up the nickname 'Britpo', which has never been entirely suppressed, despite Mairéad Byrne's spirited suggestion that the accepted abbreviation should be B&I, in homage to the defunct Irish Sea ferry company B&I Line.[2] The list has been managed by successive teams of 'list owners' (JISCmail's term); the current owners of the list being Mairéad Byrne and Ian Davidson. Despite their rather proprietorial title, the list owners have fairly limited powers. They do not censor or delete posts to the list, though they have the power to suspend or ban users who break the list's rules. There are about 240 subscribers to the list: an international grouping by no means confined to Britain and Ireland. Few of these have been members since the beginning of the list, though one or two remain. Most subscribers are 'lurkers'—people who (presumably) read the list, but rarely contribute. Regular contributors constitute a small group of maybe 10–15% of the membership.

Like most JISCmail lists, British and Irish Poets performs a number of functions. Members may use the list to discuss poetry and criticism, to ask questions, to link to websites of interest to the membership, to advertise upcoming events and publications, to review books, readings, festivals and conferences, and to post their own work. Some of these things happen much more often than others, and I'll try to suggest some reasons for that below.

When I first started to read B&I, in 2003, subscribers were greeted with a welcome message (which I quote in the title of this essay) explaining the interests of the list in the following terms:

> British and Irish Poets orients itself towards the contestation and contestability of norms and forms both in and through poetry. We recognise that ideas as to how this might and can be achieved will vary, often vigorously, and the list seeks to promote such vigour. Debatable terms such as "innovative", "linguistically-innovative", "experimental" and "new" are not out of place here. Once again their interpretation is part of the robust nature of the list.[3]

This message has now been replaced with one whose tone is informative, rather than manifesto-making:

> British and Irish Poets (B&I Poets) is a poetry listserv focused on non-mainstream traditions of Irish and British poetry, particularly in the 20th and 21st centuries. [...] The current focus of the list is on work that is often described as "postmodern", "innovative" or "experimental". [...] The capacities and limitations of categories and definitions have themselves been subjects of vigorous debate on the list, as have the possible meanings of "British and Irish", in the fluid terms of poetry.[4]

Byrne and Davidson's version of the welcome message places the 'vigorous debates' about terminology and identity in the continuous past implied by the perfect tense. This is not necessarily because of any sense that these are now settled questions, or there is no longer a need for manifestoes in poetry, but because they have excited such ire in the past that a temperate tone seems prudent. Discussions about such 'debatable terms' can become bewilderingly arcane and vociferous: the list archive for January and February 2005 records a choice example centering on the term 'academic verse'. This did mutate eventually into a genuinely valuable discussion of the value of MFA programmes in poetry. Equally often, however, such spats over terminology sputter out into mutual frustration or continue into areas very remote from poetry and poetics.

The format of an e-mail exchange lends itself to elaborate refinements of definition, but it is sometimes hard not to grow impatient with B&I's nitpicking.

Like most online communities, B&I can be bafflingly cliquish, generating with equal regularity exclusive in-jokes and protests about all the exclusive in-jokes. A more irascible exclusivity emerges when an uninformed visitor posts a message out of step with the list's interests and prejudices. A tendency to bemoan exclusion from a cultural centre dominated by identitarianism and formal flaccidity while at the same time fiercely guarding peripheral credentials is still evident in both British and Irish neo-modernism, as is a certain amount of automatic bashing of the mainstream. Status-hungry and mock-populist statements such as Don Paterson's plea for poets to be regarded as tradesmen in his 2004 T.S. Eliot lecture—'Only plumbers can plumb, roofers roof and drummers drum; only poets can write poetry'—get savaged on B&I, where a more high-minded list might consider them beneath notice.[5] Shooting fish in a barrel is fun, and by no means confined to neo-modernism. But this entertaining blood-sport has the potential to retard criticism sympathetic to neo-modernism, making it reactive and provincial when the poetry it engages is inventive and internationalist.

Despite being occasionally maddened by B&I, I continue to subscribe, always scan the daily digest that appears in my email inbox, occasionally contribute. Its archives are one of a few sites that I recommend to students and others who want to find out more about 'different' poetry. It's been going for as long as (or longer than) most people have been familiar with the Web, and as such represents a very substantial volume of comment. The new welcome message recognizes B&I's status as a resource for readers, and requests: 'Please keep in mind, when you are posting, that you are contributing to a valuable archive.' (It remains to be seen whether this memorandum will have the desired effect on member etiquette.)

There are a couple of things that don't happen on B&I, though, or don't happen much. The first of these is an undoubted blessing, the second I miss and regret, since it doesn't seem to happen very often on the Web at all. Blessings first. B&I contributors don't post their poems for comment. Posting of poems is encouraged by the list managers, but it's an invitation accepted by very few; the regular exception being the indefatigable Jeff Harrison, who posts a poem every couple of days. Critique of a posted poem is quite taboo, it seems (this is an unwritten rule), an almost unalloyed good in a poetic climate in which workshops are posited as a cure-all. Poems reside in the archives as threads in themselves, accessible but with no critical apparatus.

Also rare on B&I is the experience of close reading as a communal activity, a conversation. Neither the relatively formal, structured close study of poems which takes place in academic seminars, nor the kind of informal and spontaneous discussion which usually ends with the participants knee-deep in books pulled off the shelf to make a point, has an online equivalent on B&I, or indeed, elsewhere on the Web. The lack of practical critical conversation on the B&I list prompted me to consider some of the obstacles to establishing such a dialogue. As noted above, the e-mail exchange format lends itself to discussion of filigree precision, with sometimes exasperating results. It's just that those discussions tend to apply themselves to the vocabulary of criticism rather than the vocabulary of poems themselves. Attention to the political, social or poetic-factional implications of language use, with participants challenged repeatedly to define their terms, leads further from the original comment or query until it is forgotten altogether.

Neo-modernist poetics need not be unsympathetic to close reading in itself. Indeed, it's hard to see how it can be, when contemporary neo-modernist groupings owe so much both to Language poetry and to Cambridge formalism. And yet, in expressing reservations about the value of close reading it is precisely these formalist tendencies—the word 'academic' gets used a lot—that are identified as a problem. In response to a query I posted on B&I about the relation between close reading and neo-modernist practice, Tim Allen, editor of the online magazine *Terrible Work*, posted this:

> I would hazard a guess that there are very few such poets who have not indulged in close reading, either instinctively or through intellectual habit, of both their own and others' material. The reflexivity necessary would be a real struggle without it.

This is not to say that close reading is always beneficial —a certain type of close reading when practised by certain personalities seems to actually prevent them from writing anything themselves, or it can make them write stale and lifeless stuff, the kind of thing we used to call "academic verse"—you could recognise it a mile off. One of the problems we are experiencing at the moment, and this is another can of worms, is that in many cases current "academic verse" looks and sounds so much like the kind of thing that the avant [-garde] crowd have been producing for years, but I digress. Speaking for myself, close reading of my own and others' poetry has been vital for both understanding and practice.[6]

(That 'can of worms', inevitably, was opened, and close reading soon forgotten in the welter of definitions of 'academic' and 'avant-garde'.) This statement is interesting on a number of points. First, that close reading might be an 'instinctive' reflex for certain readers is borne out by my own experience of working on poetry with university students of English—some grasp the principles of close reading rapidly and are quick to apply them to other forms of criticism, others never accommodate themselves to it. Their protests often take the inchoate form of 'I don't like dissecting poems; it kills them', which means, I think, that the student wants to engage with the process of the poem's composition, but lacks critical vocabulary with which to do it. Approaching my query from a pedagogical perspective, Rupert Mallin replied,

> I understand critical practice but have a problem with "practical criticism." Here in my hand is The Practical Criticism of Poetry —a textbook—edited by C.B. Cox and A.E. Dyson (1969). As textbooks go it's good for its time, employing the "direct method" of seminar discussion to analyse poems. Because it works out of that discussion, contrary and contradictory opinions mix with a body of questions. OK to this point. Yet, if the poet isn't dead, the text lies there dead. Nothing wrong with dead poems at all! However, we can't engage with the practice and method of the poet thereby. Even in this textbook, the lively questioning runs into the wall of history and its weight. Indeed, despite the students' enthusiasm, even this criteria of criticism builds their critical faculties as it

closes doors on their own practice. Hence I'm nervous about
"criticism."[7]

The extent to which we still lack a shared critical vocabulary which
can articulate 'process' in poetry is illustrated by Allen and Mallin's
independent use of the same metaphor employed by the typical
frustrated student: the poem as corpse.

An opposition between poetries of 'process' and 'product' doesn't
get us much further, since almost all poems are both commodities and
instances of temporizing rhetoric. Nor does that opposition map neatly
onto the modernist / mainstream one: Neo-modernists may 'set out in
determined opposition to the idea of writing as a consumer item', as
J.C.C. Mays writes of Trevor Joyce,[8] but the close relationship of neo-
modernist poetry to small-press and limited edition publishing means
that innovative poetry often comes packaged as a desirable object;
meanwhile the referential relationship between text and world that is
a given in much mainstream work alerts us to the temporality of its
language.

There's a conflict in neo-modernist critical thinking about practical
criticism, which can be explained in a literary-historical sense by the
phenomenon Allen refers to—the partial absorption of principles
of innovative poetry into an Establishment mode. Neo-modernist
scepticism about close reading is partly oppositional: a reaction against
a critical practice that has made peripheral poetries palatable (and
susceptible to dilution by) a dominant centre. And yet close reading
remains essential to neo-modernist practice: 'the reflexivity necessary
would be a real struggle without it', by which Allen seems to mean both
self-reflexivity and intertexuality.

The response of many B&I contributors to my reflections might
be that the quality of posts to the list has declined, and that discussion
has largely been replaced by links and advertisement. Many members
have left because of this perceived drop in standards. I don't share
their pessimism, though it is clear that the list has changed. In 1996,
the subscribers shared interests and reference points to a far greater
degree than they do today. There were also far fewer online resources
for the discussion of poetry, less competition for contributors' attention

and efforts. It is in the nature of online communities to mutate, and sometimes to die off altogether, but long before they do, they generate complaints of a nostalgic nature. The earliest threads of this kind that I have found in the B&I archive date from 2001 (a more diligent eye might find earlier ones);[9] somehow the list has staggered on for another six years.

In Internet terms, B&I is elderly, and its email-list format primitive. And yet its superannuated format might be the reason for its dogged survival. An email list is not a forum, which you can choose to visit, log into and in which discussion is separated into themed threads. It is not a monologic blog, in which any comment is dependent upon and addressed, at least in the first instance, to the blogger. As long as you choose to subscribe, B&I mails will continue to come into your mailbox. Their content may hold little interest for you, or it may hold much, but they are difficult to ignore entirely. The email list offers the possibility of receiving the unexpected as mail. And an interest in the 'unexpected', better than any of the 'contested or debatable' terms—'postmodern', 'innovative', 'experimental'—unites the subscribers to British and Irish Poets.

Kit Fryatt is Lecturer in English at Mater Dei Institute, Dublin City University.

Notes
1. *British and Irish Poets*, JISCmail, <http://www.jiscmail.ac.uk/lists/british-irish-poets.html>. Accessed 10th April 2007.
2. Mairéad Byrne, 'B&I', *British and Irish Poets*, (10th October 2006). Accessed 11th April 2007.
3. cris cheek and Trevor Joyce, 'Welcome Message', *British and Irish Poets*. In Mairéad Byrne, 'Welcome message', email to Kit Fryatt, 26th November 2006.
4. Mairéad Byrne and Ian Davidson, 'Welcome Message', *British and Irish Poets* (January 2007) Accessed 11th April 2007.
5. Don Paterson, 'The Dark Art of Poetry' *The Poetry Library*, South Bank Centre, http://www.poetrylibrary.org.uk/news/poetryscene/?id=20 Accessed 17th April 2007.
6. Tim Allen, 'So much rubbish everywhere', *British and Irish Poets* (2nd February 2005) Accessed 29th March 2007.

[7] Rupert Mallin, 'So much rubbish everywhere', *British and Irish Poets* (1st February 2005). Accessed 29th March 2007.

[8] J.C.C Mays, 'Scriptor ignotus, with the fire in him now [The Poetry of Trevor Joyce]' *Dublin Review* 6 (Spring 2002) 42–65, 59.

[9] See Lawrence Upton, 'Re: british-poets list changes', *British and Irish Poets* (2nd March 2001). Accessed 17th April 2007.

'Replace the Mindset':
Tony Lopez and the Turning of Public Language

ROBERT HAMPSON

I. *Expect some slippage*[1]

In his essay, 'Innovative Poetry in English', Tony Lopez defines the British 'innovative poetry' of the last thirty years as 'liminal writings' whose 'investigations of language necessarily involve the same issues as those explored in the most recent literary and cultural theory'.[2] As examples of those issues he instances 'the social construction and the inscription of gender identity; the relations between ideology and economy, colonial history and race; the politics of language, literary form, and canonicity' (122). And he describes the investigation of language in terms of this poetry's 'presentation of language as a mediating threshold between our senses of internal and external experience' (122)—hence the term 'liminal writings'. He then outlines some of the forms this investigation has taken in practice:

> ... through strategies which delay and confound simple naturalization, through the development of procedural and aleatory techniques of composition, through the questioning of "natural" seeming speech-based and free-verse poetics, the suspension and confusion of gender identity, the deformation of advertising rhetoric, the radical revision of pastoral, the development of open and serial forms, the recovery of separate "expert" vocabularies, and so on. (122)

We can all think of appropriate examples for each of these practices. In his essay, Lopez uses this overview of recent practice as the starting-point for a reading of poems by Denise Riley, Allen Fisher, J.H. Prynne and Tom Raworth. He shows how Riley's subversion of the first person displays 'the process and the constructedness of the gendered voice' (124) in *Mop Mop Georgette*. He analyses Fisher's 'language of constant slippage and unreliable assembly' (126) in *Brixton Fractals* and delineates also some of Fisher's compositional procedures in that work such as 're-arranging word-order; inventing new word-clusters that echo the sounds of existing lines; describing the process of building the work itself; and by transcribing events happening locally at, or close to, the time of writing' (129). He demonstrates Prynne's choreographed collision of different kinds of language — economics, advertising, technical innovation — to explore the connections between the globalised economy of capital and the oppression of the producers of that wealth. He shows how Prynne's 'Punishment Routines' is 'patterned by these political concerns as they register in the formation of the language of that time' (134). He ends with Raworth's 'indeterminate and provisionally open' poetry, where 'each new line adjusts the provisional status of what went before by seeming to connect, or not, and by adding incrementally' (134), as Andrea Brady has demonstrated, with 'various kinds of social and political meaning ... evoked, left behind, picked up again, joined to other issues' (137).

I want to use this essay to approach Lopez's own work. What he says about the four poets he has selected for this essay, as we would expect, often throws an illuminating light upon his own practice. The work I have selected is *False Memory* (Salt, 2003). Two sections from this collection, 'Corneal Erosion' and 'Studies in Classic American Literature' first appeared in *Negative Equity* (Equipage, 1995). An earlier edition of *False Memory* (The Figures, 1996) contained six sections: 'Corneal Erosion', 'Studies in Classic American Literature', 'Assembly Point D', 'Blue Shift', 'Non-Core Assets', and 'Brought Forward'. *Data Shadow* (Reality Street, 2000) consisted of five further sections: 'Imitation of Life', 'Restricted Zone (slight return)', 'Speckled Noise', 'Always Read the Label' and 'Radial Symmetry'. The Salt edition brings together these 11 sections. I should say here that each section consists of ten 14-line poems. One immediate question that springs from this is whether *False Memory* is one long poem divided into sections, each section consisting of ten stanzas, or whether this is an extensible sonnet sequence. The second question is what are the principles of selection, combination and permutation. Andrew Crozier, in his review for *Jacket* of the edition published by The Figures, suggests that 'Lopez has no story to tell or opinion to editorialise; if anything he is beguiled by the tectonics of number systems'. This, however, is not an aspect of the work I want to consider here. Rather I want to consider how the poem operates through the kind of 'choreographed collisions' of different kinds of language that Lopez analysed in Prynne's work and how he produces that 'language of constant slippage' that he finds in Fisher's work. The third poem (or stanza) in the section called 'Imitation of Life' begins as follows:

> This application form should be accompanied
> By voice-mail and personal calls. Fair Athena,
> It's easier if we don't see one another (63)

The first line derives clearly from the world of bureaucracy—the official administrative language of job applications or grant applications. Subsequent lines bring in the registers of personal relationships ('It's easier if we don't see one another'), formal grammar ('For first and second persons only, and agree/Like adjectives'), classical translation ('We did not pull down the city ...'), advertising ('Forget lip gloss'), and possibly an echo of the start of Lyn Hejinian's My Life ('A moment white ...'). Part of the pleasure of the poem is the cutting from one register to another—and the constant demand on the reader's attention that this cutting makes. There is generally (but not always) a change of register at each line-end, but there is also often a cut within the line to produce an internal torque. This constructivist aesthetic produces, for example, the amusing discontinuity of the juxtaposition of classical invocation ('Fair Athena') with mundane twentieth-century personal drama ('It's easier if we don't see one another'). The poem is sensitive to the welter of discourses, knowledges and processes (bureaucratic, advertising, etc) through which we daily have to navigate and negotiate, but, above all, it registers, the coercive pressure of this linguistic context: not only the fragmentary glimpse of grammatical regulations, but also the repeated instructions that shape and construct modern subjectivity ('The application form should be accompanied', 'It's your natural charisma that should shine through', and 'Forget lip gloss, discover our new creation').

Compare this with the fourth poem in 'Speckled Noise'. Again, the poem works by appropriating and turning the language of power: 'You may wonder why our ready-gel is causing / So much excitement'. These opening lines don't merely ironise and send up the language of advertising. Like the reference to 'natural charisma' in the previous poem, the word 'excitement' points precisely to the alienated nature of the commodity culture we live in. The opening lines of the poem invoke the systems of advertising, print-media, and banking. The next four lines lay these systems bare through the juxtaposition of company liquidation, consumer special offers, and the treatment of citizens:

> Normally
> A liquidator is appointed but buyers
> Get no compensation. Simply collect 8 tokens
> And join the queue for post-war restitution
> (Don't even ask about the price of dental work).

The poem creates a sense of a society in crisis. At the same time, *pace* Crozier the internal and external cutting does seem to have a palpable intent: it conveys a clear sense of the imposed powerlessness of the citizens — fobbed off with tokens, consigned to queues, deprived of affordable health care. But even the functionaries and administrators of this system do not escape its alienation: 'Lawyers, notaries and fiduciaries have all / Just been lonely too long.' The technical language of legal professions is cut into the language of popular song ('too lonely too long'), but, as in Denise Riley's poem 'Lure 1963', the echoing of the words of a popular song suggest that even strong 'personal' emotion is inescapably mediated and commodified. The final lines juxtapose images of extreme deprivation ('No chair, no table, no straw mattress, nothing') to the availability of 'vast sums of production money' that have been 'held back', presumably in some film-making deal. The poem negotiates the language, processes and systems of a mediated and commodified culture, registering alienation and deprivation, and exposing (again and again) the structural inequalities that the production of these mediated and mediatised discourses are designed to occlude.

II. *Forget lip gloss*

In his essay on Ted Berrigan's '5 New Sonnets: A Poem', Lopez reproduces and then presents a reading of the first of these 5 sonnets.[3]

He engages with the discontinuities and incoherences of the poem, before revealing that '5 New Sonnets' had been 'mechanically derived' from Berrigan's earlier book *The Sonnets* (1964): the first line taken from the first line of the first sonnet, the second from the second line of the second sonnet, and so on.[4] This article suggests Crozier's comment on Lopez's beguilement by the 'tectonics of number systems'. I want to focus, however, on other issues raised by the article. Lopez's attempted reading of the sonnet constructs a 'speculative narrative ... sustained by formal connections that are both thematic and acoustic ... across the irregularities of punctuation and grammatical inconsistencies' (48). Lopez's own sonnets, if that is what they are, are also collaged and linguistically discontinuous, but they are, to use his own word, 'smoothed' in terms of punctuation and grammar. They are coherent on the levels of syntax and punctuation, but semantically discontinous. It is at this level that, like Berrigan's sonnets, they articulate and embody 'a poetics of discontinuity and incompleteness' (51). There is a similar play of continuity/ discontinuity on the formal or generic level. Lopez's 14-line poems, like Berrigan's, allude to the sonnet form but generally without reference to the rules of the form. As Lopez says of Berrigan's sonnets: 'there is no division into octet and sestet ... no scheme of rhyme ... and no snapping into place of dialectic synthesis, whether in sestet or clinching couplet' (48). Lopez notes that Berrigan uses the mechanical method of production in order to 'detach the composition as far as possible from expression of "self" or "voice"' (51). There is a similar rejection of the psychological 'as the locus of the poem's meaning' in Lopez's work.

Lopez's sonnets are marked by coherences and incoherences both internally and across the section of which they form a part. The first section, 'Corneal Erosion', for example, has recurrent motifs of flooding, fire, the sounding of sirens, university business, numbers (perhaps a game of bingo), building processes and procedures, a Conservative party conference, trains and aeroplanes. Thus the first poem begins: 'And I don't see how we can win. The first faint / Intermittent soundings of the sirens may be ignored.' In retrospect, the first line can be taken to refer either to a game or to the General Election — as well as figuratively

— although it is not clear who 'we' is. The second line is picked up a few lines later ('But you should vacate the building when you hear/A continuous note') and these instructions generate a narrative that returns in the second poem: 'I heard the call, looked up, went on with my work'. The interlinking of these sonnets is also foregrounded by other devices. Thus the third poem ends with a reference to 'sparse woodland', which leads directly, without any full stop, into the first line of the fourth poem: 'Or what used to be called campus development'. In the same way, the fourth poem ends with the question: 'But would you pay for a job title and office space?', which the next poem answers: 'Me neither. Though it depends what you mean by pay.' This poem in turn ends with the statement: 'Bourgeois is an obsolete type size, pronounced *berjoyce*.' The sixth poem begins: 'Of course the search committee and shortlist were bourgeois' causing a momentary hesitation between type size and social class, documents and individuals.

The separate sections of the work have their own thematic foci. The second section, 'Studies in Classic American Literature', for example, appropriately enough seems to have an American setting and invokes various American authors—Melville (and whaling), Thoreau, Robinson Jeffers, Ted Berrigan and Ezra Pound. It also recalls Joseph Beuys's performance with a coyote in New York (17) and John Lennon's 'Imagine' (15), while Keats's definition of 'negative capability' is split across two poems: 'That is when a man is capable of being in uncertainties' (13) 'Without any irritable reaching after fact and reason' (20). A later section, 'Brought Forward', similarly revolves around the Windsors and Lady Diana, necrosis, finance, a costume re-enactment of Sir Francis Drake's colonial landing, a murder, the Jones-town cult suicide and fragments of Keats's poetry relating to death. At the same time, as this second reference to Keats suggests, certain thematic materials recur not just within the same section but across the various sections of the whole series.[5] In each case, Lopez works with 'public language' in various forms: the public language of bureaucracy or advertising, but also the public language of newspapers, biographies, scientific reports and literature.

In this part of my essay, as Will Montgomery has pointed out to me, I have introduced (and discussed) a different form of 'public language' from that with which I started in part one: I have been discussing literary fragments and literary form rather than bureaucratic language. This raises a number of questions. What does it mean to use (and abuse) the sonnet form? What does it mean to cite and re-contextualise literary fragments? Is this the same kind of 'turning' of public language as the turning of bureaucratic language? Should we, perhaps, see the sonnet form (like any literary form or genre) not merely as a liminal space, mediating between the practitioner and the reader, but as a public space that perpetually invites its own re-appropriation and turning? The foregrounded and inescapable restrictions of the sonnet form invite an inventive response, while the history of the form, from Petrarch and Shakespeare through Elizabeth Barrett Browning, Christina Rossetti and Hopkins, is a history of formal variation. In the same way, are the literary citations to be seen as appropriating and critiquing a discourse that has shaped us—or are they to be seen as a form of public language that provides a site for resistance? Are they a benign form of public-private partnership? Lyn Hejinian reminds us in her essay in this collection that public life is not just civic life, but also extends to the daily life we lead. In addition, in her reading of Barrett Watten's 'Mode Z' and Wordsworth's *Prelude*, she shows how the public can be made private in order to be made public again—and also suggests, more specifically, how the citation of the poetry of predecessors creates a space of intersubjectivity that might even provide the basis for an alternative mode of sociality. I am particularly interested that Lopez should cite and recycle Keats's definition of 'negative capability', since this was originally a private communication, part of a letter to a friend, never intended for publication. But it also offers a stance towards experience, a programme that is based on negativity, on lack, as the basis for openness and acceptance. In addition, in the context of 'Studies in Classic American Literature', it inevitably brings with it D. H. Lawrence—and also Charles Olson's engagement with Keats and negative capability. It signals, in other words, a tradition of engagement and re-interpretation. Allen Fisher, in 'Confidence in Lack', also quotes this definition of 'negative capability'. In *Necessary Business*, Eric Mottram describes the 'resources' he lists at the end of his poetry collections as 'a multiple area of reference, of shared information'.[6] In this spirit, I would want to suggest again that the repeated citation of predecessors creates an alternative mode of (transhistorical) sociality, that, in turn, provides the basis for another form of critique.

III. *the price of dental work*

I want to end by considering the words provided in the title for this conference: 'poetry and public language'. As I was writing this paper, I was very conscious of the ambiguities of the phrase 'public language'. Does it mean language produced by the public or language produced for the public — the language of government, administration, bureaucracy? In what I have said so far, I have clearly assumed the latter meaning as my starting point, although I have subsequently included other language made publicly available. Philip Terry, in his paper, has provided a very concise and elegant summary of the possible relations between the two terms of the conference title.

In writing about 'appropriating' and 'turning' language, I have also obviously had in mind the situationist practice of *'detournement'*. In 'Basic Banalities', Raoul Vaneigem declared:

> The spontaneous acts we can see everywhere forming against power and its spectacle must be warned of all the obstacles in their path and must find a tactic taking into account the strength of the enemy and its means of recuperation. This tactic, which we are going to popularise, is *detournement*.[7]

In the same issue of *Internationale Situationniste*, in an essay called 'All the King's Men', Guy Debord addressed 'power's capture of language': where 'Information is power's poetry (the counterpoetry of the maintenance of law and order)', poetry is 'nothing other than liberated language, language that wins back its richness'.[8] In 'Captive Words', Debord similarly asserted that *detournement*, the Dadaist negation, the subversion of official 'public' language, must become 'a permanent practice of the new revolutionary theory', since it is 'impossible to get rid of a world without also getting rid of the language that both conceals and protects it, without stripping bare that language's truth'.[9]

The practice of *detournement*, as outlined by Vaneigem and Debord, is clearly central to the situationists' demand for 'a critical attitude to all existing conceptualisations and values, since these are necessarily the tools with which the existing reality must be undermined and must be used against the structures within which they have developed'.[10] By implication, then *detournement* in Lopez's poems performs a similarly critical function, particularly in relation to official language and the language of media and advertising.

I was also aware of the polysemous nature of the title as a whole. Were we being asked to consider, for example, poetry which adopts a public or civic voice? Could we discuss 'public language' without also discussing 'public space'? And what does it mean to discuss poetry and public language in the context of a university conference? I had originally intended to end with a consideration of graffiti, urban skateboarding, and *par cours* as attempts to re-take urban spaces. However, this original intention was itself high-jacked by another event, which got me thinking about public language and the 'turning of public language' in a different way.

I recently attended a conference on 'The Art of Partnership' organised by the London Consortium for Arts and Creative Enterprise (April, 2007). One of the speakers was a man called Charles Leadbeater, who was introduced as 'a thinker'. Leadbeater's subject was the transformative social effect of digital media. He celebrated a world in which his six-year-old son can put up a website in thirty minutes and be out there; in which there were no more experts but knowledge was co-produced (Wikipedia was his example here); in which digital media recreated the 'commons'—a public space in which knowledge, information, creative work could be freely exchanged. There are a number of attractive and a number of problematic aspects to this Utopian vision. My interest in Leadbeater, however, was sparked further by the conference biodata. Here he was described as 'a leading authority on innovation and creativity': he was a writer, a consultant, a government adviser. More precisely, Leadbeater is a former FT journalist; a former adviser to BP-Amoco; and a key figure in Demos, which describes itself as 'The Think Tank for Everyday Democracy'. In 1998, he was invited to write a White Paper for Peter Mandelson on 'Building the Knowledge-Driven Economy', and he presumably still has an input into government thinking on education and the arts.

I thought then that I would end this paper on 'public language' by looking at some of his works for insights into what might be government agendas for education and the arts—and the 'public language' of democracy and the 'commons' in which these agendas might be couched—within which our own activities are likely to be inescapably situated. I started with Leadbeater's 1999 book *Living on Thin Air: The New Economy* (Viking, 1999), which described itself as a blueprint for 'a radical modernizing project'. If I tell you that its account of 'knowledge capitalism' ('creating, disseminating and exploiting new knowledge') begins with the assertion that 'globalisation is good' and finance capital is a 'maligned force', you probably have all you need to know. An earlier pamphlet, *The Rise of the Social Entrepreneur* (Demos, 1997), provided a richer source. Social entrepreneurs, it explains, 'identify under-utilised resources—people, buildings, equipment—and find ways of putting them to use to satisfy unmet social needs'. Put like this, they sound entirely beneficial, appropriating and detourning 'under-utilised resources'. But there is also, for me anyway, an undertone of asset-stripping. (I recall from *False Memory* how 'So-called high performance/Investment funds prey on carefully selected/Undervalued companies' [107].) The four examples the pamphlet uses sound entirely benign, turning a Victorian Hospital closed down by the NHS into a centre for AIDS or a tenants' co-op expanding into a housing scheme. However, there are also glimpses of another agenda: 'They help communities to build up social capital which gives them a better chance of standing on their own two feet'. What emerges, the pamphlet suggests, is 'a modern type of social welfare for the twenty-first century' (8). I was interested that Will Rowe in his essay went back to Beveridge and the post-war creation of the welfare state. Leadbeater asserts that 'the welfare state was designed for a world that no longer exists' and is now 'in decline'; his solution is a return to the charitable provision that ran from the twelfth to the nineteenth-century. He contends: 'We need to revitalise and modernise that voluntaristic, non-statist tradition'. He goes on: innovation is 'the only hope we have of maintaining the quality of welfare while reducing its costs' (12), and the way to make services more efficient is through 'contracting out and privatisation'. Not surprisingly, he also envisions that 'Large-scale private sector companies may also become involved in social innovation through partnerships with voluntary organisations and a growing role in the provision of education and social insurance' (12).[11] In other words, the welfare state is too expensive, and the future will be charitable provision for the poor and private provision for everyone else, but this is presented in terms of 'more room for experiment and diversity' (12).

The Rise of the Social Enterpreneur also asserts what it calls 'the ethic of individual self-fulfillment and achievement' as 'the most powerful current in modern society': 'The choosing, deciding, shaping individual who aspires to be the author of their life, the creator of their identity, free within their private sphere, is the central character of our times' (14). This heroic individual is also implicit in Gordon Brown's commitment last week in his Budget speech to 'greater choice, greater competition, greater contestability and greater accountability'. Leadbetter asserts: 'social progress is measured by the expansion of individual choice within this private sphere'. He goes on triumphantly: 'This individualism is not just consumerist. It is also moral.' (14). Brown is drawing on the same neo-conservative economists to make the same re-affirmation of Adam Smith's model of individuals rationally pursuing their own selfish interests as the basis for a dynamic social order.

Will Rowe, like Lyn Hejinian, was suggesting certain epochal moments. For Britain, these were the post-war consensus that produced the welfare state—and the Thatcher election victory. This initiated the challenge to the welfare state—and an over-turning of the values behind it—that has been sustained and extended by New Labour. This has involved a certain turning of public language—'innovation', 'modernisation', 'Everyday Democracy'. It has also created the material and cultural conditions in which our own practice is situated. Tony Lopez's critical turning of public language provides, I would argue, a model for critical engagement with these material and cultural conditions.

Robert Hampson is Professor of Modern Literature at Royal Holloway, University of London.

Notes

1. Both the title quotation and this heading come from Tony Lopez, *False Memory*, (Salt, 2003), 95, 5.
2. Tony Lopez, 'Innovative Poetry in English', *Meaning Performance: Essays on Poetry* (Cambridge: Salt), 122.
3. Tony Lopez, '"Powder on a Little Table": Ted Berrigan's Sonnets and 1960s Poems', *Journal of American Studies*, 36. 2 (2002), 281–292; reprinted in *Meaning Performance*, 45–57.
4. 'Powder on a Little Table', 50.
5. The section titles point to some of these common areas: damage to the body, literary criticism, emergency procedures, science, finance, accounting, aesthetics, and consumerism.
6. Allen Fisher, *Necessary Business: J.H. Prynne, Eric Mottram, cris cheek*, *Spanner* 25 (July, 1985), 184.
7. Raoul Vaneigem, 'Basic Banalities, II', *Internationale Situationniste* 8 (January, 1963), reprinted in Ken Knabb (ed.), *Situationist International Anthology* (Berkeley: Bureau of Public Secrets), 125.
8. Guy Debord, 'All The King's Men', *Internationale Situationniste* 8 (January 1963), 29–33, reprinted in Tom McDonough (ed.), *Guy Debord and the Situationist International: Texts and Documents* (Cambridge, MA: The MIT Press, 2004),153–158, 154. By 'information' Debord means instrumental language; by 'poetry', he does not mean poems. He goes on to assert that 'for the SI it is a question of a poetry *necessarily* without poems': 'all of our descriptions of poetry have nothing to do with reactionary, old-fashioned authors of a neoversification, even when they align themselves with the least ancient of formal modernisms. The program of fulfilled poetry is nothing less than the creation of events and their language at the same time, inseparably' (155).
9. Guy Debord, 'Captive Words (Preface to a Situationist Dictionary), *Internationale Situationniste* 10 (March 1966), 50–55, reprinted in McDonough173–80, 173.
10. Sadie Plant, *The Most Radical Gesture* (Routledge, 1992), 166.
11. This model of voluntary sector and private sector taking over from the public sector has recently been imposed on the probation service. Ministers have argued the greater flexibility of the voluntary sector, offering responses tailored to local conditions, and have tended to downplay the likely outcome of private sector take-over.

The Sad Note in a Poetics of Consciousness

Lyn Hejinian

I should begin by offering some explanation of my title and then distancing myself from it a bit before, perhaps, returning to it once again. I'm comfortable with the second phrase of the title, 'a poetics of consciousness,' as an adequate description of what I practice, successfully or not. It's 'the sad note' that's disquieting; it attempts to speak, all at once, of an immensely complicated concept ('negative dialectics' in the broadest possible sense); of an historical moment, this one, to which anger, pessimism, and grief seem to me to be the only sane responses; and of an imageless affective presence—not quite psycho-social zone nor experiential register though it's responsive to both, even excessively—that's by its nature, as by intention, resistant to description and key to some of our best art, albeit not the best-selling, nor the best understood.

I got to the 'sad note' as a way to mark our *historical moment*, although the actual phrase came to me in reading about another one, though one that was also dolorous. In *The Dialectical Imagination*, Martin Jay's remarkable history of the Frankfurt School from its inception through the historical moment of Nazism and into the commencement of the Cold War, Jay quotes from, and comments on, an essay ('Gedanke zur Religion') by Max Horkheimer. The relevant phrase comes toward the end of the passage and is Jay's. 'To Horkheimer, all absolutes, all identity theories [which would resolve differences upward into a transcendent Hegelian universal] were suspect. Even the ideal of absolute justice contained in religion [...] has a chimerical quality. The image of complete justice "can never be realized in history because even when a better society replaces the present disorder and is developed, past misery would not be made good and the suffering of surrounding nature not transcended." As a result, philosophy as he understood it always expresses an unavoidable note of sadness, but without succumbing to resignation.'[1]

That was the initial sad note of my title: *sadness* as a condition of political consciousness, public consciousness, but, especially, as a condition of historical consciousness; sadness in awareness of the irreparable character of inflicted suffering, the irrevocable, irreversible force of injury and its resulting pain—which has occurred, is occurring, will occur: a comprehensive and on-going condition. This sad note has everything to do with public life but little, it would seem, to do with poetry, but there it was, loud and clear, and three or four months ago, obeying the request for a title from the conference's organizer, I put it into my title and sent it nine time zones forward, from California to England.

'Philosophy [...] always expresses an unavoidable note of sadness [...]'; can the same be said of poetry? And if so, mightn't it then be the case that that note of sadness, which is customarily felt to be the most intimate aspect of a poem, the element that speaks to the innermost emotions of the reader from the most private emotions of the author, in fact has a public source? If the answer is yes, then the sadness in poetry is public; it is historical; it is informed by recognition that suffering cannot be made right.

This is a sad thought indeed, but I don't want to give up on the last clause of Jay's exposition: we may sound the sad note but 'without succumbing to resignation.'

The term 'consciousness' of my title refers not only to consciousness of the irrevocability of suffering, but I began there, at what I hope might serve as a threshold to historical consciousness, though I am still far from being able to give a comprehensive definition of what that term means. But certainly consciousness framed thus, as historical in some sketchy, incomplete sense, belongs to the sphere of care for the world, care more in the sense of concern, worry, than in any custodial sense. And it seems inextricably death-bound.

But in evoking consciousness, I want too to offer a glimpse of the obverse side of anxious, mournful care, to evoke care in the life-bound sense of curiosity. I am reminded here, not for the first time, of the last word of George Oppen's long poem 'Of Being Numerous': 'curious.' 'Why do we want to be here,' he said, speaking about that final moment in the poem in a letter I've cited before. 'Why do we want to be here—I would say: it is curious—the thing is curious—Which may be referred to, briefly, as O's Affirmation.'[2] The O, presumably, is for Oppen. But the O must also be for Nothing, Naught, ground zero of absolute negativity, a good place from which to begin.

I deploy consciousness as a means of beginning, and as a means of moving not only forward but also outward. Consciousness is good at externalization, at objectification, not only for the sake of study but also for the sake of argument. And this brings me to the question of 'poetics,' which is, by the way, what I hope I am doing here. This conference announces its theme as that of 'Poetry and Public Language,' and certainly the question of the language of public life has emerged as one of the central concerns of contemporary poetics. Public life is also its primary arena. Poetics marks out, creates, a social space in the terrain we term poetry. I would almost say that poetics is the public life of poetry, but to do so would suggest that poetry has a private life, and I am not convinced that this is the case.

Public life is not limited to civic life, the political; public life is life in the shared world, our given on-going lived reality. Public life is waking life—alert, conscious life—and that should be historical life, life without loss of context, life dense with temporality, in which historicity overflows ontology, becoming outwits being.[3] We should speak of poetry and public life in a way that links them inextricably together, so as to be assured of poetry without contextual loss. To add poetics to the continuum of poetry is to provide contextual gain.

As I see it, poetics doesn't break with poetry. Poetics is not an autonomous sphere of cultural work, its considerations are never independent of poetry as a method. Indeed, poetics is the sphere in which poetry loses (escapes) its autonomy. Nor does poetics explain poetry— poetry contains sufficient explanations of its own, sufficient reasons. But poetics makes us conscious of poetry, or of the poetic method: conscious of its dialectical as well as phenomenological entailments and potentials.

* * *

Mode Z

Could we have those trees cleared out of the way?
And the houses, volcanoes, empires? The natural
panorama is false, the shadows it casts are so many
useless platitudes. Everything is suspect. Even

clouds of the same sky are the same. Close the door
is voluntary death. There is one color, not any.

Prove to me now that you have finally undermined
your heroes. In fits of distraction the walls cover
themselves with portraits. Types are not men. Admit
that your studies are over. Limit yourself to your
memoirs. Identity is only natural. Now become
the person in your life. Start writing autobiography.

———Barrett Watten

1

When I first read 'Mode Z' many years ago, I was puzzled first by the title
(what kind of mode was 'mode Z'?) and last by the final line (how was
I to read, or to obey, or perhaps better disobey, the command to 'start
writing autobiography'?). It appears as the first poem in Barrett Watten's
1980 collection, *1–10*, where it functions somewhat as a prolegomenon,
and perhaps also, for reasons I'll get to shortly, as a gesture of homage.
The poem is given the same initial and signal position in Watten's 1997
volume of selected poems, *Frame*. At only twelve lines, 'Mode Z' is one
of his rare short poems. But if I may, I will appropriate to my own ends
a comment that Paul Valéry made with respect to art generally and
that Walter Benjamin too has quoted and apply it to this poem: 'We
recognize a work of art by the fact that no idea it inspires in us, no mode
of behaviour that it suggests we adopt could exhaust it or dispose of it.'[4]
I have been reading the twelve lines of Barrett's 'Mode Z' for a number
of weeks now, and I have more to say in its context than can be said
here today. For this occasion, I want to concentrate on the two points
that caught my attention years ago. Is—was—Barrett Watten serious in
urging us to start writing autobiography? And why is the title of the
poem 'Mode Z'? What is 'Mode Z'?

My initial thought was that the 'Z' in question refers to Louis
Zukofsky. It's an obvious possibility, although I also recognized that the
'Z' in the title could be more or less synonymous with 'X'—as cipher,
sign of the unknown or unnamed, sign of the missing, the absent, the

displaced ('his mark'), etc. That we can't answer whose mark adds serious complications to the (admittedly thus far dubious) prospect of mode Z's being the mode of autobiography. To write the life history of a person who's unknown, who's only a cipher? The notion is almost too much of an oxymoron, though it might serve—indeed has served, one way or another—as an interesting premise for a work of fiction. Aren't the hilariously and strangely fruitfully empty interiors of Samuel Beckett's works inhabited by just such figures?

But I return to my first hypothesis, that the 'X' which is here 'Z,' is the mark of Louis Zukofsky. I know that Barrett Watten at the time he wrote 'Mode Z' already had a longstanding engagement with Zukofsky's writings and with the possibilitites that the long- and almost conspiratorially-neglected Marxist, materialist strand of Modernism offered. Louis Zukofsky's *Autobiography* was published in 1970, ten years before Watten's *1–10*. It's a short book and not even a properly literary one. It is, essentially, a musical score, Celia Zukofsky's 'twenty-two settings to eighteen poems' of his, as Louis Zukofsky describes it in his brief, one paragraph prefatory comment. Apart from the songs' lyrics (which are all short, previously published poems by Louis Zukofsky), the only writing to appear in the book are five austere one-paragraph autobiographical statements, scattered between groups of songs and no more illuminating than the authors' bio-notes one finds in magazines. The *Autobiography* in its entirely is only 63 pages long, which is downright skimpy when compared to Zukofsky's long poem *'A'*; the published version of that is 806 pages long, not counting the index. In the brief Foreword to the publication of *'A' 1–12* (1959), Zukofsky gives that, ongoing epic work autobiographical status too; he calls it *'A' / a poem of a life.'* The poem was only half done at the time, 'its last words, as he put it, 'still to be lived.' And, in one of the two epigraphs he gives to his *Autobiography,* he restates the case: 'As a poet I have always felt that the work says all there needs to be said of one's life.'

For Zukofsky, however, if the poetry is the life, in an autobiographical sense, it has nonetheless to be completed with music. I am fairly certain that Zukofsky does not intend music to serve as emotional enhancement or embellishment to words. Nor is it meant to help us bypass the thick mediation that language puts between us and, say, sublimity or beauty or, simply, experience. What's important is that music is the 'other' to speech; it is non-signification. In summing up his poetics in his famous formulation, 'an integral, upper limit music lower limit speech,' the notion of the integral is key. Drawing the term from calculus, and using the elongated S-sign that Leibniz came up with, Zukofsky's formula in 'A'-12 situates the arts of music and speech as two points on an historical continuum. The integral here charts their interrelated development; it can tell us how far the art has come.[5] And it can't come far unless speech and its other (music), signification and absence, are dialectically composed—co-posed and co-present.

The integral then is a dynamic, fluid structure—a force field, of sorts. As Paul Ricoeur, in his last, great book points out, history keeps its emphasis on change.[6] If historical consciousness is intent on keeping context in mind, then it must be regarded, at least by the measure of Ricoeur's formulation, as different from history (or historiography) proper. Historical consciousness considers change (the workings of time) but in context, where context itself is temporally dynamic. It is no static condition but, like a landscape, it is full of activity, at myriad levels, from the macro to the micro. Historical consciousness is then a phenomenology but one that aspires to be polyphonic as well as encyclopedic.

2

'Mode Z' first appeared in *This* 9, which is dated 'Winter 1978–79.' There, it comes immediately after Watten's poem titled 'X,' which seems to undermine my hypothesis that Louis Zukofsky is the primary referent and to reinstate Z as an X, or to situate the Z in a signifying system with or counter-referential implications. The letter in the title may still gesture toward Zukofsky, but in the context of *This* 9, it belongs just as much to a sequence whose trajectory has brought us to a late-alphabetical site, one from which we can project a post-alphabetical situation, which can't be signified, has no identity. Following 'X,' and passing over a missing 'Y,' 'Z' comes to serve as the sign for something beyond 'X' (the unknown).

Looking through notes from a year or so ago that I wrote in preparation for a discussion of Watten's book-length poem *Progress* in a graduate seminar I was teaching, I find the following 'talking point': 'Watten writes out of profound psychological insight and intellectual passion. Why the high level of abstraction? One answer, which is not however the only one, might be this: what could be taken for abstraction in his work, might better be understood as affect, maybe even affect so strong that it cannot (or refuses to) remain attached to any particular image, entity, thing. Things (entities, persons, situations, events) can elicit passion, even command it, but they can't satisfy it. They can't even testify to it.'

But there's more to an explanation of radical abstraction, insistent imagelessness, in a work like 'Mode Z' than that. In *The Dialectical Imagination*, Martin Jay, in talking about Adorno's abiding interest in Schoenberg, makes this comment: 'polyphonic music, the least representational of aesthetic modes, was perhaps best suited for the expression of that imageless 'other' that Critical Theory refused to define positively.'[7]

Representation is a problem and perhaps especially for history, insofar as history means to preserve for the future a site open for what must, in the present, remain as 'the *bilderlos* (imageless) tangibility of the utopian other.'[8] 'X' in math is the sign of that which is yet to be determined. Might not 'Z' too signify that promise and preserve that opening? 'Could we have those trees cleared out of the way? / And the houses, volcanoes, empires?'

Or is mode Z the zigzag course of dialectics?

3

Watten recently commented to me that the poem is a whirligig. I have wanted to wait until I've said as much about the poem as I can say before soliciting information or comments about it from him, eager as I am for help. So I stopped him from saying more, but not before he had said that he had intended it to play with people's minds. It certainly did with mine. 'Start writing autobiography'? That threw me. I took it as ironic, meaning the very opposite of what it said. Don't do that. The first edition of my book *My Life* came out the same year that Barrett's 'Mode Z' appeared as the initial poem in his *1–10*. And now a group of ten of the writers who were active together in the San Francisco Bay Area Language writing scene around the time that 'Mode Z' (as well as many other Language school works) was written is writing autobiography together. The result is *The Grand Piano*: a ten-part (ten-volume) project, subtitled 'An Experiment in Collective Autobiography, San Francisco, 1975–1980.' The project is named after a coffee house in San Francisco's Haight-Ashbury district which hosted a reading series that was one of the prominent focal points of our activities. Two volumes of the collective autobiography have been published to date. They each contain ten essays, one by each author, written independently but edited collectively by all ten *Grand Piano* authors. Publisher: Mode A.

Mode A is an imprint of Watten's This Press; it was created last year (2006) for the sole immediate purpose of serving as the publisher of our 'Experiment in Collective Autobiography,' which is appearing now some thirty years after Watten ended his poem 'Mode Z' with the command 'Start writing autobiography.'

I don't want to suggest that *The Grand Piano* is a response—a positive response—to that command, however. That's a wrong conclusion. Or rather, I'd like to consider the possibility that the command itself is a wrong conclusion. That may be the point: 'Mode Z' has an argument that proceeds strategically and intentionally to the wrong conclusion.

A proper, stable argument is a logical construct, built with propositions, each of which, whether syllogistically or dialectically or chronologically or otherwise, prepares the way for the next, until a conclusion is reached and the argument is, as we say, *made*—like an edifice. But this one, 'Mode Z' (and, though it is premature to say so, perhaps also, coincidentally, the ten-authored works published by Mode A: *The Grand Piano*), is an odd edifice, if it's a whirligig, spinning its wings.

A whirligig does not spin its wings to no effect. Any analogy to spinning one's wheels is a bad one. The *intended* activity of the whirligig is to spin; that's its virtue and key to the fun it provides, since in doing so it negates itself—not totally, of course, but its specificity gets blurry.

Its parts move too fast for our perceptual skills—we lose sight of it, even as we can see that it—something—is there. Its purpose is to become different in motion from what it is when still, changing difference (its distinctive, separate bright blades) into singularity (the vaguely halo-like blur) as it does so, and estranging perception. Admittedly, to do all this the whirligig depends on the wind; within limits, the stronger, the better.

The Grand Piano, when complete, will consist of 10 small volumes, each containing ten short essays, to different degrees grounded in memory, representing varying concerns and diverse ways of remembering and of putting things together. They reason differently and reflect different reasons. It is a collective endeavour, but the results are not collective memory in the strict sense. *The Grand Piano* is an account of a time and its multiple layers and contexts. The account is as fortuitous as it is haphazard, productive of remarkable interconnections whose very existence testifies to a poetics, as well as to a shared history that is as differently shared as it was differently created.

The project makes public private experiences of a public time, which is to say that already, from the start, it was to be constructed from incommensurate materials—separate experiences of time, event, intention, agency, and memory. As I read through the little books (Parts 1 and 2 have been published; Part 3 is virtually complete and will be going to the printer shortly), I am struck by the ways in which the contents are engaged in a struggle with history—or a struggle to achieve what I'm calling historical consciousness: a sense of significant interrelatedness; of heterogeneity and of difference—of change and singularity; consciousness of time, process, irrevocability, and imagination.

Historical consciousness is what provides us with *Erfahrungen*— the lived-through character of experiences, integrated and integrating experiences, in whose significance we participate.

Integrated experiences foster (though they can't guarantee) happiness (what the Frankfurt School liked to call 'genuine happiness'), which I think of as a sense of interconnectedness, of belonging, not so much one's own belonging as the belonging of things, a sense of the intricate vast *durée* known as the world, and perhaps most precisely, of that vast *durée*'s intricacies. That is the autobiography to write. 'The individual is thus a dialectical instrument of passage.'[9] 'Now write autobiography.'

But the trees have not yet been cleared out of the way. Nor the houses, volcanoes, empires.

4^{10}

At this juncture, to avoid misunderstanding, I need to distinguish my notion of 'historical consciousness' from T. S. Eliot's 'historical sense,' as he articulates it in 'Tradition and the Individual Talent,' that most temptingly seductive short essay; I still have the volume in which I first read it, with enthusiastic underlinings: 'The progress of an artist is a continual self-sacrifice, a continual extinction of personality.' No doubt the personality I had it in mind to extinguish was that to which I thought I was doomed by my gender, and being an *adolescent* female at the time I first read Eliot's essay, and, by dint of age, class, and ethnicity much given to self-criticism, my readiness for self-sacrifice no doubt verged on the religious, the saintly, the masochistic. It was a long time before I learned to distinguish Eliot's 'escape' from the 'negation' of the Frankfurt School.

By the end of his essay, Eliot has reframed *the poem* (the ideal poem—and it is a deeply idealist concept by the end) in such a way as to eternalize or naturalize it in relation to the past (the Anglo-European tradition with which he's determined to align himself) and provide it with a non-contextualized status. Eliot's poem is to have its own, total emotional grounds—it is to have its emotion autonomously, asocially, according to its own logic. Eliot's famous pronouncement at the end of the essay ('Poetry is not a turning loose of emotion, but an escape from emotion; it is not the expression of personality, but an escape from personality.') announces an escape from accountability. In the name of the impersonal, which he equates with the scientific, which he presents in turn as the realm of the organic, the natural, he renounces collectivity, the social, even, paradoxically, tradition (in the sense, for example, that Walter Benjamin makes of it in 'On Some Motifs in

Baudelaire') in favour of the talented individual, freed of particulars and approaching universality. By giving total autonomy to a cultural product (and denying its cultural character in favour of a natural, organic one), Eliot denies its embeddedness in social structures, its complicity with reigning ideology—something a Marxist would never do.

'The existing monuments form an ideal order among themselves, which is modified by the introduction of the new (the really new) work of art among them. The existing order is complete before the new work arrives; for order to persist after the supervention of novelty, the whole existing order must be, if ever so slightly, altered; and so the relations, proportions, values of each work of art toward the whole are readjusted; and this is conformity between the old and the new' ('Tradition,' part 1, 4th paragraph). I'll let Max Horkheimer comment on that, via a quotation from a letter of his to Leo Lowenthal, written in 1943 and commenting on the Nazis' sense of history: 'Their concept of history boils down to the veneration of monuments. There is no such thing as history without that utopian element which, as you point out, is lacking in them [the Nazis]. Fascism, by its very exaltation of the past, is anti-historical. The Nazis' references to history mean only that the powerful must rule and that there is no emancipation from the eternal laws which guide humanity. When they say history, they mean its very opposite: mythology.'[11]

5

> For I, methought, while the sweet breath of heaven
> Was blowing on my body, felt within
> A corresponding mild creative breeze,
> A vital breeze, which travelled gently on
> O'er things which it had made, and is become
> A tempest, a redundant energy,
> Vexing its own creation. 'Tis a power
> That does not come unrecognized, a storm
> Which, breaking up a long-continued frost,
> Brings with it vernal promises, the hope
> Of active days, of dignity and thought,
> Of prowess in an honorable field,

Pure passions, virtue, knowledge, and delight,
The holy life of music and of verse.
(Wordsworth, *The Prelude*, Book I, ll. 40–54)

This passage from very near the beginning of Wordsworth's *The Prelude* gives us wind enough for a whirligig (and of course some tradition). It is not until much later, in Book X of the poem, that he introduces the whirligig, which he calls a wind-mill. This whirligig is 'a fiendish toy,'[12] the toy of anarchic, maddened, blood-thirsty revolutionaries:

They found their joy,
They made it, ever thirsty, as a Child—
If light desires of innocent little ones
May with such heinous appetites be matched—
Having a toy, a wind-mill, though the air
Do of itself blow fresh, and makes the vane
Spin in his eyesight, he is not content,
But with the play-thing at arm's length he sets
His front against the blast, and runs amain
To make it whirl the faster.
(Wordsworth, *The Prelude*, Book X, ll. 336–45)

For Wordsworth, the whirligig is an emblem of the French Revolution run amuck, the 'innocent authority' (X, 350) of its purpose perverted. In 'Mode Z,' at another moment of failed revolution, Watten, with considerable perversity of his own, takes up that toy and thrusts it through the air. It's 1978—a decade after the utopian moment of 1968; if we'd known how bad things had yet to get, more of us might have taken up whirligigs.

But enough about the whirligig. 'Mode Z' is just that, a *mode*; it's a dialectical argument, far more than it's a dialectical image. And it owes more to Breton, I suspect, than Benjamin.

As a dialectical argument it has several fronts and they face both outward and inward, with simultaneous macro and micro targets of address. It argues with historical time and cultural tradition and the project of poetry, and it is unsettling at every stage of its development. It asks almost too much of us, and if the conclusion it reaches is that we should start writing autobiography, then it's no wonder we are upset. The argument has, step by step, stripped away everything on which we might ground the life we're to write. There's nothing left to point to. 'There,' 'then,' 'it,' 'they' are nowhere to be found. This is the true non-referential terrain of early Language writing, the 'sad note' of negativity.

The disruptive mode here called 'Z' is radical in a literal, as well as metaphysical, sense; it pertains to the roots of belief, to assumptions, givens. 'Mode Z' accepts no givens. 'Could we have those trees cleared out of the way?'

To clear away givens—which are always naturalized (that's definitive of their givenness)—is to reject rationalizations, modes of excuse that are addresses as much to oneself, 'the person in your life,' as to others, lies that oneself has to be the first to swallow. Rationalizations are compensatory in nature. They function as justifications, intended to align psychic structures with social structures, so that what will be allowed to happen is commensurate with one's desires. They are a product of fear—'an internalization of fears,' as Paul Ricoeur puts it; rationalizations internalize fear within one's intellectual order.[13]

'Mode Z' does not conquer fear; in fact, reading it makes me afraid. But it does work to externalize what has been interiorized. The metaphysical radicalism of 'Mode Z' is carried out as a sequence of insubordinations and alienations, literal and figurative alterations, or *alter*-ations. The achievement is alterity and, thereby, heterogeneity—and the possibility of public life.

I have never been able to paraphrase 'Mode Z'—by which I mean *the poem*, Watten's, mine, yours, whoever's: the poem of mode Z. Perhaps *that* is my 'sad note': a note, impossible to resolve into an image. 'Mode Z' fights against the image, and that fight is undertaken as much on behalf of public life as on behalf of poetry. The image in contemporary life belongs to what T.J. Clark has termed the 'ethos of deception'; the image is the coin of the realm, the commodity *par excellence*, of the culture of deception. T.J. Clark is brilliant in his analyses of what we might call the capital (in Marx's sense) of images, and scathing in his disdain for the ways in which we, 'professional twenty-first-century intellectuals, chained to their image-displacement machines like lab animals to dispensers of morphine,' have bought into them.[14] As it condenses into an abstraction, an anti-image, the ultimate argument of 'Mode Z' may be with us. Images (to cite Clark again) have 'become the very instrumentation of the market—not "capital accumulated to the point where it becomes image", to quote the famous phrase from Guy Debord, but images dispersed and accelerated until they become the true and sufficient commodities. Debord did not quite see (or perhaps he did, at the bitter end) that the spectacle would in due course be internalized, privatized, "personalized" [...,] with the image doses more and more self-administered by interactive subjects, each convinced that the screen was the realm of freedom.'[15]

Poetry today has as one of its tasks that of clearing public life of images and giving us art instead. 'Could we have those trees cleared out of the way?'

Lyn Hejinian is Professor of English at the University of California, Berkeley.

Notes

1. Martin Jay, *The Dialectical Imagination* (Berkeley: University of California Press, 1996), 47.

2. The letter is to be found in Rachel Blau DuPlessis, ed., *The Selected Letters of George Oppen* (Durham, NC: Duke UP, 1990), 402 n. 6; my remarks on it are in Lyn Hejinian, *The Language of Inquiry* (Berkeley: University of California Press, 2000), 350–51.

3. What's at stake in my advocating historicity over ontology are contemporary cultural conditions under the domination of global capitalism. There is no *becoming* in capitalism; in its mastery of the human situation, it proclaims its status as complete. This is it: the plenitude is before us, it's all here. Fully naturalized, transcendent and universal, capitalism puts an end to history.

4. Paul Valéry, as quoted in Walter Benjamin, 'On Some Motifs in Baudelaire,' in Howard Eiland and Michael W. Jennings, eds., *Walter Benjamin: Selected Writings*, Volume 4, 1938–1940 (Cambridge, MA & London: The Belknap Press of Harvard University, 2003), 337.

5. My thanks to Snehal Shingavi of the UC–Berkeley English Department for these insights.

[6] Paul Ricoeur, *Memory, History, Forgetting,* Kathleen Blamey and David Pellauer, trans. (Chicago & London: University of Chicago Press, 2004), 183.

[7] Martin Jay, 182.

[8] Ibid, 71.

[9] Adorno, letter to Walter Benjamin, quoted in Martin Jay, 207.

[10] My reading of Eliot's 'Tradition and the Individual Talent' is greatly indebted to conversation with Colin Dingler of the UC–Berkeley Rhetoric Department.

[11] Quoted in Martin Jay, 278.

[12] This is Watten's characterization of it.

[13] See Norbert Elias, *The Civilizing Process,* and Paul Ricoeur's discussion of it in *Memory, History, Forgetting,* 209

[14] T.J. Clark, *The Sight of Death* (New Haven & London: Yale UP, 2006), 122.

[15] Ibid, 184–85.

Watten & Hejinian ('What, no, begin again?'): or Poetry as Language's 'State of Emergency'

Piers Hugill

Emergence/ Emergency/ Crisis

I distinctly remember looking at the horizon, checking for the tell-tale sign of the mushroom cloud, and wondering out loud with school friends whether nuclear war might not come this week, or maybe next. At ten years of age I must have felt a casual acceptance of the possibility of imminent catastrophe. We had all been prepared for it, knew what kind of nuclear shelter was most likely to keep us alive, even if the chances of contracting radiation sickness were so high that ultimate survival seemed vanishingly remote; knew, furthermore, that war meant total planetary destruction. Apocalypse was, in a very ethereal sort of way, an ever-present reality. That must have been 1982, just before Brezhnev's death.

Jean Baudrillard, who died earlier this year (6 March 2007), became infamous when in 1991 he claimed that the First Gulf War never happened.[1] Of course those of his detractors who maintained that he was merely denying the 'efficacy' of the war in terms of real deaths, and real misery, critics such as Christopher Norris[2], were radically simplifying his central argument; that this war was one in name only, a nominated crisis, which provided the excuse for war to be declared without there actually being any real engagement between opposing forces: as he put it, not Clausewitz's 'continuation of politics by other means', but rather 'the continuation of the absence of politics by other means'.

His subsequent analysis of 9/11 is somewhat different.[3] Rather than viewing it as a non-event, Baudrillard understood 9/11 to be the 'absolute event' of its time, that is, the supreme expression of the totality of global capital in irresolvable contradiction with itself. In continuity with his previous analysis, however, was the employment made of this 'event' as grounds for a 'state of exception'; in the case of 9/11, not only the wars in Afghanistan and Iraq, but the Patriot Act, and the USA's very own gulag in Guantanamo Bay.

Giorgio Agamben recently drew attention to the 'scandalous' debate in the 1920s and 30s between Carl Schmitt, the German jurist of the Nazi era, and Walter Benjamin regarding sovereign power, and the basis of that power in the sovereign's ability (or not) to decide on the 'state of exception', i.e. that moment when the rule of law is suspended, but in which power has not withdrawn its constitutive violence.[4] Benjamin, in his responses to Schmitt, and most clearly in his essay 'Critique of Violence', tried to delineate the difference between an 'impure' sovereign power that maintains the rule of law, and a 'pure' violence that neither 'makes nor preserves law, but deposes it and thus inaugurates a new historical epoch', what we should more properly understand as revolutionary violence.[5]

The modern is likewise a moment of crisis; but also a moment of emergence, of becoming, of the unforeseeable. As an idea it has remained almost entirely elusive, not least because there has been an unfortunate tendency to try and date it, to make it synonymous with 'modernism', for example, or isolate the specific locales and dates that constitute modernity as an integral experience (Paris, or the 1920s). Its etymology has been traced to the fifth century term *modernus*. In its original form, *modernus* signified simply the new ; it was complicated in the 11th century expression *modernitas*, however, by its implicit relationship to *antiguitas*: hence it became a synonym for *nostra tempora*.[6]

In the following two centuries these two terms became subject to value judgements that eventually led to the famous debate about the relationship of modernity to antiquity which constituted the first major challenge to the Renaissance poetics of imitation, a dispute over whether contemporary poets could exceed the achievement of the ancients, or whether they were doomed simply to copy classical models in perpetuity, because everything that could be achieved in the arts already had been. 'Our' modernity has seen a continuation of this permanent *Querelle des anciens et des modernes* ever since.

There never was a when or where of modernity, but only ever an activity associated with it. Henri Meschonnic describes this activity succinctly: '[w]anting to know what modernity is, I realized that it is the subject as ourselves (*en nous*). That is the weakest point in the chain that holds art, literature, and society together ... The weakest because it is not compromised by the sign. Which it escapes'.[7] The modern, then, is that which escapes the contemporary, and therefore the maintenance of order (*le maintien de l'ordre*).

Emergence/ Emergency/ Utopia

Elsewhere Agamben has suggested that the only coherent way to distinguish poetry from prose is in the possibility of enjambment inherent in lineation.[8] Arguments about the status of 'prose poetry' aside, poetry, therefore, is marked by a peculiar structural crisis: how to end? The last line of a poem cannot be enjambed, and at just that moment the poem collapses back into prose, and the generative ruptures that kept it open are sealed once more.

Henri Meschonnic, furthermore, claims that poetic language reveals most acutely the way that the 'sign' of structuralist linguistics hides or, reduces the signifier to a mere token. It imposes a form of universalism, or false totality, which via the dualisms (form-content, nature-culture, word-thing, etc., all on the model of *signifier-signified*) of 'traditional theory', which he uses in the sense given the term by Horkheimer (to be distinguished, therefore from *critique*) prevents the emergence of the *new*, or the utopian, in favour of the *status quo* and the perpetuity of the same.

Poetry is essential to this critique of the sign, because it has always been its weak point. It is the 'weak link' in traditional theory because it is the form of discourse where it is most difficult to disguise what Meschonnic calls the *signifiant* (what might otherwise be called the 'signifier') by reducing it to the formality of the dual pair *sign-sense*. In other words, poetry is the form of discourse in which the subject of that discourse is most obviously in play. Poetry is the most embodied form of language, and hence maintains the trace of the body in its orality, its rhythm, and its historicity.[9]

The crisis in Agamben's theory of poetry seems at first sight to be very different from the crisis in Meschonnic's, but what if we consider the 'end' of the poem to be no different from the 'weak link' that Meschonnic diagnoses in the theory of the sign: in both cases there is no essential difference between poetry and prose, other than a point or moment of crisis or rupture; in one sense at least this constitutes the moment of modernity itself, which is constitutively marked by such crises, or ruptures.

Leningrad

It is an implicit thesis of Barrett Watten's theoretical work *The Constructivist Moment*, both that there are *moments* themselves that form a sequence of historical ruptures in critical thought, but also that, despite the widely circulated belief in the 'end of communism' following its collapse, the Soviet Union nevertheless represented a highly significant moment and articulation of the idea of the modern in the twentieth century. Hence, when he, Lyn Hejinian, Michael Davidson and Ron Silliman took part in a Summer School in Leningrad in 1989 on the subject 'Language—Consciousness—Society', the resulting collective work, *Leningrad*,[10] records not only a series of personal and isolated moments, but an encounter with an alternative experience of both history and subjectivity that challenged the previous assumptions of the US contingent.

But what is this Russian 'relation'? More than being just a topic of their work, the Soviet Union appears to constitute a kind of foil to Watten and Hejinian's Americanness, or more accurately, a form of particular historical subjectivity, marked by a number of important encounters, that in another context might have been trivialised as being between East and West. More than simply an expression of the problematics of a poetics of translation this meeting with Soviet poets, musicians, painters and intellectuals, constituted a reconfiguring of a whole series of concerns: most especially about the nature of subjectivity and the subject, and a realisation of this that went beyond merely ethnographic interest, into a profoundly experienced revelation of the radically historical and 'open' nature of subjectivity, itself constituting a poetics of language and its place in discourse.

Hence, one of the most profound debates held during the Summer School related to discussions held between the American and Soviet contingents over misunderstandings of the nature of the sense of subject in Russia (and Russian), at first in a schematic and structuralist account, based on the purported lack of specific grammatical forms marking selfhood in Russian; an interpretation that was later made the basis of an infinitely more sophisticated argument about the experience of subjectivity in late Soviet society. In *Leningrad*, the following exchange between Lyn Hejinian and Arkadii Dragomoshchenko takes place:

> I had been told some months earlier that many people in a Russian audience will not understand the Western notion of subjectivity … [to Dragomoshchenko] "I know in Russian you have no word for 'self' except as a passive suffix or a reflexive pronoun," I said, but he shrugged his shoulders and wouldn't talk about it. Subjectivity is not the basis for being a Russian person. Our independent separate singularity can hardly be spoken of, but Arkadii said "many people wish it". "You know," I said, "many of us wish to overcome it. We think that if we can surpass or supersede the individual self we can achieve a community." Our ideas are to some extent rooted in our Protestant past, and Russian, even Soviet, ideas are rooted in Russian Orthodoxy. A Protestant person stands entirely alone speaking to God. "Protestants", said Arkadii, "go to church to mail a letter to God, the church, it's like a post office. The Orthodox church—the building is not symbolic—it is considered to be the real body of God, and Orthodox people too are God because they are together there, not alone, and speaking, by the way, has nothing to do with it." We have our great, modern, inescapable but not universal theme of isolation and alienation. "Yes, I suppose so. You are afraid of your finitude, and we are afraid of our infinitude."[11]

An attitude later used to explain not only the Soviet tendency for passengers to expand physically on public transport, but the phenomenally high incidence of agoraphobia among the population of Leningrad and other Soviet cities (and an occasion, like many in *Leningrad*, retold in *Oxota*). This theme occurs elsewhere in Hejinian's writing. So, for example, in 'The Rejection of Closure', the essential mobility of the Russian subject helps to conceptualise a 'dynamic' theory of subjectivity that escapes totality. As Marjorie Perloff notes:

'[Hejinian's] explanation of Russian reflexive verb forms is somewhat fanciful: from Pushkin to Pasternak, after all, Russian poetry has displayed a very strong sense of personal identity, even if there is no single word that defines selfhood. Just the same, this peculiarity of Russian grammar ("the closest representation of [the] notion of the self occurs in (but only in) the reflexive pronoun *sebya* (oneself, myself), which never appears in the nominative case and is most frequently seen in the form of the suffix *sya* at the end of reflexive verbs") helps Hejinian articulate her own view that "The person ... is a mobile (or mobilized) reference point; or to put it another way, subjectivity is not an entity but a dynamic"'.[12]

The political context for the 1989 Leningrad Summer School was Mikhail Gorbachev's policy of *glasnost*, which can be glossed (and note the etymological connexion) as 'publicity' or 'public voice', and which was instituted as a leading mechanism behind the reform policies of *perestroika*. Soon, however, *glasnost* became synonymous with the idea of 'openness', and with that of 'encounter' itself: with the West, for example. The moment that Watten, Hejinian, Davidson and Silliman went to the USSR was one of seemingly rapid transition, even while it was staged within the collapsed body of the long 'Brezhnev stagnation' beginning in the mid 60s; it was the briefest of tears in history, a moment when subjectivity experienced an ephemeral moment of possibility, whether as utopia or nihilism. Certainly this appears to be a leading concern of Watten's essay 'Post Soviet Subjectivity in Arkadii Dragomoshchenko and Ilya Kabakov', in which the different historical, linguistic and ideological contexts of the late USSR and the USA produce utterly incommensurable reactions to the historical breach represented by *glasnost*. So, while '[t]he postmodern moment thus seems to be a process the West must go through, in losing the defence of reification in confrontation with its privileged other', this is not 'a primary motivation for the works of post-Soviet artists'. Rather Dragomoshchenko and Kabakov seek 'a reconstructed subject, after the fall of [Soviet] New Man ... [which is] situated precisely on the fault line between the loss of cultural memory and the epistemological inadequacies of Soviet science.'[13] The result is that 'the historical emergence of an unstable post-Soviet subjectivity makes Western postmodernism appear even more qualified in its imagination of totality, which begins to come undone without the antagonism of the Soviet state'.[14] What we have is the recognition of the radical historicity of the kinds of subjectivising and ideological processes that constitute the postmodernism of the 1970s and 80s, which Watten relates to Fredric Jameson's contextualisation of this artistic/cultural formation in the era of 'Cold War antagonism [consequent upon] the "era of national revolutions" and the Vietnam War'.[15]

The Historical Subject, or History as Subject ('Bad History')

By way of a conclusion I want to make a single claim, which is not itself dependent on any particular reading of the texts that I have mentioned in this paper so far, but which, rather, concerns what I perceive to be a general trend in the writing of Watten and Hejinian since their respective Soviet experiences, and which, in itself, may be a somewhat impertinent suggestion.

Both Watten and Hejinian have been at the forefront of an attempt to subjectivise the historical and the public in their work, or perhaps more accurately to narrate the historical and the very process of the structuration and individuation of bodies of work that are inseparable from any sense of subjectivity and social praxis. To that extent they have moved away from the 'postmodern' (bourgeois) lyric, in the direction of the production of integrally social *and* personal narratives, what we might, with Pound, as well as Watten, call the 'epic'. It is in just this sense that I would read not only *Under Erasure*, but also a text such as *Bad History*, as being a product of that Soviet experience, even though there is no obvious reference to Russian history among all the other bad histories included.

Border Country

Borders, thresholds, limina, margins, limits; rims, lips, cusps: but by means of the simple expedient of changing the metaphor from a spatial to a temporal figure, the avant garde becomes central once more to politics, and to the activity of making history.

If poetry is on the edges of discourse, its most fragile, poorly guarded region, the weak link in the whole system of the maintenance of order that constitutes ideology, especially in these hystericised days of the 'state of exception', one crisis or emergency following another, then in speaking of poetry we are always dealing with a moment of open possibility, of *glasnost*, the utopian, or apocalyptic, the moment of revolutionary possibility, or the disintegration into barbarism: in either case it is a moment of pure, or impure, violence that faces us, and a decision.

Piers Hugill is Lecturer in Creative Writing (Poetry) at the University of Southampton.

Notes

[1] The complete argument appears in *The Gulf War Did Not Take Place*, trans. Paul Patton (London: Power Publications, 2004)

[2] See his *Uncritical Theory: Postmodernism, Intellectuals and the Gulf War* (Amherst: The University of Massachusetts Press, 1992)

[3] Jean Baudrillard, *The Spirit of Terrorism*, trans. Chris Turner (London: Verso, 2003)

[4] Giorgio Agamben, *State of Exception*, trans. Kevin Attell (Chicago: University of Chicago Press, 2005)

[5] Agamben, *State of Exception*: 53

[6] See Hans Robert Jauss, 'La "modernité" dans la tradition littéraire et la conscience d'aujourd'hui' in *Pour une esthétique de la réception*, (Paris: Gallimard, 1978)

[7] Henri Meschonnic, 'Modernity Modernity', trans. Gabriella Bedetti, *New Literary History*, 23, 2 (1992), 401–430: 401. This is a partial translation of *Modernité Modernité* (Lagrasse: Verdier, 1988).

[8] See in particular his essays '*Corn*: From Anatomy to Poetics' and 'The End of the Poem', both in *The End of the Poem: Studies in Poetics*, trans. Daniel Heller-Roazen (Stanford: Stanford UP, 1999): 23–42, 109–115.

[9] A detailed account of Meschonnic's conception of 'orality' and the bodily in poetry and language is provided in his essay 'Qu'entendez-vous par oralité?' in *Les états de la poétique* (Paris: PUF, 1985): 93–133.

[10] Michael Davidson and others, *Leningrad: American Writers in the Soviet Union* (San Francisco: Mercury House, 1991)

[11] Davidson, *Leningrad*: 34–35.

[12] Marjorie Perloff, 'How Russian Is It: Lyn Hejinian's *Oxota*'
http://epc.buffalo.edu/authors/perloff/hejinian.html [accessed 24
April 2007] (para. 18 of 54)

[13] Barrett Watten, 'Post-Soviet Subjectivity in Arkadii Dragomoshchenko
and Ilya Kabakov' in *The Constructivist Moment: From Material Text to
Cultural Poetics* (Middletown: Wesleyan UP, 2003), 291–320: 318.

[14] Watten, 'Post-Soviet Subjectivity': 320.

[15] Ibid.

Climate Change and Contemporary Modernist Poetry

RICHARD KERRIDGE

Most scientists in the relevant fields agree that potentially catastrophic climate change is taking place, and that it is due to increases in atmospheric carbon produced by activities that are the basis of our ordinary lives. The likelihood is a rise in average global temperatures this coming century of between 2 and 4.5 degrees centigrade. It could be higher: 6 degrees or more, if feedback effects are severe. Recently, several 'popular science' books have attempted to imagine and explain what this is likely to mean, including James Lovelock's *The Revenge of Gaia* (2006), Fred Pearce's *The Last Generation* (2006), George Monbiot's *Heat* (2006) and Mark Lynas's *Six Degrees* (2007). They make appalling, truly frightening reading. John Lanchester, reviewing a clutch of these books, comments that:

> I suspect we're reluctant to think about it because we're worried that if we start we will have no choice but to think about nothing else. [..] We deeply don't want to believe this story. (Lanchester, 3, 6)

6 degrees, says Lynas, would produce similar ecological conditions to those that caused the end-Permian extinctions, in which about 95% of all species disappeared. Dead anoxic oceans, methane fireballs, only the polar regions habitable: this, admittedly, is at the far end of likelihood, as currently judged, but quite possible. Lovelock reports the opinion of some scientists that 'if global temperatures rise by more than 2.7° C the Greenland glacier will no longer be stable', and that 'a rise in temperature globally of 4° C is enough to destabilize the tropical rainforests' (Lovelock, 51). Both developments would produce huge feedback effects. Pearce asserts that 'we are in all probability the last generation that can rely on anything close to a stable global climate' (Pearce, 293). Like Lanchester, I find it hard to write about this as if it were real.

Some people deny that the crisis is real, but more perplexing, in a way, are those who accept, at the level of intellectual belief, that climate change is happening, but do not modify their lives accordingly. Their position is the existential and archetypal one at the heart of the problem.

Many readers of this book on 'Poetry and Public Language' will probably come into this category, as I do myself. Nominal recognition co-exists with practical disavowal. The only changes we seem able to make are ones that bring scarcely any inconvenience to our set patterns of life. These are very unlikely to be sufficient.

Such is the impasse at which we presently find ourselves. Back in 1991, Slavoj Žižek wrote about it, suggesting that environmental crisis was an instance of the Lacanian 'real', unrepresentable and therefore incommensurate with our understanding, so that no response could be adequate. Right across the range of reactions,—denial, complacency, activism, panic—responses will be inauthentic, simulated, self-dramatising space-fillers:

> What is at stake is our most unquestionable presuppositions, the very horizon of our meaning, our everyday understanding of "nature" as a regular, rhythmic process. [...] Hence our unwillingness to take the ecological crisis completely seriously; hence the fact that the typical, predominant reaction to it consists in a variation on the famous disavowal, "I know very well (that things are deadly serious, that what is at stake is our very survival), but just the same ... (I don't really believe it, I'm not really prepared to integrate it into my symbolic universe, and that is why I continue to act as if ecology is of no lasting consequence for my everyday life)." (Žižek, 34–35)

According to this view, we, most of us anyway, *cannot* respond adequately to the crisis because it is so unprecedented and incommensurable as to be unrepresentable by existing forms of narrative. The possible futures it presents us with are so excessive as to break any chain of personal narrative that might link them with the experience we have now. Ecological crisis poses a similar narrative problem to the representation of nuclear war and its aftermath: any sensibility that could be in a position to narrate these events would be so transformed by them as to be unintelligible to us back here where it hasn't yet happened.

Poetry that broaches this subject, then, will be confronted with this impasse, this gap between nominally knowing and behaving as if one knew. Overcoming that gap in time to avert catastrophe, if we do, will be an immense transformation, cultural as well as scientific and political. I want to look briefly here at what two poets in the Modernist tradition, J.H. Prynne and Tony Lopez, do with this state of affairs. They are chosen because my design is primarily to explore the proposition that contemporary neo-Modernist writing has specific equipment for reaching into this subject, as writing that keeps to the personal voice and the conventionally poetic has not. My perception that this may be true comes from little more, at present, than the observation that neo-Modernism, and the cut-up method in particular, can bring into poetic space kinds of discourse not normally available to the personal lyric.

J.H. Prynne

> [T]o the intelligentsia, to the moulders of opinion (...), "ecology crisis" is a godsend; and its minatory vision of a civilisation choked and poisoned by its own waste is the new stock in trade of the salesmen of apocalypse. In "The Ideal Star-Fighter", the only one of his recent poems which I think I understand, Prynne with just indignation rejects the moral blackmail which the ecologist's propaganda exerts and depends upon. (Davie, 179–180)

This was Donald Davie interpreting Prynne in 1973, recognising some ecological dangers but vehemently rejecting apocalyptic warnings, regarding them as moral blackmail.

The broad argument in the course of which these remarks appeared was that the post-war social democratic consensus in Britain had made solidarity the pre-eminent virtue, and that in a post-Nazi world there was no other responsible choice. Social solidarity, in these cultural and moral terms, meant a willingness to temper all forms of idealism, for fear of the intolerance they might produce. It also meant accepting the emerging norms of a mass consumer society that Britain was only just beginning to experience. These norms had to be accepted, because the alternatives—demanding forms of aesthetic and moral idealism, heroic narratives of any kind—were liable to produce intolerance. The result, for Davie, is a poetry of 'lowered sights and patiently diminished expectations' (71), honourable for what it is prepared to forego.

As an example of these honourably reduced expectations, he repeatedly cites a willingness to accept the environmental effects of mass consumer society. This becomes, for Davie, the test of the scrupulous relinquishment he admires: he seems to see it as the hardest test, and in many of his asides that touch on the fate of the natural environment—it is nearly always introduced in asides—he sounds as if he cannot really accept that relinquishment at all, or only at tremendous effort. All this was before climate change was a perceived danger, of course.

Davie's mistrust of all forms of apocalyptic vision is a defence of liberal democracy, unheroic and philistine though he finds it: a resistance to the need of apocalyptic rhetoric to claim all the space for itself. We can see this now in John Lanchester's apprehension that thinking at all seriously about climate change will mean ceasing to be able to think about anything else. Apocalyptic arguments always claim that one particular feared eventuality is too important and too imminent for us to be able to afford patience with dissent, and with other people's different preoccupations, which, from the apocalyptic point of view, are always local, provincial and ignorant. However sincerely it is held, the apocalyptic vision is a coercive, anti-democratic vision, and because it provides such a good excuse for dismissing other viewpoints, it is tempting to the cynical who seek power.

That is the kind of 'moral blackmail' Davie says that Prynne rejects in the following lines from 'The Ideal Star-Fighter', published in *Brass* (1971):

> And so we hear daily of the backward
>   glance at the planet, the reaction of
> sentiment. Exhaust washes tidal flux
>   at the crust, the fierce acceleration
> of mawkish regard. To be perceived with
>   such bounty! To put the ring-main of
> fear into printed circuit, so that from the
>   distant loop of the hate system the
> whole object is lovable, delicious, ingested
>   by heroic absorption! We should
> shrink from that lethal cupidity
>
>   (Prynne, 2005, 166)

This 'backward glance at the planet' is literal as well as metaphorical, referring to the iconic photograph of the Earth taken from the Moon in the course of the Apollo mission of 1969. Ecocritic Greg Garrard notes that this image has been used repeatedly by environmentalists. It has often been read as symbolising the smallness and fragility of the ecosystem that is our common home, though Garrard mentions other ways of reading the image: as representing the sublime triumph of technology, or the availability of the planet as abundant resource. A genuinely ecological perspective, though probably still powerfully moved by the image, will take into account the ecological cost of the way it was produced (including the links between the Apollo space programme and US military technology) and the dangers of the illusion of disembodiedness that such a photograph gives us:

> So the Earth image is contested, and, arguably, compromised by the institutions and practices that made it possible. It is, moreover, a false perspective that allows us to see what only a handful of US astronauts have actually seen, a 'god's eye view' that promises a kind of transcendental power that we, as individuals or as a species, do not possess [...]. (Garrard, 162)

A genuinely ecological, or ecocritical, perspective will thus function as a corrective to any *easy* environmentalism the image might inspire.[1]

Jeremy Noel-Tod, in a soon-to-be-published essay, makes a similar distinction between easy and rigorous environmentalisms. Quoting Davie's words about moral blackmail, Noel-Tod says that what the poem rejects is not 'the evidence of ecological damage but rather the whimsical moralism of doing "your bit" for "the planet"' (Noel-Tod, 2007). A moralism that is whimsical is one that doesn't count its own cost: an affectation rather than a real moral decision. Prynne's insistence on this distinction, and his severity towards sentimental environmentalism that doesn't really mean it, is needed much more urgently now, in 2007, when we read with climate change in mind.

This is the moral severity that runs through all Prynne's writing. His comments on L=A=N=G=U=A=G=E poetry, for example, express scepticism about the idea that a particular reading practice will function as a space outside the market economy and thus lift readers out of complicity (see Prynne, 2000). The same severity generates Prynne's poetic form, as Simon Perril has argued in an analysis of *Bands Around the Throat*, the 1987 collection in which the Chernobyl disaster of the previous year is a terrible presence. Perril finds the poetry's structuring energy to be a moral and political ambivalence towards the lyricism whose pull is tremendously powerful and essential to the writing's motivation. 'Few writers,' says Perril, 'have explored the rhetoric of lyric with such ferocity'; in particular, how difficult it is, in a consumer culture in which dissent is commodified, for poetry to take lyric flight without implicitly making a false promise of freedom. If it avoids *that*, how is it to avoid a too defeated irony? The 'lyric voice's culpability', in Perril's words, is 'its deceptive presentation of itself as immune to the very forces it is simultaneously claiming to be all-engulfing' (Perril, 1997).

Prynne longs to be able to release a lyric voice. In his work an undiminished Romantic sense of joy in self and world waits in potential, informed by an extraordinary breadth of contemporary knowledge. What restrains this joy is a scrupulous refusal to present it other than in the context of the contemporary political economy in which it has a place; hence, for example, his intercutting of fragments of lyrical pastoral with agri-chemical terminology in a series of works, notably *High Pink on Chrome* (1975). Readers encounter a lyric voice trammelled, interrupted, blocked, thrown back and encumbered with responsibility, and this obliges us continually to assess the precise cultural position of what we are doing. Without that process we can't have our lyric. Disavowal of this responsibility would be self-deception: collusion with consumer-capitalism in its placing of poetry as one of the commodities that promise the finer, more civilised life—and, by extension, with the whole practice of erasure of origin that occurs when we are sold sweat-shop products and tropical hardwoods.

Late Prynne has usually been read as a reworking of many of his previous concerns and motifs in the new context of an electronic and globalised capitalism now encroaching upon even the equivocal spaces that were once available. John Wilkinson illuminatingly describes this later poetry of flattened cadences, modular stanzaic forms structured with 'fretwork or mesh [...] the common term between textiles and electronics' (Wilkinson, 201) and long stretches devoid of humanising pronouns. In a powerful phrase, Wilkinson says that 'even the most compressed of late Prynne poetic texts are rife with bitten-off and damped down memories of earlier writing whose cadences felt deeply compelled' (Wilkinson, 204).

In refusing to mediate all his material as the narrated experience or dramatic utterance of a persona, Prynne gains access to wider sweeps of perspective than such a dramatised experience could contain. He is able to engage with the world as economic system and ecosystem. From the public sphere he takes a remarkable variety of materials: literary quotations and allusions, passages from published sources of scientific and technological knowledge, terminology from different professional worlds, media gossip, popular catch-phrases. These different elements become strangely intermediate in status. Sometimes he seems to have appropriated them with his own powerful voice, lyric or argumentative, so that they have become *utterance*; at others they seem to be what he has selected, not spoken, and sit outside his speech, separate from it, distant, sealed, not open to dialogue.

One of his most recognisable devices is the punning and splicing together of sacred and profane. Most frequently it is religious or literary-lyrical tropes punned and spliced with systems terminology from the financial markets, in a sardonic pairing, for example, of spiritual and financial investment. This pairing is a way of foregrounding the long-term structures of desire and fulfilment implied in lyric utterance, and thus of revealing the lyric as just what it pretends not to be—the product of a worldly calculation. In *Bands Around the Throat*, Perril finds a tripartite analogy. Christian hope of salvation is compared to investment in long-term financial products: a pairing familiar from earlier poems. The third term is the apocalyptic threat that structured the Cold War:

> The commodification of hope as a religious contract for the future—an afterlife bought into through a slow-maturing

policy demanding unquestioning suffering in this world—
relates back to the phrase "deterrent hope", Hope for
an afterlife—conditional upon the results of the day of
judgement, and therefore a certain quota of fear—acts like
a nuclear deterrent in its cementing of the social order by
implicit threat: that of Nuclear apocalypse or damnation.
(Perril, 1997)

Prynne's use of these parallels is complex. The pairing of Christian
hope and financial investment is a reminder that all activities have their
cultural and economic niche. There is no simple contrast between sacred
and profane, or innocence and calculation, but rather a requirement
that the value of both should be held in mind, and that the demarcation
of the spaces they occupy—in our minds, in culture, in administration,
in education, in the relationship between work and leisure—should be
questioned. Complicity should be faced—not distanced and swept up
into one huge abstraction but understood in the midst of day to day
decisions. I think it was the grand gesture of zooming out into space
and then looking back at the whole complication of one's life subsumed
in a single image that offended Prynne: a gesture equivalent to an
irresponsible lyricism in poetry.

In 'If There is a Stationmaster at Stamford S.D. Hardly So', in *The
White Stones* (1969), Prynne wrote of:

> the final
> policeman's dream
> that the quanta of wish
> and desire, too, can be marched
> off to some goal so distant
> where in the hermitage
> of our last days the
> handcuffs would seem
> an entirely proper
> abstraction
>
> (Prynne, 2005, 45)

The argument against apocalyptic fear applies also to millenarian vision,
and this poem brings the two together, ending with:

> and while
> the public hope is as
> always the
> darkened ward
> the icecap will
> never melt
> again why
> should it
>
> (46)

This last line break produces two questions: the sinisterly soothing 'Why should it?' and the teasing 'Why? *Should* it?', the latter suggesting quizzically that apocalypses have their uses. With this melting icecap, and a probing interest in the relationship between 'spirit' meaning soul and 'spirit' meaning oil, the poem now seems startlingly prescient. Yet it deploys the melting icecap as a remotely futuristic scenario, and an event contingent on geo-climatic processes outside the scope of human responsibility. How should we read these lines now, when the sliding of the polar ice sheets into the sea in the next hundred years is something that may well happen if collective humanity does not soon change its ways? And how is the warning against apocalyptic visions to accommodate valid environmental fears?

That is the essential question for an ecocritical reader of Prynne. What if the apocalyptic visions happen for once to be accurate? Where does that leave his stance? Has Prynne, whose technique might otherwise be the most promising model for an adequate poetic response, immunised himself too thoroughly?

These questions in mind, I want to go back to the 'The Ideal Star-Fighter', the poem Davie thought so anti-environmentalist. According to Jeremy Noel-Tod, what Prynne is dismissing in these lines is not environmental concern itself but a superficial, tokenistic environmentalism that marches the practical questions off into generalised concern for the planet. Noel-Tod attributes to Prynne the sort of scrupulous, self-watchful environmental consciousness described, in relation to the Earth image, by Greg Garrard. On this reading, the poem's implicit demand is for an environmentalism that makes itself real in actions. It is saying that we cannot honourably profess to be environmentalist if all it means is the affectation of a generalised mournful love.

The title, 'The Ideal Star-Fighter', comes from Wyndham Lewis's Expressionist psychodrama *Enemy of the Stars* (see Lewis, 36), in which it describes the Romantic idealist Arghol who makes a doomed attempt to escape the inauthenticity he believes has been imposed on him by ordinary social life. With the allusion, Prynne is pointing to the association between that kind of Romantic egotism and a susceptibility to apocalyptic fantasy. As Paul Edwards has explained, *Enemy of the Stars* allegorises the relationship between Romantic idealism and practical normality, revealing their violent antagonism as product of, and mask for, their inseparability (see Edwards, 139–165). Prynne is transposing that inseparability to the relationship in poetry between lyric flight and calculation, and also between environmentalist sentiment and the recognition of what one's actions reveal about own true priorities.

What has changed since 1971 is that it is now much harder to regard environmentalism as a form of nostalgic Romantic idealism. If we take seriously the threat posed by climate change, environmentalism becomes the opposite: a set of calculations of the most urgent kind that reveal our material interests. Indeed, the calculations as to how much this small action or that will add to our 'carbon footprint' seem likely to become a constant presence that will make it harder still to associate environmentalism with lyrical irresponsibility.

The calculation of material consequences features rather dis-concertingly in 'The Ideal Star-Fighter', in fact, in the many instances of moral and emotional phenomena described as if they were material events. In the first two lines there is 'a slight meniscus' floating on 'the moral/ pigment of these times'. Further on, we have 'hope converted to the/ switchboard of organic providence/ at the tiny rate of say 0.25 per cent/ 'for the earth as a whole', 'the total crop yield/ of fear' and 'glints of terror the final inert/ residue'. Emotional reactions are described as if they were the chemical reactions to which a purely materialist view would reduce them anyway, and ideological shifts are seen in the same way. This splicing, like the splicing of religious and financial discourses, is a Prynne trademark. Here it appears as a parody of scientific materialism, ferociously certain in tone. Rhetorical analogies are drawn between emotional and moral reactions, especially fear, and the reactions of pigment exposed to sunlight: in human skin, in the normal workings of the eye, in plants in photosynthesis, and in the photochemical reactions involved in the taking of photographs such as that famous Earth image. The 'politic/ albino' of the first stanza is thus someone who finds it politic to be so sensitive to light as to be obliged to remain under cover.

Also invoked are the fabulously long perspectives of astro-physics, looking backwards to the big bang and forwards to some future time when the sun has diminished to a 'white dwarf' remnant ('the final/ inert residue'). Perhaps the Earth too will have reached that condition, having been engulfed by the sun in its final 'red giant' flare up. So there is a post-apocalyptic sense here, qualifying the fearful pre-apocalyptic: the bang has already happened and we are the residue, our emotions its reverberations. This connects with Prynne's interest, throughout *The White Stones* and especially in 'The Wound, Day and Night', in the idea of a cosmic music that is the echo of the bang while the universe still expands (see Reeve and Kerridge, 37–46). There may also be some reference to 'dark matter', though the most suggestive discoveries of this came latter than 1971.

The poem certainly makes an attack on the apocalyptic imagination, as deployed by environmentalists among others, and on the political and cultural deployment of fear. 'Deployed' is the word, as these analogies between emotional and material processes mainly suggest that some sort of technological structure has been put in place to generate, divert, pool and distribute emotional energy. Hope goes into a 'switchboard', fear into a 'ring-main', and there is a point of view from which fear is a deliberately cultivated and measured 'total crop yield', this latter position of survey being the calculating and managerial counterpart of the backward look at the planet that generates so much emotional release. Such covert management of the apparently spontaneous occurs both in social ideology, where the mass media function as the grid ('the eye / converts the news image to fear enzyme'), and in the individual psyche. Unacknowledged management of this kind is also what Prynne wants us to be wary of when reading lyric poetry.

Each of these analogies suggests that fear is being deliberately generated, as a form of energy that can then be stored and directed. A grid transfers this energy from its source for use elsewhere. This is the 'hate system', with its 'distant loop', from the far curve of which the Earth is safely lovable. At the other end of the loop, we are too close to see the Earth, which dissolves into the 'dotted pigments' or microdots with which the printer forms the image. In an instantaneous shift between extremes of scale, these dots, visible *as* dots only when we are too close, are then compared to the 'granulated' appearance, from the Earth, of Cygnus, a distant constellation including some spectacular supernovae, stars already burnt up. Alternation between seeing from too far and from too near is revealed as a technique of evasion, characteristic of the apocalyptic imagination.

Reading now, I want to apply this insight to the current impasse of environmentalism, its alternation of panic and inaction. What we seem to have in the final stanza is the paradox of an anti-apocalyptic poem making an apocalyptic warning, and a not altogether sarcastic one. Prynne's mocking move is to represent the fear of apocalypse as itself implicated in the material forces that seem to be bringing apocalypse about:

<blockquote>
We
cannot support that total of dis-
placed fear, we have already induced
moral mutation in the species.
</blockquote>

(Prynne, 2005, 166)

Mounting urgency is produced using motifs from the climactic 'countdown' scenes of apocalyptic thriller movies. Something is about to happen. Pressure, as indicated by various obscure dials and measurements, seems to be reaching intolerable levels. These are the final lines:

> Do not take this as metaphor; thinking to
> finish off the last half-pint of milk,
> look at the plants, the entire dark dream outside.

If the description of moral and emotional forces as if they were material could be taken merely as metaphor, its force would be negated: the two would continue to occupy separate zones. 'Do not take this as metaphor': do not allow yourself to entertain apocalyptic fantasies as if they could exist in some purely imaginary and literary zone and need have no practical consequences. Unless you act on your apocalyptic perceptions, you are not entitled to them. That last half-pint of milk can stand now for the unchanged habits of consumption that nearly all professed environmentalists in the West still maintain.

Tony Lopez

Late Modernist, neo-objectivist poetics, when they come to environmentalism, produce an insistence on seeing one's environmentalism itself as quasi-material and part of a larger economy, so that one has to face the question of the niche one's views and feelings occupy. What shelters them, and what do they feed on? I want to examine this perspective in the poetry of Tony Lopez, whose most recent work, the prose-poem *Only More So*, includes in its array of 'found' phrases and passages some literary ecocriticism as well as other environmental material.

Cut-up has been essential to Lopez's writing from the beginning, and since the late 1990s it has become his dominant principle of composition. An austerely self-denying style has emerged, relinquishing direct utterance completely but full of indirect statement. The found materials are sentences, clauses and phrases cut away from their contexts and put together. Many are forcefully declarative statements, which gives their isolation a kind of pathos:

> Music has downsized in tune with the casual look
> Now transcending fashion as such. Radiation
> And sudden exposure to market forces

> Stripped out early consumer activity.
> Should another email arrive from Europe today
> Be sure to be clear that we have completely
> Conflicting visions of the future. Tick if you
> Would prefer not to receive this material.
>
> (Lopez, 2000a, 60)

Far from attempting to escape the jostling of discourses in public space, the poetry accepts an obligation to reproduce it. All the components have been gathered there. Favourite sources seem to include financial pages, scientific articles, political commentary, management theory, lifestyle pages, advertising and cookery, sometimes spliced with literary quotation.

A phrase from an advert, from fashion journalism or from the instructions for using new technology, is positioned where it seems to be talking about poetry, sickness, war or poverty. Obviously, there is satire here upon the way the news media commodify all these things, so that readers of a Sunday supplement will consume the shocking alongside the trivial. Those two categories, shocking and trivial, still seem categorically separate in such a reading, so that their juxtaposition is shameful, and in showing us that juxtaposition the poem calls us to change our priorities.

This basic reading of the juxtapositions never goes away, I think, but it is complicated by the way the cut-up sentences form strange continuities as well as jolting discontinuities:

> Those sweet and melancholy airs hydrate and gently smooth away all resistance, not to the absence, but to the contest of meanings in historical time. Each person will therefore be for themselves a person in the process of becoming, and beyond mere identity politics. It's a nice idea, but how do we get there, and what kind of salad are we building here?
>
> (Lopez, 2000a, 7)

In these lines from the mock preface to the sonnet sequence *Data Shadow*, bathos is registered in the movement from 'sweet and melancholy airs' and 'a person in the process of becoming' to 'what kind of salad are we building here?'. The cut-up produces sharp contrasts: between sacred and profane, open sensibility and managerial manipulation, high art and trivia. But here too there is indeterminacy, in the uncertain transitions. The abrupt comic bathos, and the way that salad phrase is so perfectly caught, communicates a principle of ironic appropriation, witty mimicry, that makes this salad something more than merely an item from the celebrity chef cookery pages; more, that is, than a piece of glossy, reductive commodity fetishism interposed to curtail other human and political possibilities.

What this reveals is that the cut-up method, as used by Lopez, is not simply a matter of the sacred (language open to diverse, changing senses and therefore expressive of liberty and unlimited potential) being exposed to the profane (the goal-oriented instrumentalist languages of late capitalism) and suffering from the encounter. Profane catches something from sacred, too, acquiring an ironical inflection that speaks back against all the compromised rhetoric. Resistance of this kind can only thrive by keeping on the move, skipping from appropriation to new appropriation. Life starts up again in these statements and phrases snatched back from commercial, managerial and even literary use, with an optimistic energy that is strange when the writing's starting-point is a linguistic landscape in which everything is already owned within the system. This writing has a paradoxical freedom of movement, opened up by the recognition that all the language on display can be grabbed and used ironically, since none of it is innocent or authentically one's own.

Lopez has always been fascinated by the ambiguous aura that statements and phrases acquire when space is cleared around them and they are made to stand alone, as conceptual art, found art, takes familiar objects and repositions them as art-objects. In Lopez's cut-up, space is sometimes cleared around a phrase as if it were on display in a gallery. Sometimes the result is piercingly funny. I laughed aloud when I first heard these lines, at a reading:

> People know
> that trees are good for birds

and not just a tool
for social disruption

(Lopez, 2000b, 10)

Lopez's own minimalism, refraining entirely from overt comment, reveals another, enemy minimalism in the paranoid reductiveness of a goal-oriented managerial viewpoint normally unwilling to concede the existence of any meanings other than its own, but here with delicious graciousness conceding one.

This poetic response to contemporary culture is a game-playing counter-move that says to power something like this: 'if you withhold all but your systematized, reductive meanings, poetry will follow suit and attempt to live on the meanings to which you accord priority, rather than bring out more open and human meanings to trot around the demarcated space you have provided'. Not that power is listening, of course, but at least this is a move that rejects the proffered demarcation. Poetry can only continue to *be* poetry by refusing, at least superficially, to be recognisable as such. That seems to be the implicit stance.

So, what can this form of poetic minimalism say about environmental crisis? The refusal to occupy the expected linguistic and cultural space, or 'niche', draws attention to the fact that there *is* a demarcated space, and thus to the relationship between that space and others (one of the statements in *Only More So*, possibly to do with computer game design, is 'We decided on the creation of a new space in which shame could be experienced'). Searching for an authentic voice means searching for autonomy and sheltered space. Implicit in the refusal to do this, therefore, is some recognition of interdependency and complicity, and by extension a sense of cultural ecology. Potentially this could lead us to material ecology, and take that too, as a scientific discipline, out of its niche, forcing it into collision with other cultural discourses.

There is something more than this. In *Only More So*, the found materials are forced together in dense blocks of prose that hem them in. There are still many instances of the comedy that comes from isolating a statement: among the types are absurd composure ('String theory has yet to make contact with the empirical universe'), pathos of understatement ('If a body lives, the eyes will unavoidably be filled with meaning and expressiveness') and bathos ('Zorro isn't going to break any new ground'; 'When radioactive rain fell on the hills and farms of the Lake District and North Wales, we decided to go home'). But the specific frustration imposed by these dense blocks is not only that every line of thought is cut off; it is also that nothing can be prominent. Nothing can stand out or makes itself heard. And some of the elements—not only the environmentalism, but also lines that seem to come from debates about torture and documentaries about the Holocaust—are such that, muffled by this crowdedness, they seem to scream silently at us.

So here is a poetic form that dramatises the way that in hearing environmental messages, and others, we fail to hear them. It doesn't offer a way out of that impasse. Neither poet does. They hold us, and themselves, very firmly there, because we don't need to be told what to do. We know, and these poets refuse to let us pretend otherwise.

Richard Kerridge is head of postgraduate studies in English Literature and Creative Writing at Bath Spa University.

Note

[1] There is a possibly unreliable transcript of a lecture given at much the same time that has Prynne speaking even more scornfully, in a knockabout way, about the uses made of this image of the Earth: 'Jeremy Prynne lectures on *Maximus IV, V, VI*, Simon Fraser University, July 27, 1971', transcribed by Tom McGauley. Available online at http://charlesolson.ca/files/Prynnelecture1.htm, downloaded 16th July 2007.

Works Cited

Davie, Donald. *Thomas Hardy and British Poetry*. London: Routledge and Kegan Paul, 1973.

Edwards, Paul. *Wyndham Lewis: Painter and Writer*. New Haven: Yale UP, 2000.

Garrard, Greg. *Ecocriticism*. Abingdon: Routledge, 2004.

Lanchester, John. 'Warmer, Warmer.' *London Review of Books* 22 Mar. 2007: 3–9.

Lewis, Wyndham. *Enemy of the Stars*. London: Desmond Harmsworth, 1932.

Lopez, Tony (2000a). *Data Shadow*. London: Reality Street Editions, 2000.

— (2000b). *Devolution*. Great Barrington: The Figures, 2000.

— *Only More So*. Part-published in *Practice: New Writing + Art* 2 (2007): 145–148. Part-available online at http://www.argotistonline.co.uk/Lopez%20poem.htm downloaded 30th July 2007.

Lovelock, James. *The Revenge of Gaia*. London: Allen Lane, 2006.

Lynas, Mark. *Six Degrees: Our Future on a Hotter Planet*. London: Fourth Estate, 2007.

McKibben, Bill. *The Age of Missing Information*. New York: Random House, 1992.

Noel-Tod, Jeremy. 'Walking the Yellow Brick Road: A Pedestrian Account of J.H. Prynne's *Poems*.' In Kennedy, David, ed. *Necessary Steps*. Exeter: Shearsman Books, 2007.

Pearce, Fred. *The Last Generation*. London: Transworld, 2006.

Perril, Simon. 'Hanging on Your Every Word: J.H. Prynne's *Bands Around The Throat* and a Dialectics of Planned Impurity'. *Jacket* 24, November 2003. Available online at http://jacketmagazine.com/24/perril.html downloaded 30th July 2007.

Prynne, J.H. 'Jeremy Prynne lectures on *Maximus IV, V, VI*, Simon Fraser University, July 27, 1971', transcribed by Tom McGauley. Available online at http://charlesolson.ca/files/Prynnelecture1.htm, downloaded 16th July 2007.

— 'A Letter to Steve McCaffery'. *The Gig* 7, November 2000.

— *Poems*. Fremantle: Fremantle Arts Centre Press/Tarset: Bloodaxe Books, 2005.

Reeve, N.H. and Richard Kerridge. *Nearly Too Much: The Poetry of J. H. Prynne*. Liverpool: Liverpool UP, 1995.

Wilkinson, John. 'Tenter Ground.' *Notre Dame Review* 22 (Summer 2006), 196–207. Available online at http://www.nd.edu/~ndr22/John%20 Wilkinson/Wilkinson-review.pdf, downloaded 30th July 2007.

Žižek, Slavoj. *Looking Awry: An Introduction to Jacques Lacan through Popular Culture*. Cambridge, MA: MIT Press, 1997.

Advertising in *The Maximus Poems*

MICHAEL KINDELLAN

What follows outlines a particular mode of public language as it appears in the first volume of *The Maximus Poems* by Charles Olson. I want to talk about advertising, first as presented in *Maximus* as an historical phenomenon, and second, as Maximus[1] finds it in its more contemporary state, suggesting throughout that Olson objects to advertising primarily on aesthetic terms, if we take aesthesis in its older sense, to denote 'a sensory link between interior and exterior worlds' (Lawrence n.p.). In *Maximus*, advertising's aesthetic disjunctions relate directly to the disconnection between citizen and a common language of genuine exchange, wherein spatial separations and temporal suspensions preserve the 'common' while attenuating the 'exchange.'

In the historical retrospect of the *Maximus*, Olson attends principally to a book called *ADVERTISEMENTS* by Captain John Smith, soldier, sailor and author, which according to Olson hit the mud streets of Gloucester in 1630, exactly seven years following its foundation by Dorchester emigrants. If we measure this duration between foundation and the publication of Smith's *ADVERTISEMENTS*, and then compare that elapse to Maximus's pronouncement elsewhere, that after seven years 'you cld carry cinders in yr hand | for what the country was worth [...] the language | has belonged to trade or to the English | ever since' (*Maximus* 408), an obvious thesis emerges. Captain Smith was refused the position of navigator by the founding pilgrims, who chose one Miles Standish instead. Smith says in *Travels and Works* that he published *ADVERTISEMENTS* because his services were refused by Gloucester's founders, inclined as they were to 'save charges, saying books and maps were much better cheape to teach them, than my selfe' (quoted in Butterick 103). Olson considers this event to be a profound dissociation.

Of course, Smith's advertisements of 1631, not 1630 as Olson contends, were more usefully instructional than those Maximus discovers in his own subsequent inspection of Gloucester, and Olson takes time in his reviews of books *about* Smith to ignore the prose of the authors and praise the care of their subject's own writing. In a 1953 review of Bradford Smith's *Captain John Smith, His Life & Legend*, Olson lauds the captain for his language's prehension of the matters it discusses. Olson remarks (circuitously, as my editorial ellipses show):

> The wild thing about the original Smith in this business is [...], the very bite in his language [...]. He knew the country [...], said it in prose like no one has since, simply that he had the first of it [...], got it into words [...]. Why I sing John Smith is this, that the *geographic*, the sudden *land* of the place is in there, not described, not local, not represented—like all advertisements, all the shit now pours out, the American road, the filthiness, of graphic words [...]. God, to get the distinction across, so that even Ezra Pound stops praising ads [...]. Even [Pound's] own act is now ad-writing, that where he got it—say Elbert Hubbard—that this age of distraction is total, that energy, as a component, is not enough, Ezra (*Collected Prose* 319–20).

Olson in fact includes Smith's entire poem 'THE SEA MARKE' in *Maximus*, which originally stood as a dedication to *ADVERTISEMENTS*; at the Vancouver Poetry Conference of August 1963, Olson said this piece 'argues a condition of poetics at the date it was written' (qtd. in Butterick 103). Its opening stanza reads:

> Aloofe, aloofe; and come no neare,
>   the dangers do appeare;
> Which if my ruine had not beene
>   you had not seene:
> I onely lie upon this shelfe
>   to be a marke to all
>   which on the same might fall
> That none may perish but my selfe (73).

The wrecked vessel functions as a macabre sort of billboard, one that recommends remoteness for safety. The message is at once caveat and council, and rehearses an older sense of the word 'advertise,' as was Olson's wont, meaning to make a public announcement of warning. And yet the poem, transposed by Olson into a new context, also warns *about* advertising, with 'shelfe' denoting not just an underwater hazard, but a place for a commodity, wrecked and ruined.

Directly following the quoted poem, Maximus asks, in section 'III' of 'Letter 15,' and what of 'the economics and poetics *thereafter*' (74). Olson admits the two are intimately intertwined. An earlier poem, 'Song 2' from a sequence called '*The Songs of Maximus*,' prefigures this admission, showing Maximus, too, assailed by the unrelenting address of corporate slither, which is aptly likened to fish guts washing the city in red:

>   all
> wrong
>   And I am asked—ask myself (I, too, covered
> with the gurry of it) where
> shall we go from here, what can we do
> when even the public conveyances
> sing (17)?

Some of the despair undoubtedly arises from a nascent inkling Maximus is himself implicated in the 'musicracket of all ownership;' Maximus initially petitions Gloucester from some distance outside it, by 'islands [incidentally, also] hidden in blood' (5), thereby adding to the demand exhausting the attentions he hopes to resuscitate. Recognition of this fact could partly explain the reduced number of letters (i.e., epistles) in the ensuing volumes of the poem. Implicit in the subsequent eschewal of letter-writing, too, is a renewed attempt to dump what Olson perceived to be a false dichotomy between literate, logical and verbal hierarchies of the *logos* on one side and the aleatory capacities of *muthos* and orality on the other—*Maximus IV, V VI* is much more fragmentary and mythological compared to the first volume's more complete historical pretensions, in respect of this development. Maximus attacks authorities of the botched public discourse with fitting hyperbole, again without self-exoneration:

>   (o Statue
> o Republic, o
> Tell-A-Vision, the best
> is soap. The true troubadours
> are CBS. Melopoeia

is for Cokes by Cokes out of
Pause

IV
(o Po-ets, you
should getta
job (75)

This passage contains a further swipe at Pound. Olson wrote to Creeley in a February 1951 letter that 'it should be no wonder that Ez., at the same time he carries on a conspiracy to reform finance... says radio commercials are the best verse now being writ' (qtd. in Butterick 107). A June 1946 entry in *An Encounter at St. Elizabeth's*, which is a collection of Olson's notes regarding his visitations with Pound, says:

> Yesterday we batted around the radio, the movies, the magazines, and national advertising, the 4 plagues of our time. I had in the morning, after the Ziegfeld Follies, been wondering how deep the effects go, had recalled that, in time terms, the existence of these 4 was short, about the span of my own life, 35 years (89).

In 'Letter 15,' Olson in fact dates the inception of national advertising as 1902, coincident with what he calls the 'American epos.' In an unpublished notebook, Olson idiosyncratically defines epos: 'epos means words—without accompaniment of song or lyre & without being acted out (contrasted to *ergon*)' (qtd. in Butterick 106), which I think complicates rather than clarifies Olson's position on the relation between advertising and poetics. The plain effect inherent in epos, which Olson elsewhere calls mere 'WORDS THEMSELVES,' marks Olson's refusal to adjust his verse even to the music of the phrase, as Pound's melopoeia might demand—Olson's line, he's famously insisted, instead conforms to the pressures of breath. Olson rearticulates his poetic programme in a brief essay called 'Logography,' wherein he says 'word writing, not idea writing, that would seem to be it' (*Collected Prose* 184). So in this sense, Olson has no quarrel with the attenuated affect of epos. And yet, it is inconceivable Olson would recoil from ergon, from activity, from work literally measured in terms of the heat of which it is equivalent, as the *second line* of the *Maximus* categorically states 'I, Maximus | a metal hot from boiling water, tell you' (5). In opposing ergon, Olson takes issue with *Aristotelian* ergon, and by association with a good deal of western metaphysics as well (he's not called Maximus for no cause), insofar as said metaphysics inscribe into linguistic structures abstract divisions which Olson wants to reject. This tradition, in audacious outline, begins at Socrates, goes via Descartes and ends up as a strange tonic comprised of the 'moral imperialism' (Butterick 104) of Elbert Hubbard, the arrogant certitude of Ezra Pound, and the simulated rural drawl of brash newspaper ads for Raymond's department store in Boston.

*

By the time Maximus arrives in Gloucester, the 4 plagues have done a good deal of harm to both social and aesthetic sensibilities. The damaged idioms and nullifying jingles of commercial language degrade public awareness, and usurp, as Robert von Hallberg puts it, human attention with a silent flood that forces the spectator into passivity (58). The *Maximus* poem '*Songs of Maximus*' offers a concise assessment:

> coloured pictures
> of all things to eat: dirty
> postcards
> And words words words
> all over everything
> No eyes or ears left
> to do their own doings (all
> invaded, appropriated, outraged, all senses
> including the mind, that worker on what is
> [...]
> lulled (17)

From Maximus's very first letters to Gloucester, he makes his disapproval explicit with emphatic apostrophe: 'kill kill kill kill kill | those | who advertise you | out)' (8). Maximus admonishes Gloucester's people to recover what they may not know they've lost, itself a rhetorical gesture that goes some way in positioning Olson's poet between Shelley's unacknowledged legislator and 'Oppen's re-visionary legislator of the unacknowledged world' (Lawrence n.p.).

The 'separation and disarticulation' (Lawrence n.p.) resulting from advertising's division of product and its promotion mirrors and induces a splitting of audience from original, and therefore, in Olson's estimation, more coherent context. Maximus is forced to concede heterogeneity is a condition of a logocentric polis: what is more, its people are practically aphasic, conditioned by 'neoned-in sound' (6) and 'spray gunned silence' (6). The advertising plastered across Gloucester is language without substantial object, and thus without excitement to action. Its people don't talk and so don't act (Olson spends good deal of *Maximus* as well as in critical prose and letters arguing a connection between genuine performances of both). We get no real sense of anything actually happening in Gloucester in the present moment, other than Maximus's writing it. Inhabitants are 'isolated persons,' 'islands of men and girls' (16), and so

> can know polis
> not as localism, not that mu-sick (the trick
> of corporations, newspapers, slick magazines, movie houses,
> the ships, even the wharves absentee owned
>
> they whine to my people, these entertainers, sellers (14)

Gloucester's diminished attention is intimately connected to abstraction, is in fact a function of it, which Olson envisages as language devoid of intimacy necessary for constitutive relations, social, political, or aesthetic, and we can see a criticism of this situation developing as early as the first poem of the *Maximus*. By 'Letter 3,' Maximus is fully conscious of the problem and incants a prayer-like appeal that inveighs directly against the 'absenteeism' in absentee ownership, against the vanished sources of now common public language of advertising:

> Let those who use words cheap, who use us cheap
> take themselves out of the way
> Let them not talk of what is good for the city

Let them free the way for me, for the men of the Fort
who are not hired, who buy the white houses

Let them cease putting out words in the public print
so that any of us have to leave, so that my Portuguese leave,
leave the Lady they gave us, sell their schooners
with the greyhounds aft, the long Diesels
they put their money in, leave Gloucester
in the present shame of,
the wondership stolen by,
ownership (13)

Maximus approves of the immigrants who come *in* to Gloucester from elsewhere, as Maximus does from Tyre, as Olson did from Worcester and from Washington, as we are told his father had; neither subtracts wealth from the city, neither takes away, but instead puts *in*. For Olson it is a primary trajectory, this coming in; those who benefit the city are recommended by the preposition 'in,' and the verb 'gave.' They are *placed*, literally, in direct opposition to ownership that destroys whatever scant coherence and value the heterogeneous city still retains because owners 'use cheap,' 'take,' go 'out,' 'steal,' even force others to 'leave.' Such figures abstract in the primordial sense in *pulling away from*.

This is not the action of Maximus, whose movement is ultimately that of arrival: Maximus comes to Gloucester 'from off-shore' at the outset of *The Maximus Poems*; he then 'set[s] out now | in a box upon the sea' (373) at the end of *Maximus IV, V, VI*; finally he finds himself back in Gloucester as *Volume Three* opens, 'writing a republic | in gloom on Watch-House Point' (377). This very action, I want to suggest, supplies Olson and his creature Maximus with a method supposedly capable of counteracting the social entropies induced by abstract universalisms. Right from the start of *Maximus*, Olson insists the primary arrangements of any person's movement in a viable polis must be localising, which is more a method than a condition, and intensive:

in! in! the bow-spirit, bird, the beak
in, the bend is, in, goes in, the form (8)

In 'Projective Verse,' Olson lays the groundwork of a literalist aesthetic, whose measures accord with rhythms of fishing trips, tides and much else besides: 'Each line is a progressing of both the meaning and the breathing forward, and then a backing up, without progress, or any kind of movement outside the unit of time local to the idea' (*Collected Prose* 246). Attention to the fact, citizen, that you are more a physiological than conceptual reality, so far as Olson is concerned, should more or less take care of what he called the 'enormous fallacy' of post-Socratic metaphysics, principally Plato's deductive reasoning and world of forms, and Aristotle's logic and classification. These epistemological frameworks form what Olson pejoratively called a 'universe of discourse,' which Creeley succinctly defines on Olson's behalf as 'abstracting, generalising systems of reference which put the immediate always at a theoretical "distance", so that reflection and representation might then be the primary human acts rather than the very "actions" themselves' ('Preface', *Charles Olson: Allegory of a Poet's Life* xviii).

In his essay, 'A Polis of Attention and Dialogue,' Jeff Wild suggests that Olson is in fact addressing people whose commonality is the quality of their attention (n.p.); Don Byrd calls such quality of attention a 'radical phenomenology [in which] fishermen provide a model for perceptual care and precision' (*Charles Olson's Maximus* 81). To facilitate this, Olson suggests a method of writing that 'relates powers of saying to powers of doing' (Lawrence n.p.). Olson puts it rhetorically in 'Letter 3' when he asks who are potential citizens in light of the universe of discourse that so perniciously divorces people from their experience? He answers promptly:

> Only a man or a girl who hear a word
> and that word meant to mean not a single thing the least more than
> what it does mean (not at all to sell any one anything (19)

Michael Kindellan is a PhD student at the University of Sussex.

Note
[1] Throughout this essay italicised *Maximus* refers to the poem, un-italicised refers to Olson's eponymous character.

Works Cited

Butterick, George F. *A Guide to the Maximus Poems*. Berkeley: University of California Press, 1980.

Byrd, Don. *Charles Olson's Maximus*. Urbana: University of Illinois Press, 1980.

Creeley, Charles. 'Preface.' *Charles Olson: The Allegory of a Poet's Life*. Berkeley: North Atlantic Books, 2000.

Lawrence, Nick. EPC/Nick Lawrence Home Page. March 2007 <http://wings.buffalo.edu/epc/authors/lawrencen/republic.html>

Hallberg, Robert von. *Charles Olson: The Scholar's Art*. Cambridge, MA: Harvard UP, 1978.

Olson, Charles. *Charles Olson and Ezra Pound: An Encounter at St. Elizabeth's*. Ed. Catherine Seelye. New York: Paragon House, 1975.

___. *Collected Prose*. Ed. Donald Allen and Benjamin Friedlander. Berkeley: University of California Press, 1997.

___. *The Maximus Poems*. Ed. George Butterick. Berkeley: University of California Press, 1983.

Wild, Jeff. 'Polis of Attention and Dialogue.' EPC. 2003. March 2007 < http://epc.buffalo.edu/authors/olson/blog/wild.pdf>

Robert Duncan: Poetry and the Vietnam War

Catherine Martin

Late in October 1971, Robert Duncan wrote to his fellow poet, Denise Levertov on a subject that had preoccupied their letters with a growing intensity in recent weeks: the Vietnam War. There was a pronounced difference in the political commitment these two poets made to the anti-war movement. While Duncan followed the anarchist belief that the individual should resist any attempt to be co-opted into a movement which compromises their own volition, Levertov was actively engaged in the peace movement, supporting her husband, Mitch Goodman, who was indicted for resisting the draft law in 1968. Yet what exercised Duncan's attention was not this difference, but the question of the poet's responsibility to engage with and imagine this war. Against the kind of poetry Levertov's commitment had driven her to write, Duncan insists the poem should be more than the record of action that takes place outside it—in fact, the poem should be the action:

> as workers in words, it is our business to keep alive in the language definitions as well as forces, to create crises in meaning [...] in which we are the more aware of the crisis involved, of what is at issue (*Letters* 661).

The crux of his argument with Levertov over the war is—for him—a fundamental difference in the way they conceive of the poem and its relationship to the world. In the same letter Duncan reminds Levertov of the principles they had jointly espoused in their earlier work, which were inspired by a ground breaking document of mid-century American poetics, Charles Olson's 1950 manifesto, 'Projective Verse'. Foremost in Duncan's mind is Olson's proposition: 'FORM IS NEVER MORE THAN AN EXTENSION OF CONTENT' (Olson 614). Duncan writes, 'Our initial breakthrough was [...] concerned [...] with form as the direct vehicle and medium of content', clarifying: 'Which means and still means for me that we do not say something by means of the poem but the poem is itself the immediacy of saying—it has its own meaning. It is as immediate as the dream' (*Letters* 668). What he objects to in Levertov's recent work is not merely her prioritization of content over form, but her failure to engage with this content in her poems. For Duncan the poem is less the vehicle for a prior meaning which he wants to express through it, than an ongoing event in language which allows the writer to discover through its process meanings which were not intended, but are nonetheless illuminating about the subject at hand.

As his reference to the dream suggests, for him the poem is always the ground for revelation; for an insight into the present situation, which is achieved through an associative probing of the words of the poem not unlike Freudian dream-analysis. This is what Duncan means when he says the poem 'has its own meaning'. His perverse habit of reading through puns, coincidence, connections contrived via sound resemblance and error can be infuriating and even, as Levertov accuses, coercive. Yet in its best instances in his earlier work it had resulted in a poetry where dense networks of interlinked allusion worked to recover a cultural memory which Duncan perceived had been lost from the discourse of public life.

Duncan's belief that Levertov had departed from a shared poetics can be traced back through their early letters. Their friendship began in 1953 when Duncan sent a punning tribute, 'An A Muse Ment', to the young poet whose work he had admired in *Origin* magazine. 'An A Muse Ment' recognizes as a point of commonality their shared assumption of the poem as an exploratory vehicle. It emphasizes that for their 'Pound, / Williams, H.D., Stein, Zukofsky [...] surrealist / Dada staind' generation, each line of the poem involves a crisis of attention, that the movement from one line to the next involves a process of negotiation or revision which casts the certainty of the last into doubt:

> A great effort, straining, breaking up
> all the melodic line (the lyr-
> ick strain?) Don't
> hand me that old line we say
> you dont know what yer saying. (*Letters* 3)

These lines might remind us of Robert Creeley's characteristic use of the line break's potentially estranging effects. But these hesitations, which elongate possibility and prevent thought from being curtailed, are also frequent in Robert Duncan's 1960 collection, *The Opening of the Field*. Here the fragile, restlessly shifting alignments of meaning he contrives in the pauses between lines work to evade stasis, making any terminus or conclusion provisional. Individual lines cannot long withstand the pressure of enjambment, but are constantly compromised by the coexistence of other phrases. This formal commitment to provisionality, to the poem's ability to respond rather than to insist upon an incontrovertible position, was something Duncan believed Levertov and he shared.

Peter Middleton has written very convincingly of the war as a crisis in Denise Levertov's aesthetic, where she runs up against the limitations of her 'organic form' as a mode of responsiveness. Her reliance on revelations that emerge from particular observations of the world, he argues, means that 'historical events like the war can't be easily presented [...], because such vast historical developments do not offer meaningful first hand experiences or narratives, through which such events can be understood' (Middleton 9). Yet reading through Duncan's poetry of the same period, I'm struck by a similar sense of crisis in *his* assumptions about poetry. Duncan's 1968 volume, *Bending the Bow*, offers itself as a narrative of the way the Vietnam War enters his writing life. The escalation of the conflict in Vietnam coincides with the development of a new poetic sequence he calls 'Passages'. This open-ended series extends and expands the ambition of his earlier field poems in its receptiveness to, in Olson's terms, whatever might enter its radius of perception. As Duncan says of the series: 'I want to open my work up to material that lies just beyond my recognition of use as I work' (*Letters* 466).

In 'Passages 2: At the Loom', Duncan imagines the poetry of this new experimental series germinating from a complex intertextual occasion. Remembering the 'hwirr thkk' of 'Kirke's loom', as Pound remembers Odysseus listening to it in *The Cantos*, Duncan implies the poem is generated through its own efforts to accommodate this alien, undigested material (*Bending* 11). His image of the mind as 'shuttle among / set strings of the music' suggests such material is absorbed through a rhythmic working-through, as the regular back and forth motion of the loom brings it into the 'set' confines of the poem:

> my mind a shuttle among
>   set strings of the music
> lets a weft of dream grow in the day time,
>   an increment of associations,
>   luminous soft threads,
> the thrown glamour, crossing and recrossing,
>   the twisted sinews underlying the work. (*Bending* 11)

Yet Duncan recognizes the attendant danger of the poem's transformative process, and of rhythm's seductive pull towards stasis and uniformity. If the poem grows through 'an increment of associations', the challenge is not to tie up or resolve these threads, but, as he explains to Levertov, 'to *disconnect*, to unweave—towards a much more fugitive, inconclusive relation' where the integrity or strangeness of the object is left partially intact (*Letters* 468). Interestingly, the poetic process as Duncan depicts it is here is at least partially involuntary: the poet 'lets' the weft grow in the permission he gives to threads of connection that are tangential, coincidental.

It is here that the difficulty with Duncan's self-imposed obligation to write 'about' the Vietnam situation lies. In what ways can the war trespass upon the margins of the poem? And in what ways can the poem hope to transform or absorb it? Looking back to Duncan's writing of the late 50s and early 60s, we see how his interest in the ways the poem might be, in the words of 'Often I am Permitted to Return to a Meadow', 'given' or bestowed, can lead to a powerful and effective political critique (*Opening* 6). I'm thinking here of 'A Poem Beginning with a Line by Pindar', Duncan's long 1959 poem, which acts to repair the damage done to a shared or 'public' language by the degraded political rhetoric of the then government. The poem figures the discourse of the state as blunted and historically irresponsible, simulating a stumbling, aphasic speech to represent a rhetoric that refuses to comprehend the human impact of their nuclear capabilities:

> The present dented of the U
> nighted stayd. States. The heavy clod?
>   Cloud. Invades the brain. (*Opening* 63)

These stuttered malformed words gesture ironically to a historical awareness occluded by the government's apparent failure to remember the atom bomb's devastating effects in Hiroshima.

If the poem offers any resistance to this rhetoric and logic, it is through its own involuntary process; its receptiveness to what lies 'at the margins of thought' (*Opening* 62). 'A Poem Beginning with a Line by Pindar' begins, as its title suggests, with the unwilled intrusion of a remembered line from Pindar's 'First Pythian Ode' into the narrator's consciousness. The rest of the poem grows through dream-like 'increment of association' from the images and ideas this line throws up, weaving an errant path through subjects as seemingly diverse as the political dilemmas of Poundian modernism; the deficiencies of recent American presidents, ancient Greek mythology and the history of the American west. Yet if in this way, Duncan follows in Olson's terms, the 'track the poem underhand declares *for itself*', a greater degree of autonomous agency for the poem is implied by the permission Duncan gives to the animacy of language itself to determine the poem's direction, in the homonymic movement from word to word (Olson 614). Read against the invasive climate of cold-war America, and particularly against the state's efforts to determine and police meaning, Duncan's stipulation to Levertov of the necessity to 'keep alive in the language definitions' and to 'create crises in meaning', has greater potency (*Letters* 661). 'A Poem Beginning with a Line by Pindar' is led by the logic of the pun where meaning leaks and exceeds the restraints put upon it. Such linguistic disturbances are in this poem specifically related to the homo-erotic desire from which it germinates, a desire pathologised by the state as a threat to national security, in need of containment and scrutiny. That Duncan also uses the metaphor of disease to describe the poem's self-germinating momentum seems no coincidence in an era when conservative politicians were linking homosexuality with communism, as Jane Sherron De Hart observes, reconceptualising 'homosexuality as a contagious disease spread by communists to weaken the nation from within' (Sherron De Hart 125). Duncan succeeds in turning this connection around, allowing the infectious logic of the words of his poem to gesture toward the hidden history of those whom he identifies elsewhere as 'the people of a dream secretly at work in the nation, of an other nation within and below and behind and above the public identity of America' (*Caesar's Gate* xix).

Duncan's Vietnam era poems do similarly, though more self-consciously, attempt to put back into circulation words that have become partisan. But what's more striking about these poems is their reiterated sense of experiencing the war as a crisis in language: as a failure of his own poetic vocabulary. I want to suggest that this crisis derives precisely from the contradiction between the poetics of invasion avowed in his letters to Levertov, and practised so successfully in his earlier work, and the more deadly threat posed by the Vietnam war: that it will invade artistic consciousness and make the imagination complicit with acts perpetrated without consent on its behalf.

'Passages 13: The Fire' is the first poem to explicitly address the war, though it does so in typically oblique fashion through a meditation upon Piero di Cosimo's 1490 painting, *A Forest Fire*. The poem begins by expressing doubt about its own abilities. As Albert Gelpi suggests, the poem views di Cosimo's painting as a superior 'demonstration of how the magic of the visionary imagination can in fact suffuse the violent painting with a "charm'd" and glowing "stillness"' (Gelpi xviii). This is a magic, the narrator in comparison feels he cannot sustain against the onslaught of 'the daily news: the earthquakes, eruptions, / flaming automobiles [...] the wars against communism' (*Bending* 42). If the word blocks that preface and conclude the poem, hedging it in protectively, do reach the 'pastoral stillness amidst terror, sorrow' that Duncan aspires to, they do so only at the price of emptying language of any trace of the contemporary world, by immersing the reader in the purely relational pleasure of these words (*Bending* 43). There is an endless, reiterative enjoyment to be had from the simple juxtaposition of words in these blocks that can potentially be read in all directions, enclosing the reader in the 'charmd field' of Duncan's vision (*Bending* 42). Freed from discursive pressures, the poem finds some release in this unpurposive use of words, and in the cleansing valence of freshness and coolness that attaches to them.

Yet this is not the linguistic responsibility Duncan charges Levertov to uphold. The 'stillness' of these echoing grids derives exactly from their exclusion of the exterior. The only reference they make to human interaction are in the disembodied and a-historical nouns: 'harbor', 'coin', 'hand', 'foot'. Similarly, the separateness of the squares—oddly anterior to the rest of the poem—renders them insoluble with the moral wranglings that the central portion of the poem contains. Failing to transform or work through a political anger that finds its only outlet in the cartoonish excess of Duncan's depictions of Nixon et al lying in the UN, these blocks perform a ritualistic cleansing of language, but only by retreating to what has not been tainted by the war.

I say these word-squares act like protective screens because it is as if Duncan's formerly receptive aesthetic puts him at risk of trauma or coercion. It's no longer a question of giving in to 'the intent of the poem' (*Bending* 137); rather he fears that the war, not the poem, might be using him for its own ends. Instead, his letters to Levertov insist on the sanctity of individual volition, and likewise 'Passages 26: The Soldiers' asserts that 'The first evil is that which has power over you' (*Bending* 115). The Passages series ostensibly keeps alive Duncan's wish that the poem should provide a transformative space where 'the presentations of our actual life reappear as entities creative of a dream' (*Letters* 531). However, the analogy *Bending the Bow* makes to dreaming is closer to the protective function Freud describes in *Beyond the Pleasure Principle*, where the dream works to master retrospectively an overload to the sensory system caused by a shock or trauma. The crisis these letters and poems attest to results in a larger change in Duncan's work, evident in the subsequent *Ground Work* volumes where intertextuality takes on a darker tenor in a period of paranoia, suspicion and surveillance, and where, as William Rowe has recently argued, the poem is confronted with what it cannot process: the unconsumed materiality of history, embodied in the image of a napalmed child, a 'catastrophe incommensurate / with meaning' (*Ground Work* 75).

Catherine Martin is a PhD candidate at the University of Sussex.

Works Cited

Duncan, Robert. *Bending the Bow*. New York: New Directions, 1968.
— *Caesar's Gate: Poems 1949–50*. Berkeley: Sand Dollar, 1972.
— *The Opening of the Field*. New York: New Directions, 1960.
— *Ground Work: Before the War*. New York: New Directions, 1984.
Duncan, Robert and Denise Levertov. *The Letters of Robert Duncan and Denise Levertov*. Ed. Robert J. Bertholf and Albert Gelpi. Stanford: Stanford UP, 2004.
Gelpi, Albert. 'Introduction: The "Aesthetic Ethics" of the Visionary Imagination'. *The Letters of Robert Duncan and Denise Levertov*. Ed. Robert J. Bertholf and Albert Gelpi. Stanford: Stanford UP, 2004. ix–xxv.
Middleton, Peter. *Revelation and Revolution in the Poetry of Denise Levertov*. London: Binnacle Press, 1981.
Olson, Charles. 'Projective Verse'. *Postmodern American Poetry: A Norton Anthology.* Ed. Paul Hoover. London: Norton, 1994. 613–21.
Sherron De Hart, Jane. 'Containment at Home: Gender, Sexuality and National Identity in Cold War America'. *Rethinking Cold War Culture*. Ed. Peter J. Kuznick and James Gilbert. London: Smithsonian Institution Press, 2001. 124–55.

Cluster Poems—Scepticism in Lyn Hejinian's *The Fatalist*

Peter Middleton

Montage, open field, parataxis: these terms could elliptically describe the sequence of three generations of American avant-garde theories of poetic form. Each mode represents the poem as a cluster of similar yet distinct elements; the formal paradigms differ as the assemblage of the poem becomes successively less integrated into a synthetic unity. Montage in a Poundian Canto holds the proximal ideograms in a close dialogue. Open Field poetry relies on the collective effect of what might be disparate materials to integrate into an overall semantic field that emerges from the sum of the parts and holds them in its guiding formation just as an electromagnetic field organises a space. Paratactic poetry exemplifies the Webster's *Third New International Dictionary* definition of the cluster: 'a number of similar things grouped together in association or in physical proximity (a ~ of houses)'. It seems unlikely however that contemporary poets will be espousing a 'cluster poetics' any time soon because this neutral word, that for the OED describes collections of plants, creatures and other familiar items, has been co-opted into medical and military discourse with highly negative connotations. Epidemiologists study 'clusters' of people with the same disease. A 'cluster fuck' is a situation in which everything is going wrong, and some commentators claim that it means specifically a situation where too many officers, who wear oak-leaf clusters on their uniforms, are creating a confused leadership. Then comes the 'cluster bomb', such as the 'Sensor Fuzed Weapon' developed by Textron, that delivers a group of small air-borne missiles or sub-munitions with devastating effect, and was used in the military 'Operation Iraqi Freedom,' itself surely a cluster name. It is no wonder that poets have not called their poems 'cluster poems'. Poets have to be on their guard, sceptical of the accuracy of public language and its capacity to describe our complex political landscapes where verbal sub-munitions mine the path. Yet I like to think that poets might have found the term cluster useful, since its pejorative associations allude to explosive and transgressive actions, and to a dysfunction that results from an excess of functionality—too many officer authorities, too many authoritative meanings, clustered together. Such effects have been the aesthetic aspiration of many avant-garde poets of the past few decades, who have also been acutely aware of the role of such ideologically saturated terms as 'cluster bomb' in public language, to the extent that much of the most visionary work has been devoted to a writing-through of this clustering of language. At the recent 'Poetry and Public Language' conference in Plymouth, the work of two American poets, Lyn Hejinian and Barrett Watten, became the focus of a collective investigation of the poetics required by contemporary linguistic conditions within public culture. In this condensation of my paper for the conference I discuss the scepticism that permeates contemporary poetics in relation to a widespread mistrust of the languages and epistemology of public information about current history, and the capacity of any poetic discourse to represent this difficult history adequately.

*

Lyn Hejinian offers an allegory to explain such scepticism. As children growing up we 'discover that words are not equal to the world, that a blur of displacement, a type of parallax, exists in the relation between things (events, ideas, objects) and the words for them—a displacement producing a gap.' Our human condition, we learn with disappointment, is to be scepticism, and childhood trust in words vanishes along with belief in magic or Santa Claus. Human 'psychology' is founded on 'our overwhelming experience of the vastness and uncertainty of the world, and by what often seems to be the inadequacy of the imagination that longs to know it.' Poets suffer this scepticism with particular acuteness, aware of 'the even greater inadequacy of the language that appears to describe, discuss, or disclose it.' (*Hejinian 2000*, 48–49) This is a scepticism that is not due to some individual cognitive failing (say lack of education, failure to read the newspapers, personal isolation, or dyslexic relations to language), nor is it due to social anomie (perhaps state censorship of information, corporate secrecy, or poor communications infrastructure). This would be a fundamental condition and not for instance a problem experienced by a few poets living in one city, or even poets writing in opposition to a recent war. This I think is the radical doubt that Andrew Joron is troubled by in the opening to *Fathom* where he begins his prefatory essay by asking dramatically why poetry seems to stop mattering to us. 'What good is poetry at a time like this' (15), he asks, and we might expect him to blame the deficiencies of public culture, but he resists this, it is not just the times that are out of joint, poetry is fundamentally 'inadequate' because 'poetry forces language to fail.' (15) He doesn't commit himself to saying what this failure consists of, whether it might be a failure of mutual understanding, a failure to represent some reality, or a failure of reasoning. Public language is haunted by a primordial lament, and this is why 'poetry, before taking action, listens to the speechlessness of words' (16). To which I think one could also reply: poetry ought to listen to the helplessness and speechlessness of people who can articulate their outrage at injustice and yet are prevented from making their speech and writing public by the structures that manage public discourse. Is his scepticism about language getting in the way of an analysis of why 'American poetry is a marginal genre whose existence is irrelevant to the course of Empire' (18) as it pursues 'sacred and profane wars of vengeance'? (24)

Linguistic scepticism has been such a widespread feature of essays on poetics by generations of poets since 1970 that it goes almost unremarked. The many discussions of authorial subjectivity, diminished referentiality, and the productive agency of the reader, almost always assume some belief similar to that of Hejinian in her essay 'The Rejection of Closure' (Hejinian 2000). In his insightful discussion of the sociality of Language Writers of the 1970s and 1980s in *The Constructivist Moment*, Barrett Watten is at pains to avoid ahistorical generalisations about signification and offer a materialist, historical reading of the recent American avant-garde, yet even here the analysis teeters between universalism and historical explanations when discussing this issue. The Language Writers, he tells us, were shaped by 1968 and by the 'traumatic experience of negative totality in historical crisis that cannot be represented' (79), and the emphasis seems to fall on the rigidity of the abstractions—this is a *totality* that *cannot* be represented—as much as on the contingent history.

Watten's balancing act is widely practised. Such abstract scepticism co-exists with a scepticism of a much more local kind, for instance about the reliability of discourses of public information about government, politics, war, and the economy. War has been our climate of change for the past fifteen years as a cycle of apprehension and horror has been played out in spectacles of destruction in the newspapers and on television as we witness in Robert Lowell's words, 'small war on the heels of small war,' (16) a cycle accompanied by fitful, vague news of genocides elsewhere, all the more terrible in their nebulousness, and too often, like the Congo genocide, Rumsfelded into 'unknown unknowns.' Hejinian may believe that 'words are not equal to the world' but sometimes the world itself is the direct problem and poetry has to try and manage to be up to the task of representation. In the preface to *The Best American Poetry 2004* that she edited, she reflects on the 'sorry year of 2003' that made her feel 'panics of frustration and fear' and asserts that poets had to respond: 'I cannot imagine a person, not to mention an artist and especially not a poet, who in the year 2003 could in her or his work have simply disregarded what's been going on.' (11) She chooses poems that try to best the scepticism generated by recent historical events and their media representations, poems that 'make sense in a year that one can scarcely make sense of.' (13) Making sense encompasses being meaningful, discovering sense and even creating it during a historical period in which confusion, unintelligibility, opacity, secrecy, and lies permeate the news communication media to the extent that many people conclude that the best available histories of recent events 'scarcely make sense'.

What does it mean for a poet to make sense in the face of a loss of meaning? How is is possible to believe that words are not adequate to the world, and that this particular world of today actually creates conditions that prevent ordinary citizens including poets from finding words for contemporary events? Julian Baggini writes that many people respond to contemporary events with 'a kind of intellectual despair, a suspension of judgement based on the idea either that there is no truth out there or that we can't know it anyway.' (47) He counsels a moderation of expectations, a recognition that 'lack of absolute certainty is unavoidable . . . but that is no reason to believe that we can't pursue truth and knowledge.' (47)

Baggini perhaps makes it sound too easy to resist scepticism, for as we have already seen, for poets at least it has deeper roots than the radical doubt created by current affairs. Stanley Cavell, the great contemporary critic of scepticism in its various forms, always insists on the persuasiveness of sceptical arguments, and the persistence of scepticism at the edge of our everyday experience. In *The Claim of Reason* he admits that sceptics have a legitimate worry: the fear that 'something is, or may be amiss with knowledge as a whole' (140) and that therefore there is 'something which *must* be accounted for.' This they believe is an inescapable condition at the very heart of things, not something that could be alleviated by a better press or more honest government. They worry that the tomato or the table on which it rests might be an illusion, or like Descartes that instead of sitting by the fireside they are actually dreaming it. Cavell describes their dilemma in a manner that illuminates that of the sceptic about news reports: 'After all, consider how little of anything, or any situation, we really see.' (143) The second section of Hejinian's poem *The Fatalist* meditates on such scepticism, acknowledging that 'there are always those / who say that all reality is an illusion.' (16) The poem alludes in the next sentence to a philosophical tradition stretching back to Descartes of arguing that we appear not to be able to tell whether we are dreaming or not:

Sure, while we seek to grasp deep sleep from which we wake
our own reality shrinks the totality of reality (a cosmos
from which little heroines are perpetually trying to escape)
which is infinitely extensive. We're left with a sense
of murky doings, whether it is possibility or impossibility that's lodged
there is hard to say. The overblown soundtrack (and the voice-over
narration by Tom Hanks) would suggest that everything that lies
between the outer infinity of the cosmos and our own brief spot
in it harbors power, freedom (they are much
the same). The ensuing show is awful. (16)

Disbelief in the news media makes people imagine 'murky doings' behind the images of the 'doings' of governments, armies and corporations. What the poem calls 'the desperately ungraspable vastness of meaning / everywhere' is deeply troubling as the line-break above also hints by leaving us with the momentary phrase, 'everything that lies'. The scope of this universalising category 'everything' and 'everywhere' is left undefined, though it seems implied that this scope extends to the global polity. It can't be more precisely outlined because, as the poem says much later, 'that would require us to view the world / and that's impossible.' (60) Hejinian here sketches the contours of radical doubt that trouble many thinkers, especially the uncertainty whether this is a transcendental condition or a historical moment. Cavell is clear that what he calls the traditional epistemologists are mistaken in the arguments they use to justify the belief that a radical uncertainty about the world is the only valid attitude to it. He believes that they start with a specific instance of doubt and then ignore its contingency in order to generalise it as a fundamental condition, and in doing so they violate ordinary usage (218). It is not so much the world that lacks meaning, it is the claim itself whose phrasing has become meaningless because when words and sentences are removed from their contexts, 'the point of saying them is lost' (207). Cavell concludes however that there does remain a validity to scepticism, 'namely that the human creature's basis in the world as a whole, its relation to the world as such, is not that of knowing, anyway not what we think of as knowing.' (241) Epistemologists one might say are right to fear that we cannot know the world fully in language but make too much of this, wanting the world to be more meaningful than it can or need be. It may not be language that is failing us.

Is this fair? Martin Heidegger devoted much of *Being and Time* to an exploration of these dilemmas, especially the moments of disorientation that trouble our ordinary sense of being in the world. Robert Pippin in a subtle essay on Heidegger's notorious interest in *das Nichts* or the 'nothing' argues that Heidegger arrives at this weird notion of the 'nothing' because he wants to explore the strangeness of a particularly modern experience, the loss of meaningfulness in the world: 'The totality of involvements of the ready-to-hand and the present-at-hand discovered within the world is, as such, of no consequence; it collapses into itself; the world has the character of completely lacking significance.' (Heidegger 231; Pippin 69) What are the world and being like that this can happen? Pippin is at pains to say that this does not mean that the everyday is merely incomprehensible. Tables and tomatoes are still tables and tomatoes. The problem is, 'that for Heidegger mattering just "fails" in a way that reveals the utter contingency and fragility of it succeeding when it does' (75) and he therefore presses the question, 'what is meaning that it can fail'. As Pippin points out, the dizzying total scepticism that Heidegger identifies is historically all too explicable. For those who think that the news media and the governments or corporations prevent us making sense of events, it is only by 'tarrying with the negative' (77) as Hegel puts it, that the narrative of *geist* is possible. Pippin however, like Stanley Cavell, another philosopher of scepticism, doesn't want to be too quick to tidy away such radical doubt. Similar ambivalence to scepticism is evident in the poets. Joron's essay strives to avoid making it seem that the problem is for instance merely a deficit of reliable news coverage or lack of imaginative stamina, however much these might be important parts of the failure of the world's meaningfulness, and however much it might be worth campaigning to right such breakdowns, because he wants to retain the imaginative power of scepticism.

Both Hejinian and Watten also balance the two demands. Watten's thesis in *The Constructivist Moment* is that the negativity of the avant-garde is more complex than has been generally recognised. His generation of poets, helped by the example of Clark Coolidge, saw 'Coolidge's construction of poetic language as a form of reconstituted objectification' and were helped 'to break the mold of the author-centred lyric toward a more socially reflexive poetry.' (138) Another way of saying this would be that these poets sampled the lexicons of public language and experimented with reconstructions that would move beyond the stasis of trauma, and the immobility of those abstractions. Hejinian also has suggestions for resisting capitulation to scepticism. Poets can give space to the productivity of language, treat its promise of knowledge reflexively, trace the contours of desire in its syntax, and treat scepticism as an opportunity to 'distinguish our ideas and ourselves from the world and things in it from each other.'(Hejinian, 2000, 56)

Tacit in these formulations by Watten and Hejinian are complementary poetic strategies for handling scepticism that derive from different approaches to public language, whose implications can be glimpsed in the contrast between the rhetorical modes (the theoretically driven discourse of 'reconstituted objectification' or 'socially reflexive' and the deliberately ordinary discourse of 'the world and things in it'), as well as in the opposition between the impersonally public range of the 'socially reflexive' and the everyday intimacy of 'our ideas and ourselves.' This complementarity toward public language is a feature of the poets who share such scepticism about language over the past half century. But what do we mean by public language? If all language is in some fundamental sense public, what makes some of it seem especially so? When we talk of public language we probably have several features in mind: speech and texts whose accuracy or sincerity are not easy and perhaps not possible to evaluate; vocabulary and phraseology that an individual would never use for ordinary intimate or private conversation; the specialised discourses of scientists, economists, politicians, bureaucrats at one end of a spectrum that extends to computer gamers and street gang members at the other; speech delivered to large co-present audiences who may be strangers to one another and the speaker; texts written to be read by strangers to the author; and the entire discursive activity by which a large society in which most people are only ever part of a public and not in direct communication with each other. This is not an exhaustive list, but already it shows that the concept of public language will inevitably bring shifting perspectives and a measure of reflexivity too. The most visible aspect of public language is the swirling mix of unintimate vocabulary that spills out constantly into our lifeworld through advertising, newspapers and magazines, and television, with the specialised discourses of scientists, gangs and bureaucracies, a linguistic explosion as gorgeous in its oil spill iridescence as any rich poetic diction of the past. Scientific vocabulary today, for instance, is quite amazing, a dense use of neologisms, every possible nominal extension by prefix and suffix, all in the service of a compacted proposition.

Oil slick pollution or iridescent vision? The implications of divergent stances towards public language can be grasped further by looking in some detail at two contrasting passages from relatively recent texts by Hejinian and Watten. The first is taken from *The Fatalist*, a text that Hejinian describes as generated from a large body of her own letters, lectures and other unpublished writings, and some texts by friends and correspondents. It is written in the form of sections of varying length averaging about 30 lines of paratactic sentences set out as free verse. Some sentences are grammatically well-constructed, and others are made of apparently unconnected appositional clauses.

> back and forth. Perhaps this is just a form
> of emotional defiance. It is directed
> against the news media. I tell them nothing
> especially when a festive element is added
> to the space with gladiolas and dahlias. We speak (46)

These two sentences, 'Perhaps this is just a form / of emotional defiance. It is directed / against the news media.', articulate a common reaction to the reporting of world political events of the past twenty years, especially the wars, genocides, and the so-called terrorist attacks on Western lives and property. What is the use of poetry in a public culture where the languages of politics, economics and militarism are many decibels louder, have cluster vocabularies that can be delivered with apparent precision to the sites of fear and desire throughout the globe? Is poetry anything more than defiant emotionalism, and can poets tell those commanding these languages anything? The tone of this poem is not despairing however and even this fragment shows why. Each sentence has a counter-proposition to offer that emerges from the semantic manipulations of the line-break that persistently creates resistances to the dominant meanings that shadow alternatives to them. 'Perhaps this is just a form'—and therefore not so vulnerable to the governing rules of truth, knowledge and fact. 'It *is* directed'—and not an aleatory or reactive utterance. 'I tell them nothing'—the poet reserves understanding for those who step beyond the glare of the media. 'We speak'—we speak a renewing flowering vitality, they merely mediate commodified novelty, and the language that the poem identifies as what we 'speak' is derived from the linguistic exchanges that form the life-world of everyday ordinary intimacy rather than the more public and less sayable languages of institutions.

Contrast this section of the poem with the following passage from Barrett Watten's *Bad History*, a series of prose poems that mingle autobiographical and political reflections in a prose that is also paratactical, though at a higher level of integration so that most sentences are grammatically complete.

> Consider the etymology of words such as *Patriot* and *Scud*—
> *Scud* is not an acronym for anything (like *SAM* is an acronym
> for "Surface-to-Air Missile") but a kind of media-initiated
> synthetic image that combines a self-evident scudding across
> the surface of the water toward its heat-blistered target with
> a racial characterization of the kind of agent person it is—
> scum of the cracked earth spitting up to erupt over and come
> back to thud. To the same ground where we were sitting still
> and waiting for it? The poet didn't want to think about that
> ground, so pleased he was with the spectacle of a disbelief
> that called into question any criterion for an historical event.
> (9–10)

In this passage from a section entitled 'The 1980s', the first sentence displays poetical vigour in a manner that poets widely endorse. This, the sentence reflexively indicates, is what poets feel they are good at, tracing verbal nuances through scholarly knowledges, homonymic and other sonic resonances, visual associations, historial allusions, in order to open a reader's eyes to the world as it really is. The missile is a poetic weapon whose very name heaps indignity on its target as it negates the target's ethnicity with its thudding scud on that muddy dud crud of a phonemic *Ud* the enemy Id. The second sentence notices that the trajectory of this projectile irony has closed the loop and threatens its own launcher whose privileged position suddenly seems under attack. Is this satirical venom going to poison its creator? From the start of this prose poem the poet has been defining himself through his 'disbelief' in whatever war is currently 'the' war and gradually disbelief, whose suspension we are meant to recall Coleridge named as the precondition for poetry, so that the poet chooses 'not to believe in' the war 'really having happened.' But he has to believe in the war in order to choose to continue in disbelief, so maybe he does actually believe in its actuality, the ground of his disbelief. Unalloyed skepticism about the war, the government reports of military successes with Scud and Patriot missiles, turns out to be a self-destructive response, and one with odd homologies with the demands of poetry.

Both *The Fatalist* and *Bad History* bring considerable scepticism to the encounter with public language even as they question their own stance. *Bad History* ends with a risky prose poem, 'The 1990s' that is nothing but the most meretricious public language, the discourse of property investment. Lyn Hejinian's text is wary of such public language. The passage before the one I cited earlier goes like this:

I knew that a month ago. For relief (physical relief
for the men, comic relief for the women) there was a soccer match
that lasted all through the wild third evening. A famous Russian
    tripped
over the foot of a Polish poet. This was captured
by C waving my camera. He will not cross
a bridge (should he come to one). J was loudly snorting and tears ran
down my cheeks. L was whooping and A held his head. C rocked
back and forth. Perhaps this is just a form
of emotional defiance. (46)

Hejinian works hard to resist exemplary quotation, and in this egalitarian space of propositions all are equal and no overarching sovereign synthesis rules. Her habitual poetic vocabulary, as this example demonstrates, averts itself from the kind of language that Watten pins up for his readers in *Bad History*, and instead derives its semantics from the intensity of everyday usage. This passage shows how much her words such as 'emotional defiance' are rooted in the actions, beliefs and feelings of specific individuals rather than theoretical debate.

At the risk of exaggeration I have emphasized the contrast in the use of public vocabulary in order to suggest that scepticism about public language in contemporary poetics is manifest in two apparently divergent poetic strategies towards public language—exposing its corruptions by alienating the language as Watten does in placing it in a poem or purging such discourses altogether from the zone of the poem. Poets in the modernist tradition have markedly diverged on the issue of how to engage with the cluster language, the euphemisms, the neologisms, buzz-words, fashionable idioms, corpse-free military solutions, and jargon, that permeate public culture in its many forms. Most of this public language is divested of challengeable warrant, it is a language that no person can be held to account for other than through legal processes that consider it in relation to abstract organisational entities. The lexicon also tends to be highly controlling in the reasoning and affect that it can elicit even before it is constructed into coercive syllogisms. For that reason alone many poets steer away from its lexicon. A poet such as Robert Creeley for instance avoids words and phrases that are not commonplace and replete with the density of everyday history, and many other contemporary poets do likewise. The use or avoidance of public language makes clear demarcations between poets. Working through public language you have John Ashbery, Allen Fisher, Susan Howe, Bruce Andrews, or Andrea Brady; resisting it to varying degrees you have Robert Duncan, Robert Creeley, Fanny Howe, Ric Caddel, or Caroline Bergvall. Public languages bring with them certain difficulties of articulation. The lexicon often lacks vernacular complexity, its semantics are either too fungible or deliberately aversive, and because they are not in constant motion within our intimate lives they behave more like found objects in a poem than as forms of utterance forming life. Poets who use them tend to place them in highly charged fields of anger at injustice, display the implicit claims to knowledge or authority made by these words, or treat them as inherently ironic when put where poetic diction is expected. Their practice raises difficult questions. Is irony through exposure to juxtaposed contradicting language still an effective aesthetic when measured as critique? What sort of struggle for authority occurs in the space of the poem when different discourses meet? Can the poem indicate how these discourses of political novelty operate in the logical space of reasons?

I promised more questions than answers. The question of public language is a crucial one for us all, as poets and as citizens. In the words of *The Constructivist Moment*, what are the implications of a poetics such as Jackson Maclow's that are 'based on an ethics in which expression is seen as the reflexive enactment of values held in common by communities'(35)? What happens when such reflexiveness seems blocked, when commonality gives way to radical skepticism? In this paper I have traced some of the strategies currently employed by poets to negotiate with scepticisms that range from fundamental doubts about the adequacy of language to those provoked by the mendacity of our public communications when as Hejinian says in *The Fatalist*, 'the so-called "war on terrorism" has sapped energy from every discussion even those at tables sheltered from the rain.' (54)

Peter Middleton is Professor of English at the University of Southampton.

Works Cited

Baggini, Julian. *Making Sense: Philosophy Behind the Headlines*. Oxford: Oxford UP, 2002.

Cavell, Stanley. *The Claim of Reason: Wittgenstein, Skepticsim, Morality, and Tragedy*. New York: Oxford UP, 1999.

Heidegger, Martin. *Being and Time*. Translated John Macquarrie and Edward Robinson. Oxford: Blackwell, 1962.

Hejinian, Lyn. *The Language of Inquiry*. Berkeley: University of California Press, 2000.

—. *The Fatalist*. Richmond, California: Omnidawn, 2003.

—. *The Best American Poetry 2004*. New York: Scribner.

Joron, Andrew. *Fathom*. New York: Black Square Editions, 2003.

Robert Lowell. *Near the Ocean*. London: Faber, 1967.

Pippin, Robert. *The Persistence of Subjectivity: On the Kantian Aftermath*. New York: Cambridge UP, 2005.

Watten, Barrett. *Bad History*. Berkeley: Atelos, 1998.

—. *The Constructivist Moment: From Material Text to Cultural Poetics*. Middletown, Connecticut: Wesleyan UP, 2003.

'Umbilical Stump Still Pulses': Public Language and Number in the Poetry of Rae Armantrout

WILL MONTGOMERY

This paper addresses two aspects of the large topic of public language in Rae Armantrout's work. First of all, I will discuss the poems as a response to contemporary American media culture. Second, I want to consider the social ramifications of the incidence of number in Armantrout's writing.

In interview Armantrout has said:

> I keep asking what happens to the subject—the "cogito"—in a society where perceptions are commodities, already shrink-wrapped. The Information Age seems to be a place where The-White-House-Under-Fire competes with Russia-on-the-Brink for the slot on the nightly news half hour. Don't those topics sound like the names of race horses or cartoon super-heroes? Sometimes I wonder whether the powers behind the government are really trying to destroy the pre-conditions for thought.[1]

What can a poem do in response to this position, besides simple monitor the media-led cartoonisation of political discourse? In my view, the co-incidence of private and public registers in Armantrout's writing offers some room for manoeuvre, some scope for a critically conceived dissensus.

Armantrout's brief, downbeat memoir *True* contains some indications of the fault lines between public and private speech that open up in her poetry. They show her as a small child encouraged by both parents to see herself as '"male-identified" and an outlaw—little Jesse James'.[2] And they show her as an adolescent infatuated with the myth of the Old West, saving up money to fund an escape across the border to Mexico, where life was, allegedly, closer to what it had been in the heroic days of the cowboys.

Armantrout writes of her childhood adoration of Billy the Kid, who assumed the central position in a pantheon of rebellious male idols. This was consciously set up to rival her mother's admiration for various conformist males, mainly ministers. Billy the Kid was a 'fetish figure' for the young Armantrout.[3] It was unclear, she remarks, whether she identified with such rebellious males or was 'romantically attracted' to them.[4] What *is* clear, however, is that putting popular myths to her own uses provided Armantrout with a little leverage on an oppressive familial environment that she gradually realised was rather representative of the culture as a whole. The first sentence of *True* stakes a claim for the importance of such questioning of her own experience:

> Many people must see their lives as somehow exemplary. I tend to see my early life as an example of the pathology of "Middle America" at mid-century. [5]

In self-deprecating, low-key prose, Armantrout's memoir makes it clear that the 'pathology of "Middle America", as exemplified by the Armantrout household, was a pathology of religious conservatism, racism and sexism. Armantrout's poetry is a highly oblique attempt to expose the hidden linguistic wiring of that culture's contemporary manifestations.

Disney, another 'exemplary' aspect of mid-century American cultural life, is part of the picture for the young Armantrout.[6] *Fantasia* inducts her into the world of Stravinsky. And, later on, Disney's presence stands over an early date with her future husband, Chuck Korkegian:

> I kept asking where he was going, but he wouldn't say. We ended up at the Tiki Room in Disneyland. That evening was symbolic for me. It seemed that Chuck would open up the Unknown. It seems ironic now that the Great Unknown was represented by Disneyland. But I romanticised his unpredictability, his unconventionality, even his poverty.[7]

The ironic perception that the 'Unknown' might be represented by Disney seems especially pertinent here. The friction generated between large ideas—the cogito, the Unknown—and popular culture is one of the motors of Armantrout's poetry. Cartoons and cartoonishness are as much a feature of the writing as the coercive discourses it purports to resist.

One example of this in the work can be found in Armantrout's use of the compressed language of tabloid-style headlines and TV listings (there's even an early poem, from her 1978 book *Extremities*, entitled 'Footnote to the Television Notes').

In the poem 'Visualizations', for example, the line 'Boy Wins Love With Tall Tale' sits in inverted commas at the top, its isolation intensifying the oddness of the decontextualized phrase.[8] Moving through several twists and turns, including some acerbic material on 9/11 as a media event, the poem concludes with another headline, 'Umbilical Stump Still Pulses'. This combines horror-film schlockiness with an echo of the *tale* or *tail* that opened the poem. The revolting pulsing stump might even be an expression of the amorousness announced in the first line. In a poem that discusses the recursive nature of cognition—'We double back/ to form thoughts'—the repetitive messages of contemporary American culture are scrambled and re-directed by Armantrout's rapid edits.

In another poem from the same volume, *Up to Speed*, a telegraphic snippet of re-wired sci-fi uses this doubling motif to monitor her culture's self-absorption:

In the shorter version,

tentacled
stomach swallows stomach.[9]

The culture's tendency to summarise, to reduce complex plots and arguments to stark outlines that barely make sense is satirised in both poems through figures of doubling.

For what remains of this paper I will discuss number as a social question in Armantrout's work, taking a cue from 'Visualizations' when it asks: '...frequency/ is a matter// of counting up to what?'

Ones, twos and threes are the basic figures around which Armantrout's poetry unfolds. (Three, for my purposes, implies the group—more than two.) Armantrout, an only child, seems equivocal, at best, about solitude. Two is an unworkable proposition. Three, needless to say, feels like a crowd. Her writing hosts three communicative impossibilities:

- the singular 'I' of the speaking subject that appears to enunciate the poem;
- the dyad, arguably proper to lyric;
- and the trio that represents the collective.

My thesis is that Armantrout's writing invites us to contemplate and to reject all of these positions but ends up with a sceptical embrace of communicative potential in all three arenas.[10]

Armantrout's recent book *Next Life* contains several poems that consider, explicitly or implicitly, the figure of Echo—the mythical figure condemned first to repeat the end of people's sentences and then, spurned by Narcissus, reduced to nothing but voice.[11] Echo and Narcissus offer us two models of captivated doubling: the merely imitative and narcissistic delusion.

As Armantrout suggests in an interview with Tom Beckett, couples are not in a happy situation. Rejecting love as mutual misrecognition, she concludes that '...there is no reciprocity or simultaneity. I think a lot of my work says that.'[12] In the same interview she talks about the solitary activity of the writer as an 'autoerotic' experience that the writer desires—and fails—to duplicate for the reader.[13]

So the singular comes to grief, a failed autoeroticism that can't help looking outside itself for duplication. Couples come to grief through a failure to find a mutually sustaining fantasy. Where does this leave the threesome?

Many of Armantrout's poems ask this question in various ways. The poem 'Two, Three', from *Next Life*, puts it at the centre of its enquiry:

Two, Three

Sad, fat boy in pirate hat.
Long, old, dented,
copper-colored Ford.

How many traits
must a thing have
in order to be singular?

(Echo persuades us
everything we say
has been said at least once
                                before.)

Two plump, bald men
in gray tee-shirts
and tan shorts

are walking a small bulldog —
followed by the eyes
of an invisible third person.

The Trinity was born
from what we know
of the bitter

symbiosis of couples.
Can we reduce echo's sadness
by synchronising our speeches?

Is it the beginning or the end
of real love
when we pity a person

because, in him,
we see ourselves?[14]

The poem starts with a 'found' image of a boy in a pirate hat and
quickly moves to the key conundrum: 'How many traits/ must a thing
have/ in order to be singular?' The poem asks, in other words, whether
plurality can be the guarantor of singularity.

In the poem, the notion of singularity is dismissed with the figure
of Echo: there is no originary utterance; we are all caught in an echoic or
Narcissistic loop. Armantrout then broadens the picture: there are two
men—a gay couple, perhaps? However, they are not a self-contained unit.

They are observed by the 'invisible third person', a playful invocation of the Holy Spirit—and also the third party that stands for the larger groups that couples belong to.

Couples cannot isolate themselves and they do not coincide: would we be happier if desire was co-extensive, if we could synchronise what the poem calls 'our speeches'? Is finding oneself in another an act of narcissistic absorption or a failure of love? The reader is implicated as the singular origin of the text and, as observer, with the 'invisible third person'. The three first-person subject positions, 'I', 'you', and 'she/ he' are rehearsed in condensed fashion in this poem. All are found 'wanting'—in both the lacking and desiring senses of the word.

Armantrout's poems reflect an uneasiness with various kinds of identification. A position of solipsistic self-containment is rejected. The speaker cannot speak, the writer cannot write, in a vacuum. The dyadic encounter of love or the archetypal love lyric fails too: the 'bitter // symbiosis of couples' is rejected as a failed endeavour—an ambivalent narcissistic overspill always contaminates the relationship with the desired object. It fails also because there are never simply two—the implicit privacy of the duo folds into the public life of the collective. The trio fails too. It cannot come to represent the collective because any attempt to assign it a singular identity—'humanity', perhaps, or 'America'—will necessarily compromise the fundamental fact of difference.

Despite this description of various kinds of 'failure', I want to suggest that Armantrout's writing is sceptical rather than pessimistic. She is writing about the difficulty of reconciling private experience with the experience of the collective—of, in other words, 'being numerous'. As for George Oppen, this is a genuine dilemma.

One of the poems in *Next Life*, 'Us', contains the line 'Car called Echo',[15] which is itself an echo of Oppen's perplexity about the collective in 'Of Being Numerous':

> [...] How talk
> Distantly of 'The People'

Who are that force
Within the walls
Of cities

Wherein their cars

Echo like history
Down walled avenues
In which one cannot speak.[16]

With Oppen, the question is poised between, on one hand, the fantasy of a fully realised, finite and bounded subjectivity and, on the other, the difficulty of imagining a collective. So '...the shipwreck/ Of the singular' is held up against the '...madness in the number/ of the living'.[17] Perhaps, worries Oppen, the poet's utterance amounts to little more than 'A ferocious mumbling, in public/ Of rootless speech'.[18] Or perhaps there is a saving perception of connectedness between disparate singular perceptions:

Or sees motes, an iron mesh, links

Of consequence

Still, at the mind's end
Relevant [19]

In Armantrout's case, this contemplation of the one and the many becomes a contemplation of the one, the two and the many. In other words, she imagines a dyadic encounter, possibly erotic, that is neither a perfect interiority nor a plausible collective. One version of this might be the possibility of lyric.

Armantrout's writing implies a negative co-option of Oppen's 'links of consequence'. It is often built on the ironic détournement of the over-familiar. The space of non-compliance carved out by the writing depends not on the words themselves but on the play of context and register. This allows Armantrout's writing to suggest a kind of negative affirmation of community, even as it rejects monadic, dyadic or collective solutions to the predicament she finds us to be in.

The poem 'Upper World', from *Up to Speed*, is a good example of the way in which Armantrout's poems can look back at their own unfolding. [20] The sombre opening—'If sadness/ is akin to patience'—slips into cheery bathos with the sudden tonal shift of 'we're back!', another incidence of echo or doubling. The play of registers becomes clearer in the second part of the poem, as it moves from the lines 'every name's Eurydice,/ briefly returned from blankness' to 'High voices/ over rapid-pulsing synthesisers/ intone, 'without you' —// which is soothing.' As motifs of absence and mythic loss accumulate in the poem, the virtue of patience, announced in the first line, is stranded somewhere between a Penelope-like fortitude and the commodification of feeling in popular music. The reference to Eurydice, moreover, hints at the perils of looking back—of seeing again, of doubling or Echo. The entire poem grows out of the significance that the change of direction in the first three lines retrospectively accumulates.

When Armantrout writes: 'Here and there were like/ one place// But we need to triangulate,/ find someone to show' we find the movement from the single ('here') to a dissimilar dyad ('here and there'), followed by the impulse to establish a trio: the 'need to triangulate'. 'Triangulate' is Clinton-era jargon for distinguishing one's position from both poles of an established debate: Republican and Democrat; Conservative and Old Labour. So a presentational trick of numbers exists in the poem at the same time as a more abstract shifting up the gears from single speech act through dialogue to witnessed dialogue. The language of political dissimulation undercuts this potentially utopian movement.

Again, I would argue that there is more here than a mere witnessing of what Armantrout has called the 'interventions of capitalism into consciousness'.[21] My point is that in refusing to accept either the solitary utterance, or the idealised mutuality of dialogue or the collective (Oppen's 'city'), Armantrout's poetry presents us with a curiously affirmative communicative ethics. In these poems, in other words, the one and the many are endowed with communicative potential through the endorsement of a mutual dependence that is guaranteed by shared conditions of difference and insufficiency, not similarity.

In the absence of a satisfactorily complete utterance in this writing, irony offers a model of a language that finds its force in repetition. The 'degraded linguistic environment' of contemporary American culture is re-voiced in these poems.[22] Oppen's 'iron mesh' of connectedness becomes a mesh of irony. Denise Riley's suggestion that Echo is the 'initiator of the ironic' seems extremely pertinent here, as does her suggestion that 'iteration can explode a category from within'.[23] The poems' radical compression—Armantrout has always favoured the short line—intensifies this quality of extreme linguistic self-consciousness.

Despite the abundant scepticism, there is optimism in this writing. Its apparent stress on negation, its refusal of subject positions (singular, double, multiple), its love of hesitation, its emphasis on a language that, iterated to death, embodies its own self-critique—these factors allow it to imagine a space in which the problem of the one and the many, in its many modulations, is kept provokingly in suspension. Armantrout invokes a notion of community that is based on the denial of 'commonality'.

Will Montgomery is Research Councils UK Research Fellow at Royal Holloway, University of London. Poems by Rae Armantrout are reprinted by permission of the author.

Notes

1 Hejinian, Lyn. 'An Interview with Rae Armantrout'. *A Wild Salience: the Writing of Rae Armantrout*. Ed. Tom Beckett. Cleveland, OH: Burning Press, 1999: 12–26 (25).
2 Armantrout, Rae. *True*. Berkeley, CA: Atelos, 1998: 17.
3 *True*, 34.
4 *True*, 34.
5 *True*, 13.
6 See again Hejinian interview, 25: 'I find cartoons more frightening than cute. They're often a shorthand way of embodying subjectivity and its contradictions'.
7 *True*, 50.
8 'Visualizations'. *Up to Speed*. Middletown, CT: Wesleyan UP, 2004: 48–49.
9 'Entanglements'. *Up to Speed*, 17–18.
10 My thinking in this respect is guided by the work of Jean-Luc Nancy, particularly his *Being Singular Plural*. Stanford, CA: Stanford UP, 2000.
11 Armantrout, Rae. *Next Life*. Middletown, CT: Wesleyan UP, 2007.

12 Beckett, Tom. "'My Poetry isn't Built on Hope": An Interview with Rae Armantrout'. Beckett, 104–114 (106).
13 Beckett interview, 104.
14 'Two, Three', *Next Life*, 7–8.
15 'Us', *Next Life*, 35–36 (35).
16 Oppen, George. 'Of Being Numerous'. *New Collected Poems*. Ed. Michael Davidson. New York: New Directions, 2002 (171).
17 Oppen, 166, 172.
18 Oppen, 173.
19 Oppen, 187.
20 'Upper World', *Up to Speed*, 35–36. The title derives from the closing lines of another Oppen poem, 'A Narrative'.
21 Hejinian interview, 26.
22 Beckett interview, 110.
23 Riley, Denise. *The Words of Selves: Identification, Solidarity, Irony.* Stanford: Stanford UP, 2000 (157, 156).

Language Poetry on the Vertical Bias and the 'Re-visionary' Poetics of Lyn Hejinian

SUSAN NURMI-SCHOMERS

In a terse cultural-critical retrospective on the emergence of the written word, the German poet, philosopher and aesthetician Walter Benjamin traces the process by which the written word began to 'lie down,' whereby 'upright inscriptions' and the public media they depended upon were gradually replaced by manuscripts resting on slanted lecterns before, with the advent of the printing press, the written word began to 'bed itself.' Looking at his own age, Benjamin diagnoses a regaining in dominance of the vertical over the horizontal, with film and advertisements 'forcing the written word completely into the dictatorial vertical dimension.' As he remarks, 'the thick flurries of transmutable, colourful, contesting letters which alight before [the reader's] eyes lessen his chances of penetrating the archaic tranquility of the book.'[1] If we agree not to take Benjamin too literally, the metaphorical terms which he uses to trace changes in practices of inscription and reading prove to be quite valuable for the inquiry at hand, for he delivers the overarching opposition it aims to explore: that between verticality and horizontality or, to put it in terms of aesthetic strategies, 'verticalism' and 'horiziontalism.' Benjamin sets up a double equation: one which correlates horizontality with reading in the private (if not to say, intimate) realm, and verticality with 'public letters.'

If we entertain Benjamin's notion that film plays a key role in the new, public 'contestation' of letters, it would seem promising to explore the opposition between 'verticalism' and 'horizontalism' from the perspective of cinepoetic aesthetics. Let us do so and turn to Sergei Eisenstein for illumination, whose engagement in a heated controversy over how to standardize cinema screen dimensions is enlightening in this context. In advocating the introduction of what he called the 'dynamic square,' Eisenstein saw a way to escape from what he lamented as 'passive horizontalism,' to remedy the 'exclusion' of 'all the possibilities of vertical, upright composition,' equating the horizontal bias of the standard screen with the '"narrative" type of picture' found in the 'nineteenth-century pre-Impressionist period,' labelled by him as 'the worst period of painting.'[2] One could argue that the opposition which he brings into play here—verticality versus horizontality—is correlatable with a second, equally fundamental one: that between contiguity and continuity, with continuity and horizontalism constituting the parameters of narrative modes of writing and contiquity and verticalism defining anti-, or non-narrative art.

And indeed, contiguity is a fundamental element of Eisenstein's montage aesthetics, which he discusses in three theoretical frameworks: in terms of language, the physiology of retinal perception and Marxist dialectics. In his 1923 manifesto entitled 'The Montage of Attractions', Eisenstein encourages film to veritably attack the viewer, administering successions of shocks to create the desired mood, which is to say, to agitate.[3] As he puts it programmatically in 1925, '[i]t is not a "Cine-Eye" that we need but a "Cine-Fist."'[4] According to Eisenstein, individual shots do not produce the desired effect; a jarring *juxtaposition* of shots, their 'inter-action' does; it is in this way that qualitative 'leaps' onto ever higher levels of cinepoetic form are to be achieved.[5] Eisenstein's dynamic, dialectical notion of montage demands disruptive contiguity rather than harmonious continuity. Dixon characterizes Eisensteinian montage as follows:

> Montage was based and founded on the notion of Collision, where previous shots within the sequence deform and set adrift expectations of Reading by the viewer in both a formal and semiotic fashion. The Montage is the construction and the process of the unfolding of images in sequence based on opposition, resistance and defamiliarization. [...] Whereas each individual frame of the film medium exists as a still image it is only through the oppositions which occur in the montage that the potentiality of the infinite possibilities of the photographic frame may generate a specific grammar and actualize the semiotic function of film.[6]

In various, often collective, pieces on poetics, the 'Language Poets' call for the creation of a kind of explosive contiguity in and through words similar to that which Eisenstein strives to effect in and through—or should one say?—in between film shots, the common aim being to keep the art work open for multiple connections, to create a kind of charged space of interaction between page and reader, viewer and screen. As it were, the text, be it filmic or verbal, presents itself as a site of public 'contestation,' with the reader or viewer engaging in a kind of public meaning-making.

This cursory 'spotlighting' of a complex body of credos, convictions, strategies and practices must suffice here to establish the framework for a closer appreciation of one poet's critical work—Lyn Hejinian's collection of essays and prefaces to essays entitled *The Inquiry of Language*.[7] Looking at this body of critical inquiry in its 're-visionary' aspect, I invite you to consider yet a potential opposition: that between line and sentence. The point of departure for this newly identified opposition is Hejinian's remark, made in the preface to her 1988 comment 'Line,' in which she writes that having worked for 'a prolonged period [...] with sentences,' she 'was eager suddenly to disrupt their integrity, escape their confines.' 'For me,' she reveals, 'the 'new sentence' had taken on declarative properties so pronounced that they were [...] beginning to sound like imperatives [...].' (131) In his 1987 essay entitled 'The New Sentence,'[8] Ron Silliman had explored the relationship between line and 'new sentence.' He characterizes the latter as involving an interiorization of external poetic devices such as rhythm and linebreak in the sentence, this being a process which generated an 'internal presence of once exteriorized poetic forms.' (62) The 'torquing' effect Silliman was after,—an effect, he notes, which 'in poetry is most often accomplished by linebreaks,'—had 'moved into the interiors of prose.' (63) As Silliman claims, 'the torquing which is normally triggered by linebreaks, the function of which is to enhance ambiguitiy and polysemy, has now moved directly into the grammar of the sentence. At one level, the completed sentence [...] has become equivalent to a line.' (63) A new sentence is thus 'a sentence with an interior poetic structure in addition to interior ordinary grammatical structure.' (63) From this standpoint, only line and 'old sentence' can be seen as oppositional.

In her preface to 'Line,' Hejinian takes a somewhat different view; here she sees line and sentence (not labelled as 'old' or 'new') as having 'overlapping but not identical semantic ranges, with a sentence offering a complete (i.e., 'whole') thought while a line need not (and often adamantly does not).' (132) What interests me most in this context is her observation that

> [b]oth lines and sentences make a demand for other lines and sentences, linkages, but [...] in different ways and according to different syntactic and logical operations. Sentences may incorporate articulation of this kind *within* themselves, whereas principal articulation occurs *between* lines rather than inside them. (132; my emphasis)

Hejinian seems to be rediscovering the line as a form of order with a potential for doing what Silliman looks to the 'new sentence' for. As she observes,

> [a] poem based on the line bears in it a high degree of semantic mutability. [...] The integrity of the individual line, and the absorbing discontinuities that often appear between lines— the jumpiness that erupts in various sections of the work (whether the result or the source of disjunctive semantics)— are so accurate to my experience that they seem inevitable. And so, at this point, it seems logical to me to write with them. (134)

Hejinian's acknowledgement of the line's capacity to 'discontinue the sentence without closing it,' the line being defined as 'the primary unit of observation' and the 'measure of felt thought,' brings Eisenstein's aesthetics of discontinuity to mind,—an aesthetics founded on the frame as cinepoetic 'cell unit.' In readdressing the opposition which informs his aesthetics, one might ask oneself: in what respect might the sentence be consistent with the paradigm of horizontality, the line with that of verticality? To explore this question further, I want to return to Hejinian's notion of articulation and the differences in its forms and functions *vis a vis* line and sentence. In doing so, a new opposition seems to suggest itself: that between interior and exterior articulation, with the latter being understandable in two senses: for one, as something which is exterior to the text, i.e., as something which happens *in the space between* words, lines and/or sentences, and secondly, as a kind of performative 'inter-action' *between* them. In claiming that 'whatever is going to happen with sentences does so *inside* them' and recognizing that sentences 'offer possibilities for enormous *interior* complexity,' Hejinian seems to confirm the oppositional relationship between line and sentence in terms of interior and exterior articulation, but in the same breath she identifies, significantly, the possibility of sentences being 'opened *outward*, through the intervention of lines' (132; emphases are mine).

In this context, another opposition must be addressed: that between temporalization and spatialization, with line-ordered writing being perhaps correlateable with the latter and sentence-oriented writing in the sense of the 'old sentence' at least appearing to be correlatable with the former. In writing about the line, Hejinian remarks on the 'tension set up by the co-existence of beginning and end at each point,' a tension which 'excites the dynamics of the work' and 'is vital,' she says, to her 'thinking within it.' (133) To this I might respond: co-existence of beginning and end is afforded by two things: brevity and visual 'co-habitation.' Line-ordered writing lends itself to visualization and thus spatialization and materialization in ways which sentence- and paragraph-ordered writing does not. The latter depends on interiorization, not exteriorization, and with this on memory more than presence. The 'bedding down' of the written word as observed by Benjamin constitutes a move in the direction of interiorization and a committing of text to memory—short-term and long.[9] The move back in the direction of 'upright inscriptions' implies a return to exteriorialization, spatialization, materialization. One might say the verticality of rune stones, monuments and the like— of writing 'carved in stone'—reappears, and with it, writing re-enters the public sphere, but not in the sense of monolithic commemoration, declarations and statements of intent, but rather public contestation of meanings and signification,—meanings and signification, mind you, which are somehow removed, through new forms of spatialization and materialization effected to certain strategic aims, from any sphere of 'author-ity.' One might call this the realm of 'Language Poetry.'

For all this talk of opposition, let us now contemplate possibilities for synthesis and / or fruitful collision of line and sentence which Hejinian sounds out in her *Language of Inquiry*. Hejinians' comments on a 'notebook project' entitled 'Language and "Paradise"'—a kind of 'exegesis, amplification, and adjustment to' her poem 'The Guard', she says—are illuminating. As she writes,

> [t]he decision to examine the poem at the level of the sentence rather than the line was not arbitrary. It is primarily at the level of the sentence, in the moves from one to the next, that the themes of the poem develop; it is at the level of the sentences that one can follow the prevailing current. But this isn't to dismiss the effect of the line (and the line break) on these sentences. [...] The dynamic of the line is different from that of the sentence, and the interplay between the two produces countercurrents, eddies, backwaters, and swirls. The sentence and the line have different ways of bringing meaning into view. (60)

In the differences between line and sentence would seem to lie possibilities for collapsing the oppositionality of temporalization and spatialization in poetry. Hejinian speaks of the 'counterpoint between line and sentence' as something which 'establishes two series of durations,' and which in doing so 'brings temporality into spaces.' (62–3) In identifying certain oppositions, Hejinian simultaneously explores the poetic potential for exploiting them. She writes:

> although it would be inaccurate simply to equate lineation with space and sentences with time, still it seemed to me that in 'The Guard', where the writing includes an aesthetic (and therefore psychological) encounter between lines and sentences as between times and spaces, it was desirable to use a form that reflected the resulting rhythmic complications. I wanted to see the work in motion against itself, so to speak, to establish the inward concentricity, the pressure, the implosive momentum that stands for the struggle that is enacted in the poem. (63)

When Hejinian welcomes spatialization and materialization as effects of writing, speaking in one context, for example, of writing as a 'material manifestation, an embodiment of desire for reality,' (26), she would seem to be subscribing to 'verticalism.' Other efforts to characterize writing, such as the image of it as offering a 'picture of knowledge *underway*' (22; my emphasis), suggest a 'double bias.' I cannot help but think that in Hejinian's meta-reflection on 'The Guard' her calling attention to certain passages which evidence such a 'double bias' are being held up as exemplary of a 're-visionary' poetics. To certain passages Hejininan attests, namely, an 'attempt to cast time into visual and hence spatial imagery,' stating that the 'idea [had been] to point out vertical and horizontal traces of time's passage or of events which could only occur over time.' 'Recognizing the occuring inherent to things,' she writes, 'recognizing that they could only exist after "taking some time"' had 'produced an increasingly dense accrual of moving images, [...]. What I was after was [...] an impression of temporal heterogeneity, not timelessness but a strange simultaneity, a current array of disparately time-bound things.' (66) This image suggests a 'verticalization' of what is otherwise presented 'horizontally,' a 'piling up', or 'pile-up' of 'time-bound things' on a vertical axis.

In the preface to her essay 'Language and "Paradise,"' Hejinian makes explicit reference to the Russian formalists in speaking of the essay's 'paratactic and "plotless" structure' while embracing a Shklovskian 'delaying of coherence' (59–60) in what looks like an attempt to apply 'verticalist' strategies for her project of poetic meta-reflexion. And yet, in relishing the 'counterpoint' of line and sentence in certain poetic passages themselves, in realizing the exploitative potential of 'currents' and 'countercurrents,' Hejinian seems to have found poetic strategies for 'delaying coherence', which utilize both line and sentence—as 'ways of bringing meaning into view' which prove capable of interaction. Seizing upon the metaphor of language as current, one could speak of counter-forces which come up against each other, retarding flow and producing a 'damming-up' effect with an ensuing shift from a horizontal to a vertical bias,—an effect similar to the aforementioned 'pile-up' phenomenon described by Hejinian, albeit in other terms. To these ultimately 'verticalizing' strategies might be added the creation of 'a fragility of sequence,' this being something which, in Hejinian's eyes, allows 'the particular character of diverse individual things' to become 'prominent,' with their 'heterogeneity' in turn 'increas[ing] the palpability of things.' (67) Sequence, arguably an operation on the horizontal bias, must be fragile, must be open to 'verticalism' if things are to become 'palpable,' but 'verticalism' must be open to what one might call 'tempered horizontalism' as well. Such a conclusion one might draw in closing.

Susan Nurmi-Schomers teaches at the University of Tübingen, Germany.

Notes

1 Benjamin, Walter, *Gesammelte Schriften*, eds. Rolf Tiedemann and Hermann Schweppenhäuser. Frankfurt/Mn: Suhrkamp, 1991, vol. IV, 103; my translation.

2 Eisenstein, S.M., 'The Dynamic Square' (1930), in *Selected Works*, edited and translated by Richard Taylor (Bloomington: Indiana UP / British Film Institute, 1988), vol. I: *Writings, 1922–34*, 207 and 210–11.

3 Cf. Eisenstein, 'The Montage of Attractions' (1924), in *Selected Works*, vol. I, 33–38.

4 Eisenstein, 'The Problem of the Materialist Approach to Form' (1925), in *Selected Works*, vol. I, 64.

5 Cf. Eisenstein, 'The Dramatury of Film Form' (1929), in *Selected Works*, vol. I, 161–180.

6 Dixon, Steven, 'Formalism and the Language of Film (film screening): Sergei Eisenstein,' lecture held at Bergen National Academy of the Arts on March 3, 2007; cf. http://www.khib.no/index.php/khib/kalender/forelesninger_og_presentasjoner/formalism_and_the_language_of_film_film_screening_sergei_eisenstein, 1 (accessed: May 30, 2007).

7 Hejinian, Lyn, *The Language of Inquiry*, Berkeley: University of California Press, 2000, 131. In the following, passages cited from this collection of essays will be identified by the page number placed in parentheses in the text.

8 Silliman, Ron, 'The New Sentence,' in *The New Sentence*, New York: Roof Books, 1987.

9 Psycholinguistic research has shown that our short-term memory has the capacity to retain the content of an average-length sentence; it is as if it were designed to process this form of syntactical organization.

Praxis Not Gnosis: Geoffrey Hill and the Anxiety of Polity

CHRISTOPHER ORCHARD

In his collection of essays entitled *Style and Faith* (2003), Geoffrey Hill considers the question of polity. It is, he suggests, 'at its most basic level as also in the most elevated language of response, that of entitlement to speak, one's right to claim authority, albeit as a private person contending in—and with—a public matter' (86). Hill continues with an unacknowledged citation from Milton's *Areopagitica*: 'They who to states and governors of the Commonwealth direct their speech, [High Court of Parliament], or wanting such access in a private condition, write that which they foresee may advance the public good' (86). Milton's awareness of how pamphlet writing serves as an apposite and compensatory forum for writers who are excluded from the privileged loci of public disputation continually informs Hill's poetry and prose as he debates not only the issue of a poet's entitlement but also his capability to articulate personal concerns about public matters affecting Britain in the 1990s. This paper will specifically examine Hill's dilemma in acknowledging this indebtedness to polity in seventeenth century writers, specifically Andrew Marvell, while expressing both his self-loathing and contempt for those with whom he himself is trying to contend.

In *The Triumph of Love* (1998), Hill responds to the interlocutor of the previous sonnet who asks for a couple of illustrations to 'take a fix on your position' by identifying the influence of 'Milton—the political pamphlets' (130). For Hill this means as much the relationship between the poet and the addressee as it does textual content. Hence in his collection, *Canaan* (1997), Hill invokes Milton's audience in *Areopagitica* by addressing three poems to the same political body, 'The High Court of Parliament.' This verbal echo suggests the diachronic appeal of the politically engaged poet whose commitment to discourse is based on an ardent belief in the ability of poetry to contribute to public policy: 'I'm convinced that shaping, voicing, are types of civic action.' (*The Triumph of Love* 70). While Hill's literary influence is palpably Miltonic, his belief in the relationship between polity and poetry embraces earlier proponents. In *The Triumph of Love*, Hill admits the influence of the 'Italianate-Hebraic Milton' but couples him with Sir Philip Sidney, both of whose voices were 'pitched exactly / somewhere between Laus Deo and defiance' (70). This spiritual/secular nexus is proposed as an ideal discursive position for the engaged writer who can offer a pious context couched in the style of polemic aggression, a strategy that Hill practices of course in works ranging from *Mercian Hymns* to *The Orchards of Syon*. But Sidney's true fascination to Hill resides in the transference of conviction from the private world of thought to the public world of discourse. In his *An Apology for Poetry*, Sidney, echoing Aristotle, announces, 'it is not gnosis but praxis must be the fruit.' Sidney's position accounts for Hill's belief in the poet's right to intervene in public matters: 'Active virtue: that which shall contain / its own passion in the public weal—do you follow?—or can you at least / take the drift of the thing?' What is noticeable here is the irascible persona, one that typifies Hill's adversarial engagement with a reader whose intellectual capabilities he continuously questions. This is not simply a nod towards the polemical style of Milton. Hill sees himself as an inheritor of a larger Sixteenth and Seventeenth century tradition of those writers who have the capacity and desire to 'contend', that is, to quote the OED of which Hill is fond, to 'dispute keenly.' In the essay 'The eloquence of sober truth,' Hill notes the preponderance of disputation in seventeenth century critical responses to Thomas Hobbes: 'These writers are not monolinguists, nor are they determinists or mechanistic dialecticians; they engage with the (hostile) other as a contending voice among others. They recognize their own contentiousness, their own partiality, and thereby acknowledge, in a sense, their parity, their common partaking in that condition, that innate incompetence, which Hooker had called "this our imbecillitie."' (*Style and Faith* 91) Although Milton can barely contain his condescension towards entering the world of public discourse, the 'troubled sea of noises and hoarse disputes' (*Reason of Church Government*, II), the disputation with which he is engaged is precisely what Sidney means by praxis.

That the praxis of polity is disputation is problematic for Hill though because of the discrepancy between the success of Seventeenth century practitioners and his own efforts to follow in their tradition. A case in point is Hill's third and final 'To The High Court of Parliament' poem in *Canaan*. Hill opens his poem by situating, along seventeenth century examples, his own attempts at engaging in polity. In a text that considers effective literary models of critical engagement in public discourse, Hill's first query is 'who could outbalance poised Marvell'[?]. Hill's choice of poet is occasioned partly by the way in which his admiration of Marvell's rhetorical skill is suggested by the word 'poised.' But the choice of poised also suggests Hill's desire to follow literary antecedents and participate in the public forum of current political debate. For Marvell's use of this word in 'The First Anniversary of the Government under His Highness the Lord Protector' (1655) originates in Cromwell's address to Parliament the year before. By appropriating Cromwell's imagery, Marvell demonstrates, through the praxis of polity, how the poet can participate in a common political rhetoric and either dispute or support a government's public policy.

Marvell composes his poem at a time when several poets expressed public misgivings about the Protectorate. Milton had already expressed *his* concerns in *The Second Defence of the English People* the year before. As Nigel Smith points out in his introduction to Marvell's poem in the Longman edition, 1654, the first year of the Protectorate, had been marred by a series of crises, suggesting the instability of the state. On 14 September 1654, in the painted chamber at Whitehall, Cromwell, addressing Parliament, expresses his disappointment with their lack of enthusiasm for the Ruling Instrument of December 1653 that had established government in a single person and successive Parliaments: 'I thought it was understood, that I was the Protector, and the Authority that called you, and that I was in possession of the Government by a good right from God and men... If this be so, why should we sport with it? With a businesse thus serious? May not this character, this stamp, bear equall Poyze with any hereditary interest...?' (26) For Cromwell, the word 'poyze' means that the Protectorate was of equal political merit to the hereditary succession that it had replaced. Marvell picked up on this word and used it as part of a larger architectural metaphor to describe the way in which Cromwell had succeeded in achieving a harmonic political state. Earlier in his poem Marvell describes the Instrument of Government as a well constructed polity where factions are praised as a necessity for a strong state: 'the resistance of opposed minds, / The fabric as with arches stronger binds.' The free Senate is the protecting weight, a play on the protecting role offered by Cromwell in his new position. Later in the poem, Marvell depicts Cromwell as the careful architect of the state:

> Choosing each stone, and *poising* each weight,
> Trying the measures of the breadth and height;
> Here pulling down and there erecting new,
> Founding a firm state by proportions true. (emphasis added).

By sharing the word, 'poise', Marvell could publicize his support of Cromwell as the careful, deliberative architect who experimented with principles of governance in order to create a well-balanced state while criticizing those who had questioned his right to rule.

So why would Hill use 'poise' to describe Marvell? In recalling an architectural metaphor that describes the idealized Protectoral political design, Hill can offer an ironic contrast with the policies of the Conservative government constructed within the edifice of Barry and Pugin's Houses of Parliament. Cromwell's artful mediation of disparate factions is offset by contemporary obscurist politics that separates the politicians from the people. But while it is partly to praise Marvell's commitment to praxis in engaging with Cromwell, the word also identifies how praxis works in a poised or confident poet while expressing the difficulties of this praxis for the less self-assured contemporary poet who wishes to contribute to current political debates. Hill recognizes the relevance of polity through praxis which Marvell exemplifies when he states that such discourse has 'significance... for us as much as for seventeenth century thought' (*Style and Faith* 90). Such a diachronic understanding of the relationship between praxis and polity would explain why Hill positions himself within the same tradition as Sidney, Milton and Marvell. However, Hill's difficulty is the physical distance between him and those who should be the subject of his praxis. In this final poem addressed to the High Court of Parliament, Hill may very well have a *j'accuse* air about him: the dichotomy, the withering stare, the finger pointing of the YOU and the us and them, the politicians separated by the Thames 'from the people: / as 'thy' high lamp presides with sovereign / equity, over against us...' But he himself is physically immobilized: he is at a literal and metaphysical distance from the political edifice. It is a monolith of deception that lies across the Thames from where he stands; it is 'over against us, across this/densely reflective long-drawn, procession of waters.' It is Hobbes' leviathan, looming large, turned into a sinister spectral presence, literally a monolithic monstrous representation of deception and lies. Such impotency begs the following questions: can any modern poet speak for democracy? Does anyone have the Marvellian desire or the ability to engage in matters of state?

In *An Apology for Poetry*, Sidney argues that such engagement in polity required a passionate commitment: 'And how praxis can be, without being moved to practise, it is no hard matter to consider.' (emphasis added) But this is precisely Hill's dilemma. Hill cannot fulfill this role because he sees himself in possession of a post-lapsarian oratorical ineptitude, part of that 'imbecillitie' that he identifies with Hooker. By copying Marvell's 'poised,' Hill indicates his desire to engage in praxis through polity. However, his poetry, particularly *Canaan* is characterized by Hill's constant evocation of historical figures—landscape artists, reformists, theologians—whose presence is sorely missed precisely because they alone have already perfected the art of active virtue. Hence Cobbett, the Parliamentary reformer, possesses a 'singular' pitch in talking about labour laws and Parliamentary reform. Hill wants to suspend Cobbett's rhetoric in a historical stasis because of his perfection of eloquence: 'I say let stand the entire deposed authority of vision just as it fell.' This attitude of an artistic *ne plus ultra* occurs with his address to John Constable whose landscape paintings state emotions so opaquely: 'Anxious griefs, grievous anxieties, are not be sublimed through chiaroscuro. Knowing this, you framed it clearly. To mourn is to mourn.' Artists of clarity, in other words, take a stand, are defiant and yet confident in how they see and articulate the world around them. In contrast, Hill is an apologist for his indecisiveness, constantly acknowledging the criticism of the unseen interrogative interlocutor. For example, he concedes: 'you are right, of course; I neither stand / my ground nor run. In whatever direction kinesis takes me, it is no distance' (*The Triumph of Love* 102).

So does Hill have the staying power to participate in the high standards expected of the artist committed to praxis? In *Canaan*, he asks in his third poem to Parliament, 'Who can now speak for despoiled merit,/ the foul catchments of Demos.' The poem starts with a hyphen as if Hill is having a conversation with another or rather, I would suggest, his own eidolon as he bemoans the fact that there is simply no modern equivalent to the rhetorical brilliance of Marvell, the poised orator. Similarly, Hill recalls Milton's 'ideal' speech, Gillray's incisive caricature while Wordsworth 'can hardly be bettered.' There is even nostalgia for the elixir salesmen with their confident patter. Throughout his poetry, Hill is always searching for their contemporary equivalences: 'Who shall restore the way, reclaim lost footage, / achieve too late prescient telegraphy,/ take to themselves otherness of common woe.' Who indeed?

In *The Triumph of Love*, Hill ends his sequence with a question and answer: 'What ought a poem to be? Answer, a sad and angry consolation.' Hill may be able to reconcile himself to this Boethian thought of comfort, that he at least put in the effort, but there is also the modern thought, embedded in this word, of getting the consolation prize, of being the runner-up, of being unsuccessful, failing to match up to the *ideal* censure of Milton, and the *poised* rhetoric of Marvell. And so, always, the eidolon, the phantom shade that haunts his own Genius is Milton, Marvell and those other disputative Renaissance writers who perfectly aligned praxis with polity. In contrast, Hill is in despair, bemoaning the state of England's political, moral and spiritual decline, and looking for the contemporary poet prophet, Amos, the loquitor of ethical and cultural malaise who can speak for 'a spectral people/raking among the ash.' And when he cries out in *Speech! Speech!* (2000): 'Enforcer! What will you have? What can I freely give you? (5), it is less the voice of the seventeenth century haranguer/ pugilist poet at work than the exasperated poet of despair, exhausted by the gift that he recognizes he has 'over-employed'. Hill frequently refers to endurance, as if he possesses it, but there is also extreme fatigue here, as if he barely has enough energy to push through. In the third mysticism and democracy poem of *Canaan*, Hill admits that the truth is 'difficult to follow [because] exhaustion is of the essence.' While he may desire to use a noble vernacular, Hill's infuses the rigor of his style with the tone of futility: 'Where has it got us? Does it stop, in our case, / with Dryden, or, perhaps, / Milton's political sonnets?—the cherished stock/hacked into ransom and ruin; 'the voices of distinction, far back, indistinct' (*The Triumph of Love* 36). There is no doubt that the impetus for wanting to be the modern equivalent of Swiftian misanthropy is there. In 'Cycle', he asks, 'Are we not moved by 'savage indignation'? But clearly this is not enough when you face the crass masses: 'We thought, hoped rather, he might be dead. Too bad. So how much more does he have of injury time?' This thinking in terms of extra time added on after the game is finished is the football fan's rhetoric imposed on the poet's consciousness about his own mortality. It is the dismissive response of a thuggish nation, Thomas Nashe's 'rubbish menialty,' those who Hill might wish to subject to the government's ASBOs.[1] This cultural yobbishness is only exacerbated by a self-loathing encapsulated in the image of Hill the old age pensioner, stripped of respect and immobilized by the indignities of the ailing body. When he muses, 'Take out supposition. Insert suppository,' (*The Triumph of Love* 105) what else is this but an editorial enema, a colonic irrigation of the textual corpus?

In the end, Marvell's 'poised' is both a reflection of the calm, collected persona of Marvell himself as he addresses Cromwell while engaging in praxis but also the characteristic of his poetic style. In contrast, Hill possesses a self-disgust, the deconstruction and destruction, borne through self-loathing less in Las Vegas than in Bromsgrove, of his own doubt about whether he can represent the dissenting poet's voice that offers advice to a corrupt government administration. And while there is no doubt that Hill is moved as passionately as Milton in engaging in public disputation with various political administrations, he also knows that Euripides' epigraph that precedes Milton's 'ideal' censure in *Areopagitica* draws a decisive line between those who have the capacity to and deserve to engage in polity and those who are unable to and should therefore be silent: 'This is true liberty, when free-born men, / Having to advise the public, may speak free, /Which he can, and will, deserves high praise; / Who neither can, nor will, may hold his peace.' When you are the *senex sapiens*, who needs to be pricked for his inability to forgive himself, can you hope to have enough poise not only to pursue the gnosis of a poetic tradition but be able to engage in its praxis? For Hill, this remains the perpetual dilemma of the contemporary political poet.

Christopher Orchard is Associate Professor of English at Indiana University of Pennsylvania.

Note
[1] Anti-Social Behaviour Orders, first introduced by the British government under the Crime and Disorder Act (1998).

Works Cited

Hill, Geoffrey. *Canaan*. London: Penguin, 2001
—. *Speech! Speech!* London: Penguin, 2000.
—. *Style and Faith*. New York: Counterpoint, 2003.
—. *The Triumph of Love*. London: Penguin, 1998.

Emily Dickinson and Contemporary Poetry

ROBIN PEEL

I would like to start with two fundamental questions posed by Virginia Jackson. How do we know that Emily Dickinson wrote poems? How do we recognise a poem when we see one? In *Dickinson's Misery* Jackson confronts these questions by forcing us to review some of the assumptions we make about writing and the way that we read the printed word. For example, she identifies the modern 'lyric' as the genre which from the eighteenth century onwards was a form of poetry 'thought to require as its context only the occasion of its reading'. [1] The development of this genre coincides with the marginalisation of poetry, she argues, but also the arrival of influential editors, reviewers and critics. A supposedly unmediated form emerges at a time of great mediation by the publication industry and the academy. Dickinson's work, published (with one or two exceptions) only after her death in 1886, has a resonance for contemporary poetry more interesting, I wish to argue, than the familiar refrain that Dickinson is a 'modern'.

In this short paper I will rehearse very briefly the reasons why Emily Dickinson looks so contemporary, before arguing that though a retrospective reading inevitably notices features that make her work seem very close to much newer practice this 'recognition' can be distracting. Instead I will be arguing that Dickinson's work can usefully be read alongside the reporting and practice of *science*, and that this relationship can also be productively applied to a reading of contemporary poetry.

Let me approach this from another angle. Dickinson's works seems to anticipate some of the features of writing we associate principally with twentieth or twenty-first century poetry, whether modernist or postmodernist, Situationist or Surrealist, Concrete or Language. We might take for example the practice of producing home-made booklets with no intended commercial publication or circulation at all, or in Dickinson's case no agreed circulation whatsoever, beyond that of the chosen recipients. Her work might seem to anticipate Frank O'Hara's postcard poems or, with her herbarium in mind, Theodore Roethke's interest in botany. We might observe an anticipation of John Ashbery's linguistic playfulness in her work. We will probably see all these things, but largely because it is natural to identify with familiar names those features we wish to make familiar. After all, that is why there is a Plymouth in America, and a Perth in Australia. Consideration of the relationship between Dickinson's writing and the practice and reporting of *science*, however, focuses on the science/epistemology interface which just possibly might provide a useful way of thinking about contemporary poetry. The important question becomes not 'how do we know a poem?' but 'how do we *know*?'

It is not difficult to see why Dickinson has been read as a proto-modernist. The reputation comes from her seemingly *bricolage* method, her refusal to engage openly with the big public issues of the time, and her poetry's sense of fragility, dislocated perception, terror and bewilderment, as in 'I felt a funeral in my brain' (F340). It is the last stanza which for many is most striking:

> And then a Plank in Reason, broke,
> And I dropped down, and down –
> And hit a World, at every plunge,
> And Finished knowing – then –

Helen Vendler argues that it records the collapse of the sequential in Dickinson's poems (the 'and then, and then' of the previous work), and that it prepares us for the poems using the voice of someone who is dead ('A fly buzzed when I died', 'Twas just this time last year I died' and so on).[2] The (provisional) last line records an end of perception, and an end to knowing. Lee Upton, in *The Muse of Abandonment*, sees Dickinson's 'stylistic condensations' and her 'omission of context' as influences on Charles Wright, Jean Valentine and James Tate.[3] More recently, in *The Door Ajar*, Thomas Gardner has traced connections between Dickinson and Jorie Graham, Susan Howe, Marilyn Robinson and Charles Wright[4]. Other critics, such as Marshall Walker, have argued that Dickinson's sense of autonomy makes her modern.[5] It is exactly this kind of disintegration and fracturing we associate with a modernist sensibility. David Porter, in *Dickinson: The Modern Idiom* argues that Dickinson's 'stroboscopic idiom' is a precursor of the modern.[6] Porter points to her use of the vernacular, of ellipsis and her 'modernist knowledge of the mind's hidden places'. These are seductive readings. On the other hand, it takes Dickinson out of history, where it could be significant that 'I felt a funeral ' appears to have been written during the psychological turmoil of the American Civil War. It is given a date of 'About summer 1862' by Franklin. Like Joanna Dobson, I think it diverting, but distracting to read this and other poems ahistorically, as anticipations of modernism.[7] But I do see considerable virtue in returning to it as a revelation of the sudden inability to *know*. The word science comes from a root which means knowledge, and Dickinson poems interrogate epistemology, and the practice of close observation. The ante-bellum explosion in the popular reporting of science emphasised how much we might learn through such observation. We might even get back to the perception available to Adam and Eve before the Fall, some optimists argued. I don't think Dickinson believed this for a moment, however.

Dickinson's verse and contemporary poetry both draw on a *public* language in the very obvious sense that the words and forms used are recognisable by the *publicus*, even if individual poems are sometimes opaque. This is not the private code of a Pepys diary, or the specialist language of a science such as chemistry. Dickinson did not *make public* her poems, but in using the hymn form she used a very public structure. What then of Dickinson the Postmodernist and Contemporary poet? The writing seems often to be without a centre or subject, and there is a playfulness in some of her work, which involves an element of collage, or the writing and *filing* of lines inscribed on scraps of commercial paper, such as a chocolate wrapper[8] or, less inscrutably, the cover of a book.[9] Peter Middleton's description of British postmodernist poetry as a version of 'Postmodernism as play, as withdrawal from political ideologies and commitment' might suggest a kinship between Dickinson's poetry and some contemporary practice.[10] The original form of Dickinson's poem 'A poor torn heart' illustrates this, with its cut out pictures secured onto the manuscript.[11] Sewing on pictures cut from books changes the writing with which it is juxtaposed. Here there are pictures cut from her father's copy of *The Old Curiosity Shop*, used to complement some lines beginning 'A poor torn heart':

A poor – torn heart – a tattered heart –
That sat it down to rest –
Nor noticed that the ebbing Day
Flowed silver to the West –

Nor noticed night did soft descend –
Nor Constellation burn –
Intent opon a vision
Of Latitudes unknown.

(F 125)

Jackson discusses another example.[12] A US stamp, with a locomotive (Dickinson's father had helped the railroad to Amherst) and two names cut from *Harper's New Monthly* ('Georges Sand' and 'Mauprat') are surrounded by the lines which form poem 1174 in Franklin, from 1870. Are the stamp and leg-like words an *avant garde* collage or, as Jackson speculates, a reminder to go to the post office? They seem to bear no relation to the subject of the writing, even though the writing has been deliberately inscribed around the little collage. The poem, which possibly chronicles a moment in a privy when a spider scurried towards Dickinson's more intimate parts begins as follows:

Alone and in a Circumstance
Reluctant to be told
A spider on my reticence
Assiduously crawled.

(F 1174)

The poem itself is mysterious, and the context even more so. It raises the fundamental question: should we be reading it at all?

The Perils of Print

Why have editors converted this writing into print, against Dickinson's express wish? If we look at the opening of poem 2 in the Johnson edition of her work, still published by Faber today, we see the following:

There is another sky,
Ever serene and fair,
And there is another sunshine,
Though it be darkness there;
(J 2)

But this 'verse' was not written like this. Here is this writing in its original context, a letter from Emily Dickinson to her brother Austin[13]:

> Dont think that the sky will frown so the day when you come home! She will smile and look happy, and be full of sunshine *then*—and even *should* she frown upon her child returning, there is *another* sky ever serene and fair, and there is *another* sunshine, tho' it be darkness there—never mind faded forest, Austin, never mind silent fields—*here* is a little forest whose leaf is ever green, here is a *brighter* garden, where not a frost has been, in its unfading flowers I hear the bright bee hum, prithee, my Brother, into my garden come!
> Your very aff
> Sister

It is editors who have made it into a poem. Later editors returned it to its original form, but by then it had entered the academy as verse.

The appropriation of Dickinson as a modern writer has encouraged such practices. The fascicles (Dickinson's home-made booklets) and the collages might superficially seem to bear kinship with the hand-produced books of the London avant-garde presses of the 1970s and 80s, such as anti-copyright Bluff books, or even the work of Dickinson's American admirer, the contemporary poet Susan Howe, who experiments with text and context. We have now been primed to see these connections. To rephrase T. S. Eliot, contemporary art changes all the art which preceded it. We read Dickinson as a contemporary poet because we now think we see what she was doing.

But let me return to my argument that we should read sideways, and not backwards (or forwards). In *My Emily Dickinson* the contemporary poet Susan Howe, who if anyone is in a position to assess Dickinson's proto-modernist or post-modernist credentials, actually takes us away from the twenty first century and sideways in the ante-bellum period to the Nat Turner insurrection, James Fennimore Cooper and the image of Childe Roland.[14] Howe is the first to acknowledge Dickinson's Puritan heritage and the influence of writers like Jonathan Edwards. And this brings us on to the subject of Dickinson and Science, and Dickinson's avoidance of print publication.

Dickinson the Scientist

Dickinson was suspicious of science, but had a powerful investigative inclination. Scientific discourse and enquiry provided her with an important set of metaphors for observing nature and her own writing as an experiment. Charles Anderson illustrates this by looking at the variations in an 1876 poem 'A little madness in the spring' (F 1356; J 1333) which begins:

> A little Madness in the Spring
> Is wholesome even for the King,
> But God be with the Clown –
> Who ponders this tremendous scene –
> This whole Experiment of Green –
> As if were his own!

The manuscript shows that Dickinson considered various alternatives to the original line 'This sudden legacy of Green', alternatives which included 'Apocalypse', 'Experience', 'Astonishment' and 'Periphery', before finally settling for 'This whole Experiment of Green'.[15]

The parallel between scientific investigation and the private, metrical writing which Dickinson assembled in her fascicles is unsurprising when we consider the pervasiveness of scientific enquiry in the ante-bellum period, as reported in magazines, newspapers and journals. The presence of Edward Hitchcock, the astronomer turned geologist who was also President of Amherst College, and the collections that were gathered in the College, added further to the strength of the scientific culture surrounding Emily Dickinson. Even within Puritan traditions, as the young Jonathan Edwards' studies of flying spiders had shown in the 1700s, there was a strong precedent for treating the natural world as a legitimate and rewarding place for Christian observation. That, after all, was what Natural Theology argued, and the enormous popularity of William Paley's *Natural Theology* (1802), arguing that the natural world provided just as much evidence of a maker as a watch does, was evidence of a powerful Christian desire to give legitimacy to scientific study. [16] Emily Dickinson was not persuaded by this argument, but she was not immune to it.

This contingency between Dickinson and science reminds us that even if she wished her poetry to be part of a private language, it was inescapably linked to a public language to which she was heir. Our world is even more dominated by scientific theory than was hers, and our twenty-first century present is a strange looking-glass world in which there is once again a huge collision of science and faith, just when in the western world it looked as if science and rationalism had triumphed. Writing along this epistemological fault line has enormous implications for contemporary poetry, whether or not the individual writer expresses interest in it or not.

In her study of cultural encounters *Open Fields* Gillian Beer includes as an epigraph the following definition from the Concise Scientific dictionary:

> *Field*: A region in which a body experiences a force as the presence of some other body or bodies. A field is thus a method of representing the way in which bodies are able to influence each other
> *Concise Scientific Dictionary* (Oxford UP, 1989)

Beer argues for the importance of lateral encounter, the 'crossings we make as readers between fields. Instead of reading back to Dickinson through the lens of contemporary poetry, I would like to propose that we read across from her work to science and back again, and that if that is useful for work produced then, it might be equally useful for work produced now. I don't just mean the obvious relationship with science, with an artist in residence like Laurie Anderson at NASA in 2003 going on to produce something like 'The End of the Moon'. Instead I wonder if it would be productive to think about the shared epistemological practices of investigative science and investigative poetry, and the mind altering effects of scientific theory in its particular disciplines, such as geology and optics, as a provider of metaphors.

Let me try to illustrate this with one example from Dickinson. It was the telescope which allowed astronomers to see worlds not visible to the naked eye, and Dickinson demonstrates an awareness of the physics of light and telescopes in her poem 'The Admirations and contempts of time' (F 830, J 906) in which she uses the image of compound vision to illustrate the new way of seeing that comes to us as we slide into death. Our perception changes, as

> ...what We saw not
> We distinguish clear –
> And mostly – see not
> What We saw before –

This is not a scientific observation. It can be called an epistemological one, a metaphysical one, or at its most obvious level, a theological or spiritual one. But to illustrate it Dickinson draws an analogy with the working of the telescope and microscope, in which light passes through lens after lens, magnifying its object at every stage as it passes from convex to concave, as has been discussed by Hiroko Uno.[17] Olmsted's *A Compendium of Natural Philosophy* describes the compound microscope as a device with two lenses both convex (unlike Dickinson's poem, which refers also to a 'concave Witness'), one called an object glass and the other an eye glass.[18] The object glass magnifies the object and the eye glass magnifies the image.[19] The translation of this into metaphor is where art meets science.

But if art affects our reading of science, does not science affect our reading of art? Do we not read the opening of the new Jorie Graham poem 'Embodies'[20] differently because we have some theory of global warming?:

> Deep autumn & the mistake occurs, the plum tree blossoms,
> twelve blossoms on three different
> branches, which for us, personally, means none this coming spring

or perhaps none on
     just those branches on which
     just now
lands, suddenly, a grey-gold migratory bird – still here ? ....

Whether or not Graham is alluding to this contemporary scientific belief, the potential metaphor is there. I use this as a random illustration, from something which has very recently entered the public domain.

The perceptions of science and the perceptions of poetry are not of a separate order. Science has its own sublime, and poetry its own laboratory methods. Emily Dickinson was sceptical of the achievements of both, but that did not stop her practising them, and it should not discourage us from considering them as we respond to poetry in 2007.

Robin Peel is Senior Lecturer in English at The University of Plymouth. The Dickinson poems are reprinted by permission of the publishers and the Trustees of Amherst College from The Poems of Emily Dickinson: Variorum Edition, *Ralph W Franklin, ed, Cambridge, Mass: The Belknap Press of Harvard UP, copyright © 1998 by the President and Fellows of Harvard College. The Dickinson letters are reprinted by permission of the publishers from* The Letters of Emily Dickinson, *Thomas H Johnson, Ed., Cambridge MA: The Belknap Press of Harvard UP, Copyright © 1958, 1986 by the President and Fellows of Harvard College.*

Notes

1 Virginia Jackson, *Dickinson's Misery: A Theory of Lyric Reading*, Princeton, NJ: Princeton UP, 2005: 7.
2 Helen Vendler, *Poets Thinking: Pope, Whitman, Dickinson, Yeats*, Cambridge, MA: Harvard UP, 2004.
3 Lee Upton, *The Muse of Abandonment: Origin, Identity, Mastery in Five American Poets*, Lewisburg: Bucknell UP; London: Associated UP, 1998.
4 Thomas Gardner, *The Door Ajar*, 2006.
5 Marshall Walker, 'Modernisms: Emily Dickinson' in Graham Clarke (Ed), *Emily Dickinson Critical Assessments*, Volume 4, 2002: 121–123.
6 David Porter, *Dickinson: The Modern Idiom*, 1981.
7 Joanna Dobson, *Dickinson and the Strategies of Reticence*, 1989.
8 Jackson, 2005: 238–239.
9 See Jackson, 2005: 65–66.
10 Peter Middleton, 2004: 770.

11 The manuscript can be seen on the website 'Dickinson cartoonist' www.emilydickinson.org.cartoon/carindex.html. It is the copyright of the Houghton Library, Harvard University.

12 See Jackson, 2005: 168.

13 *Letters*, 1986: 149.

14 Susan Howe, *My Emily Dickinson*, Berkeley, CA: North Atlantic Books, 1985.

15 Charles Anderson, 1960: 80.

16 William Paley (1802), *Natural Theology, or Evidence of the Existence and Attributes of the Deity, collected from the appearances of nature*, Oxford: Oxford UP, 2006.

> Paley's book begins with the famous opening analogy: 'In crossing a heath, suppose I pitched my foot against a *stone*, and were asked how the stone came to be there. I might possible answer, that, for any thing I knew to the contrary, it had lain there for ever: nor would it perhaps be very easy to shew the absurdity of this answer. But suppose I found a *watch* upon the ground, and it should be enquired how the watch happened to be in that place, I should hardly think of the answer which I had before given that, for anything I knew, the watch might have always been there. Yet why should not this answer serve for the watch, as well as for the stone?' (Paley, 2006: 7)

17 Hiroko Uno, 'Optical Instruments and "Compound Vision" in Emily Dickinson's Poetry', *Studies in English Literature*, Volume LXIV Number 2, June 1988: 227–243.

18 Denison Olmsted (1837), *A Compendium of Natural Philosophy*.

19 Denison Olmsted (1837), *A Compendium of Natural Philosophy*, 1840: 547.

20 Jorie Graham, 'Embodies', *London Review of Books*, 8th March 2007: 24.

Abbreviations and Acknowledgements

F – R W Franklin (Ed), *The Poems of Emily Dickinson*, Variorum edition in three volumes, Cambridge, MA: The Belknap Press of Harvard UP, 1998.

J – Thomas H Johnson (Ed), *Emily Dickinson: The Complete Poems*, London: Faber and Faber, 1970.

Letters – *The Letters of Emily Dickinson*, Thomas Johnson, Ed., Cambridge MA: The Belknap Press of Harvard UP, 1986.

Works cited

Anderson, Charles. *Emily Dickinson's Poetry: Stairway of Surprise*, Westport, CT: Greenwood Press, 1960.

Anderson, Laurie. 'The End of the Moon', Multimedia performance piece 2005.

Beer, Gillian. *Open Fields*, Oxford: Oxford UP, 1996.

Dobson, Joanne. *Dickinson and the Strategies of Reticence*, Bloomington and Indianapolis: Indiana UP, 1989.

Franklin, R W (Ed). *The Poems of Emily Dickinson*, Variorum edition in three volumes, Cambridge MA: The Belknap Press of Harvard UP, 1998.

Gardner, Thomas. *A Door Ajar*, Oxford: Oxford UP, 2006.

Graham, Jorie. 'Two poems by Jorie Graham', *London Review of Books*, 8 March 2007.

Howe, Susan. *My Emily Dickinson*, Berkeley, CA: North Atlantic Books, 1985.

Jackson, Virginia *Dickinson's Misery: A Theory of Lyric Reading*, Princeton: Princeton UP, 2005.

Middleton, Peter. 'Poetry after 1970' in Laura Marcus and Peter Nicholls (Eds). *The Cambridge History of Twentieth Century English Literature*, Cambridge: Cambridge UP, 2004: 768–786.

Olmsted, Denison (1837). *A Compendium of Natural Philosophy*, New Haven: S Babcock, 1840.

Paley, William (1802). *Natural Theology, or Evidence of the Existence and Attributes of the Deity, collected from the appearances of nature*, Oxford: Oxford UP, 2006.

Patterson, Rebecca. *Emily Dickinson's Imagery*, Amherst: University of Massachusetts Press, 1979.

Porter, David. *Dickinson: the Modern Idiom*, Cambridge, MA: Harvard UP, 1981.

Uno, Hiroko. 'Optical Instruments and "Compound Vision" in Emily Dickinson's Poetry', *Studies in English Literature*, Volume LXIV Number 2 June 1988, The English Literature Society of Japan: 227–243.

Upton, Lee. *The Muse of Abandonment: Origin, Identity, Mastery in Five American Poets*, Lewisburg: Bucknell UP; London: Associated UP, 1998.

Vendler, Helen. *Poets Thinking: Pope, Whitman, Dickinson, Yeats*, Cambridge, MA: Harvard UP, 2004.

Walker, Marshall. 'Modernisms: Emily Dickinson' in *The Literature of the United States of America*, Basingstoke, 1983; reprinted in Graham Clarke (Ed). *Emily Dickinson Critical Assessments Volume 4* Robertsbridge, England: Helm Information, 2002: 121–123.

State Secrets:
Names and Fetishes in Barry MacSweeney's *Jury Vet*

WILLIAM ROWE

> *There is no future*
> *In England's dreaming*
> . . .
> *When there's no future*
> *How can there be sin*
>   ('God Save The Queen', The Sex Pistols)

It has become common practice to criticize current terminology of war as euphemism. But there's a sense in which this idea is a fantasy, because to think that the State could call what it does by its true name is to fall into the same imaginary transparency that the state propagates. The names given in the theatre of war are part of the reality produced by those who have greatest power over time and space. Since they cannot be denied, they enter and corrupt us insofar as we are forced to speak them even in the attempt to deny them. In the second place, they are part of a particular language whose desire is to be purely operational, purely logistical, and that can be traced back to adoption of 'operational research' by the military in the Second World War. The final aim is a discourse that does not need to include anything unknown or meaningless—what escapes from concepts—but instead instates a totality by actually producing one, one whose subject is the isolated, paranoid individual, i.e. the social subject of advanced consumer society.

With Barry MacSweeney's *Jury Vet*, one of the things I want show is how his work displays particular theatres of meaning, such as law courts, fashion shows, and 'behind' them the State itself. Though I'll want to argue that the idea that the State is located 'behind' is a type of fantasy.

But before that, I want to say more about the problem of hyper-instrumental naming. It depends of course on the politics of fear, by offering a language that gives the assurance of control, because it's a language of 'scientific' precision, and because it's all embracing, in that its terms can contain any 'enemy'. In short, the all-embracing language offers a fantasy of security from that fear that it invokes. What I will want to draw attention to, though, is who has the power to name and what are the effects of naming.

To want to give a more correct name, one that corresponds more accurately with a proper description of objects and events, in order to counter the state's use of 'euphemism' (of which there's no lack of examples from the first Gulf War to the present), runs the risk of missing the fact 'that a word is connected to an object or a set of objects through an act of "primal baptism"', i.e., that though there is an arbitrariness in naming—since it 'will not', to quote Mallarmé, 'abolish chance'—it still sticks to the object. Because it includes a component of desire—in the case of Pentagon nomenclature, one of its components would be the desire for mastery—the purely operational appearance of the terms themselves hiding the factor of identification on the part of participants.[1]

Rimbaud dramatises this naming as baptism, makes it a feature of a scenario where image is spectacle: in his 'Promontory-Palace', in *Les Illuminations*, there are 'faint eruptions of Etnas and glacier crevasses of flowers and waters … the curved fronts of Scarboro or Brooklyn "Royals" or "Grands" … this hotel chosen from the history of the most elegant and colossal buildings of Italy, America and Asia.' In the magic lantern show, tourism and advertising make a hologram that proffers a new world-territory to the gaze.

Instead of giving us realism, so as to return p(a)laces to their proper descriptions, Rimbaud gets inside the fetishistic names and images and pushes them to a limit—which could be called the appearance of the hyper-real *avant la lettre*—where a certain type of negation starts to occur: the beginnings of a release from that regime of naming, in its relation to a particular historical construction of temporality, the time of 'the consumption of images'—or 'the image as consumption of time.'[2] Using a more correct name or pointing to the incorrectness through ironical distance, would not produce the negation. As Guattari put it, 'a meaningful world' is the result of the conjunction of 'two kinds of formalization': that of language and that of 'power formations as the producers of signified content.' (169)[3] So that it's not a question of correct or incorrect names but the power relations that run through naming as such. If that is the case, there is nothing inherent in language to stop it: only revolutionary will can.

But first, I want to say something about the significance of the title *Jury Vet*. The ABC trial began in November 1977: the defendants' names were John Aubrey, John Berry and Duncan Campbell. The background was the revelations by former CIA agent Philip Agee who the Home Office was attempting to deport to the USA. Campbell wrote an article in *Time Out* about the illegal spying activities of the British Secret Service (at GCHQ). Campbell was charged with 'for a purpose prejudicial to the safety or interests of the state, collecting information concerning defence communications that might ... be useful to an enemy.'[4] The security services tried to protect the identity of one of their witnesses by calling hum Colonel B, when it was fairly common knowledge that his name was Col. Johnson. Campbell's defence included the fact that all the information he had used, to deduce the existence of a secret communication infrastructure, was in the public domain (in phone directories, for example). The secrecy, therefore, was a staged effect, something that Labour wanted to hand on to the next inheritor of the State, who turned out to be Thatcher. The vetting refers to the fact that the Defence discovered that the chairman of the Jury was a member of the SAS: this led to a retrial.

MacSweeney worked as a journalist and had been involved in reporting on the case. Thus the phrase 'Jury Vet' is both a headline and shorthand for necessary knowledge, and in the book, written between September 1979 and October 1981, it appears as a heading to several sections, indicating specific types of action: 'JURY VET MEETS CANDACE BAHOUTH', 'SOCIAL WORK TODAY: JURY VET SCANS THE RIOTS', 'JURY VET TESTS HER MEMORY', and so on, so that the book presents itself as an investigative action.

When he introduced JV at a reading at Goldsmiths College in 1982, MacSweeney said: 'I wanted a title that was national and would reflect the way I was feeling at the time which was that life is very much made up of secrecy, betrayal, various codes, passions which can be quite meaningless except in the act of doing them and their result.' The statement could apply equally well to a fashion show, a court of law, and the State, which are the theatres of appearance that the writing engages. It also speaks of where desire might break away from codes. The State refuses to name Colonel B, having given him a new name. The world of fashion shows and the fashion journalism of *Vogue* and *Cosmopolitan* produce an endless stream of new names:

> CHARTREUSE blanquette, shirt lavender, frayed
> mustard thongs. Brown heels on JOSE
> Blue heels on JANE. (107)[5]

BM's work as a journalist included covering fashion shows, and some of the edge of this language, as it shimmers in the poem, is the static-photographic holding of bodies, all the life gone into those surfaces:

> STARLIT BRAS
> & shimmy lichen
> gumboots (buckles
> & studs) (109)

It's a language capable of wrapping round everything:

> *Rain trench*
> *Rainjacket.* Warm
> lined lichen green
> zipped &
> buckled.   GOLD dropping
> chunky, clip-ons. Easy satchel. YOUR NATURAL

> SLENDER WAIST

The point is, there is no nature left outside the fashion fetish. The language is total. *The poem doesn't criticise that language for being exploitative.* It criticises those types of critique by shamelessly enjoying the language of fashion. But it does subject it to inquiry—by pushing through to the other side of enjoyment and asking what is it that this language names, and what is the pain in it.

I've mentioned Rimbaud's magic-lantern show as a theatre of appearances that *Jury Vet* calls as an ally in complicity, to probe the theatre of appearances. When I say theatre of appearances I mean the push beyond phenomenology to cosmology or history, as say with the Cave of the Nymphs, which the Neo-Platonist Porphyry expounds out of an episode in the *Odyssey*. It's a scene which displays the production of text/image out of a combination of sexual generation, cosmology and metaphysics. It conjoins making and reading of image, so that the gaze of the receiver is inscribed in the image. Walter Benjamin, in the scene of his 'Theses on the Philosophy of History', is doing something similar, with the wizened dwarf, which is theology, hidden under the table, ensuring that the puppet called 'Historical Materialism' will always win the chess game. Theology, in JV, corresponds to the image of redemption on the other side of the sex fetish: the 'shimmer' is an index of the medieval poem *Pearl*, in which the shining surface holds the opposition between a dream of redemption and a dream of money.

JV takes the fashion show as mirror of production. The main things that are produced are fetishes. And of course we have various theories of fetishism including Marx and Freud and so on. But before engaging with any of them, let's look into the types of work that MacSweeney's text does in its handling of the fashion image. I call it types of work, because there are various different things that it does. One of them has to do with being, asking the image to teach the one who is seeing:

      BLACK & ZEBRA
  twopiece on much-ribbed Chrissie,

             full-stockinged
             STAR.

I HAVE SEEN THIS FAR.

          ─────────

YOU MUST
      teach me all there is to know
           of
  pinstripe boxjacket tuxedo woman's pillhat

> velvet waistcoats,
> &
> Cup Court Shoes (107–8)

To ask the fashion-objects for their secret. The standard masochist situation, where the female chastiser is wearing furs or maybe a teacher's outfit, is that despite appearances the one who's doing the teaching is the one in the male position: he's the instructor.[6] But as you can see, with *Jury Vet* this arrangement is reversed.

A second reversal or détournement is that dirt and lust demand to be heard:

> Sachet sex Sue.
> Lanolin love.
> Talcum toes.
> Powder puff.
> I'll vet your writhing slit
> FOREVER (101–2)

Writhing – perhaps writing: 'I am with you in / TOTAL SIGNATURE'. What is overstepping the mark is to touch and not just anywhere but the genitals.[7] The vetting gaze, turned to expose the origin of sublimation, the life behind the photographic image. To write with or from that. And, to take submission all the way, beyond pleasure into prayer:

> Love bossette,
> hear my low prayer.
>
> HEAR MY VERY LOW PRAYER.
>
> Burn the venom from this heart.
>
> Suck down the spanner flak
> and Let me strike quimfolds Now.

Words like quimfolds work by substitution of the glamour terms with lust—a sort of dirty language of the real. 'Love the Dirt' (109).

What are the limits of JV's language/world? There are many objects but few types of object, therefore it's a desert. These objects are ruled by one type of operation, as was Operation Desert Storm (of first Gulf War), which reduced memory to a desert. (The digital memory bank of battle engagements, claim its makers, is total and will last thousands of years). What is the difference between that reduction and lyrical condensation?

Tone difference is that the fashion fetish does not answer to now-time: 'If I cannot do it Now I'll do it / with Someone Else. // AND SOON.' (112) Its time is Rolex time:

<blockquote>

She wore a kingfisher suede cape

& the added machismo of a man's big silver stretch strap Rolex

> Which
> tells
> the
>
> Time
>
> *On her Ankles of Fire.* (109)

</blockquote>

There is a point at which the fashion image dissolves:

> Blot
> love
> come
> now.
> (113)

Becomes shapeless like a blot or dispersed like dots ('Fuck dots / grab the scene').

The language of the medieval poem *Pearl* is thrown against fashion-naming:

YOU THE SHIMMERTEXING PEARL
WITHOUTEN SPOT OR BODY BRUISE

So the inquiry is both into *who* is named by the fashion words but also who is being addressed, the one in whom their meaning is completed. And not just who but also what: what is the substance this nomenclature seizes upon? The language of *Pearl*, and also of Wyatt and Chatterton, speaks of a time other than the amnesic present of the fashion image.[8] This other language, played into the fashion fetish, dislodges its hold and prevents it from completing its meaning in the shimmering object of circulation; exposes its command:

> She gold pelt pulled down
> somehow. Be
> SIGNIFICANT (105)

Instead of a value embodied, the gold standard (abandoned in 1968), what we get is 'Be/SIGNIFICANT', the command to keep producing meaning, never mind the content. The signified falls into the signifier, announcing the post-modern. But the poem presses against that condition. If, as Benjamin says, a fetish is a congealed dream, then inside the fashion fetish is a dream, not just of the renewal of desire but of the renewal of names. At the Goldsmiths reading, MacSweeney hinted at how the SM attraction of 'this Vogue, Cosmopolitan, varnished, erotic, economic cruelty' speaks of a failure of desire.

The poem brings about a collision, between naming as significance at any cost, a pornography of names, and the word as beseeching, as prayer, as repair. The two meet at a point of extreme breakdown and erasure:

> BE LOGGED) LOVED (eaten tongue, cudded, yanked
>   over, nailed,
>   crashed in, out of, detrunked, weeded,
>   baked heavy, licked)
> Occulist, tilth binder, clit swampee, dog hound bayer,
>   undreamed,

pilled out, underside velvet, fuck snot. She washed
bruises,
O river rinse her virgin body clean. Beck bubbles
I pleaded (105)

This is not the Surrealist point of encounter between opposites ('life and death, the real and the imaginary, the past and the future [...] the high and the low' etc.),[9] where contraries feed on each other endlessly without negation, but a determinate negation, that brings about a change in the historical place of the subject.

If sublimation means 'Saluting stars & eating shit earth,' the poem has not just put it on display, but has brought it back to the disgust that it substitutes with 'higher' aims, but not as a formal condition of all sublimation (civilization, as Freud says) but rather as a sign of a particular historical conjuncture where social desire is shown to have become a particular, unbearable, violence. The poem both preserves and negates sublimation (the conditions of the production of social desire). Sublimation depends on the signifier as that which permits the object of desire to change: hence the frenzy of naming.[10]

In an essay on fetishism and the State, Michael Taussig puts forward the idea that the State is not the reality behind the mask of political reality but 'the mask that prevents our seeing political reality'.[11] This, he says, 'not only delineates the State in the cultural construction of reality but delineates that reality as inherently deceptive, real and unreal at one and the same time.' In JV, here's the State, that keeps the secret of its own secret (its obscenity) by ostentatiously fabricating secrets, and there's the fashion scene with its creation of names and images, and its command, 'be SIGNIFICANT'. JV probes the working of the fetish. '(wool, acrylic flamingo two piece on xerox / Sue / shredding letters from a shredded / heart), torn, / let's go public, flattered in bedrooms & on / floors' (109): reproduction and control of information, in place of what is called the heart, public space produced by display of objects of desire. Thence the political subjectivity of advanced consumer society: public intimacy.

But JV presses further, seeks to find the flesh inside the clothes, the 'wild poppy pain' (101) inside the fetish signification that is the random and unformed where it first meets symbolisation. I.e. it takes us to the underlying and more general process of sublimation, which makes sociability possible, and turns it round, back to the body that rejects the command 'be SIGNIFICANT' – call it the body without organs or the trauma inside the symbolic order: it's not the development of a theory but the capabilities of a language that's at stake. And the decision is to write *with* the fetish: 'CERISE DRAGONETTE [...] / I am with you in/ TOTAL SIGNATURE.' (102) Until the negative emerges out of that sustained act.

> No pink clues
> as
> fuck seeds
> dance
> &
> rage.
> (103)

The various codes, with their theatre of public secrecy, fall away, as 'pink clues', the book unwriting the feminine and the state. Time outside the consumption of images has no 'language or concept.'[12] These moments are not frequent, but recur, serially, without development. Unlike the earlier *Odes*, where each poem stood singularly, and moved towards this time of sheer expenditure, this longer work locates itself in relation to historical, rather than seasonal and biographical time.

It is well known that *Vogue* magazine was part of the contract that put women back in to the home after the Second World War: the promise of glamour for consumption. This was one of the socially conservative features of the postwar settlement. Sir William Beveridge wrote in 1944: 'All men have value when the State sets up unlimited demand for a compelling purpose. By the spectacular achievement of its planned economy war shows also how great is the waste of unemployment.' This was the basis for the larger pact of 'welfare capitalism'.[13] Hayek's plans to overthrow it, which also date from the 1940s, came to fruition in 1979 with the Thatcher government. I note all of this rapidly, because the question I want to raise is not about the politics of the postwar settlement but the types of intersubjectivity that characterised that period, more specifically changes in the communicative fabric of society that became apparent with Thatcherism but had begun before.

JV registers and probes certain specific breaks in the communicative pact—i.e. consensual rationality. Philip Larkin's well-known poem 'High Windows' gives an index of what the consensus permitted: a transparent regime of conversation, where whatever was named could be found in the name, even though—or precisely because—spoken from antagonistic positions. Antagonistic evaluations—meanings—could be expressed in the same word. This is the world of *Look Back in Anger* or *The Loneliness of the Long-Distance Runner*. Beckett was more radical. But where what Larkin sourly calls 'the long slide to happiness' involved desublimation ('When I see a couple of kids / And guess he's fucking her and she's / taking pills'), then the pact is broken, speech is not transparent, transparency can only be wordless: 'Rather than words comes the thought of high windows.' And so the space of transparency indicates its genealogy of Victorian education and religion – i.e. reaches back to Matthew Arnold. That theatre of appearances has become empty but Larkin's poem hangs on to it.

JV responds to the break-up of the postwar consensus not with nostalgia for the Victorian/Edwardian cadence but with another past: Blake, Chatterton, Wyatt, *Pearl*.

> THEE WASP WITH NAKED FOTE STALKING IN MY
> CHAMBRE.
> THEE WHOSE BRITTIL DERTES ARE PINKSNOW
> TOES PEEKING FROM EACH DOVEGREY
> BORDEAUX SHOE!! (129)

And this is followed by 'Thee nonsense crawl has slaundered love,' where the garment of spectacle has fallen away to reveal unredeemed abjection. Why does the poetic subject in this book so often occupy a place of abjection? And why is that the place of love (slandered)?

A promise of love broken runs through the language: 'all / the / piss-filled / clouds // gather brimming at my brow' (128) and the response is not irony, regret, resentment but humility and anger: not to engage in any ironical distance but to enter humiliation and pain and speak from there so as to clog and sabotage the fashion system that images participation in market democracy. 'I kissed my Errors as they came. / Sucked sick real. / Tears flowing on the bastard zero ground.' (112) The sabotage of the tone and cadences of 'understanding' is a type of punk aesthetic. There's nothing to understand. 'Bastard Zero Decade wakes you UP.' (126)[14] The action required is to jam the circuits: 'let's make some fucking noise' as one punk band said.[15]

The difficulty that JV registers, as an experiment in language, is to get beyond the clogging, sabotaging, jamming into fuller negation. How to achieve that when the full word is the one that empties the symbolic: 'fuckdust', 'fuckdots'. That breaking down into dust and dots gives mere pulsed punctuation *before* meaning. I say *mere* pulsed, but there are two sides to this. There is a passive being punctuated, and an active exuberant will to sabotage, exuberant because it gives time pulsed and expended by the living body, and not the dead commodity, the dead community. Not yet a new political substance but the beginning of a place where it may emerge. MacSweeney's insistence on necessary negation makes Hardt's and Negri's idea of the multitude as a new political subject seem premature.

Let's look at how the negations work. In a complex section headed 'FACING FAX: DOCILE ADJUSTMENT TO DAILY HORROR', JV pitches itself against Murdoch journalism and the passive participation written into its operation:

> Happenings come fast. Fat flows thick. Spew spews.
> Wheat porridge glue.
> THIN dehiscent fuckdust streams
> their eyes
> when coming pollen Sun
> says Yes I Love You, But
> Don't Be Bright. (115)

Alongside the metaphoric level (fat, spew, glue), language that is both reductive and abjectly magical: 'spew spews' stops any displacement, i.e., the dream faculty, and thus mimics the dead fixity of Operational Research language. No displacement: no dream: no life. Sun as cosmological body, and as populist newspaper that decides elections. 'Don't be bright' as submit or as don't learn. The secret made, the secret out (*dehiscent*: gaping open (anatomy), bursting (of seed pods)). 'Fuckdust' as making blind, or as 'thin', breaking down into particles, and therefore dissolving the glue of participation. The price of 'facing fax' is high: 'Bitter / sallow / bricks of lime / & suicide.' Fuckdust is both the point of danger (capture by the phantasmagoria of populist power) and the point of negation. JV locates Margaret Thatcher at that point: 'HER DEMOCRATIC RATHOLE MOUTH DELIGHTS THE GUESTS // & DRIVES // THEIR SECRET MUSIC SPARE.'

A section called 'SOCIAL WORK TODAY: JURY VET SCANS THE RIOTS' shows social work to be premised upon restoring the broken pact, and thus on immobilisation:

> Manila folders burning on her quiet desk
>   with skinhead children eaten
> to the marrow bone,
>   beyond the poxy dole queue grind.
>   [. . .] petrol bombs Come Down
>   on Plastik Spastik Oxfam Tins
>
> & skyblue pandas burn and blaze
>
>   in the stinking urban wind. (120)

Against charity, with the World War Two memory of bombs falling, burning police cars. The same embrace of immobilised time and fire is to be found in the erotic:

> Neck chains.
>
> Blot
> love
> come
> now.
> (113)

Rimbaud's hyper-real panorama show has become the screen of neoliberal participation politics: 'No council coalbunker for us Now / that we enjoy the palaces / of ULTRA REAL.' (114) The script is mass glamour, whereby the Parisian revolutionaries end up in London fashion: 'Chanel. Estee Lauder. Clinique fumes. / [. . .] ghastly / Bang / of sans culottes / in velvet west end beds,' (117) the state power secret now operating as participation . The mediation is the language of advertising and tabloid headlines, and it covers everything, readers complicit in the immobilised dream. Insofar as participation in meaning-fetish is everywhere, the poem is everywhere: a public language.

In the final section, negation is gathered together into the word 'Thee', as against 'She', name of a magazine, of course. Into that mode of prayerful address and its collision with She, are gathered not just the effects of reification but the purchase of speech upon reality or the referential state of the language. In the past, the poem finds a different language, a Benjaminian image of a utopian future. And in the gap, between precapitalism and capitalism, subject and object, prayerful address and command of commodity, the subject is broken apart, participation is thrown against something else, which is the stab of pain inside the fetish ('She undressed at dawn. / She kept her shoes on.'), and is also the fullest negation: 'Your single body's a striking SOVIET!' (119).[16]

William Rowe is Anniversary Professor of Poetics at Birkbeck College, University of London. Poems quoted from Barry MacSweeney's Wolf Tongue *(Bloodaxe Books, 2003) are reproduced here by permission of Bloodaxe Books Ltd.*

Notes

1 Žižek, Slavoj. *The Sublime Object of Ideology*. London: Verso, 1989: 90, 93.
2 Debord, Guy. *The Society of the Spectacle*, New York: Zone Books: 1995: 112.
3 Guattari, Felix. *Molecular Revolution*. Harmondsworth: Penguin, 1984: 169.
4 http://en.wikipedia.org/wiki/ABC-trial Consulted 22.5.07.
5 Page numbers refer to MacSweeney, Barry, *Wolf Tongue*, Tarset: Bloodaxe Books, 2003
6 Deleuze, Gilles, *Masochism*. New York: Zone Books, 1991: 22.

7   Walter Benjamin describes the principle of advertisements as 'Look, but don't touch.' Buck-Morss, Susan, *The Dialectics of Seeing: Walter Benjamin and the Arcades Project*. Cambridge, MA: MIT Press, 1991: 85.

8   Benjamin stresses the amnesic effect of fashion. See Buck-Morss, Susan, *The Dialectics of Seeing*, 98.

9   Breton, André. *What is Surrealism: Selected Writings*, London: Pluto Press, 1978: 129.

10 Lacan, Jacques. *The Ethics of Psychoanalysis*. New York: Norton, 1992: 293.

11 Taussig, Michael. '*Maleficium*: State Fetishism', in *Fetishism As Cultural Discourse*, edited by Emily Apter and William Pietz, 217–247. Ithaca, NY: Cornell UP, 1993: 220.

12 Debord, *The Society of the Spectacle*, 114.

13 Sinfield, Alan. *Literature, Politics, and Culture in Postwar Britain*. Oxford: Blackwell, 1989: 14, 20.

14 For Benjamin, the point is to wake up from the dream. See Buck-Morss, *The Dialectics of Seeing*: 210–212.

15 The Dead Kirks. Thanks to Sean Bonney for pointing this out. See also the Sex Pistols in 'Seventeen': 'we like noise, it's our choice.'

16 In the final lines, where the poem signs itself off ('JURY VET', with double underlining), 'There is no end to Thee' is followed by '((This is She))', the double parentheses indicating the degree of non-equivalence, the impossibility of resolution, and how much rushes into it.

Public Poetics: The Manifesto of the Poetry Society (1976)

ROBERT SHEPPARD

Public language is customarily contrasted with private language, and I will be touching on this distinction at various points, as I look at both the poetry and poetics emanating from what Peter Barry calls the 'Poetry Wars' of the mid-1970s, in his book of that title, to which this paper is deeply indebted. (Barry 2006) However, I will be looking at another version of *public* language, whose opposite is not strictly speaking *private* language at all, but *professional* language.

I'm thinking with the distinction that the socio-linguistician Basil Bernstein makes between restricted code and elaborated code, though I'm not going to focus on his use of the distinction in his work on class, language and socialisation, but its use in considering the language of specialism and specialisation. He explains: 'Restricted codes have their basis in condensed symbols, whereas elaborated codes have their basis in articulated symbols'. (Bernstein 1980: 64) The distinction I am aiming at can be seen by considering the differences between the 'condensed' language of a peer-reviewed scientific paper and the more 'articulated' explanatory language of a serious popular science TV programme dealing with similar matters. Restricted code, in a slightly different sense, also belongs to the 'priesthood', as it were, the private languages of the initiated, the hip, the cool, or, in the case of the school of British poetry of the 1970s, the marginal or even the abject.

Before I examine this literary history, I want to focus upon the notion of 'poetics', that which makes us conscious of poetry, as Lyn Hejinian suggests in her essay in this volume, and that which haunts our dreams of its numerous definitions, as Barrett Watten reminded us in his playful poem 'Correlation of *Paterson*, book 1'. I want to define poetics quite precisely as a speculative writerly discourse, developed by writers themselves. Poetics is the product of the process of writers' reflections upon writing, and upon their acts of writing, gathering from the past and from others, and casting into the future, speculatively and conjecturally, even provocatively on occasions. Poetics exists for the writer and for others in a hoped for writerly community, to produce, to quote Rachel Blau DuPlessis, a 'permission to continue'. (DuPlessis 1990: 156) It involves a theory of practice, a practice of theory—its conjectures are often provisional, its trajectory nomadic, its positions temporary. Poetics does not always, or often, call itself poetics, since it can be mercurial and intermittent and it can appear in a variety of guises.

I am aware that my sense of poetics privileges the individual voice or the small voice of a private group, a restricted code of, and for, professionals. The existence of the artisitic manifesto as a para-literary genre, as a more public mode, is a test case for my definitions and elsewhere I have characterised the manifesto as generally inimical to the speculative and conjectural quality I associate with poetics. Poetics may be contained *in* a manifesto, but the restricted code of talking to the poetry community, to the practitioners and their first readers, in what Bourdieu calls the field of restricted production, is destabilised by the manifesto's compromised standing-forth as articulated public language.

Mary Ann Caws, in the introduction to her anthology, *Manifesto: A Century of Isms*, suggests that manifestos share some of the qualities I associate with poetics. 'The manifesto moment positions itself between what has been done and what will be done,' she says, a Janus-like posture between reflection and speculation. (Caws 2001: xxi) Like some poetics, 'its form creates its meaning'. (Caws 2001: xx) While she sees 'a manifesto [as] generally, by mode and form, an exhortation to a whole way of thinking and being rather than a simple command or a definition', poetics is less of an exhortation, and never a command, though it can involve definition; it is however, always an invitation to new ways of conceiving art. (Caws 2001: xxvii) Caws' taxonomy identifies other qualities more at variance with the speculative and conjectural impulse. She tells us that 'The manifesto is by nature a loud genre', (Caws 2001: xx) 'immodest and forceful, exuberant and vivid, attention-grabbing.' (Caws 2001: xxi) Poetics tends not to be coercive in this way. It is less about force than exploration, often of difficult evanescent possibilities that sometimes defy definition; it is a *credo* for the incredible, a stutter rather than a battle cry.

The art manifesto is an historical form, of course, much associated with the antagonisms of modernism, as Caws demonstrates; think of the Imagist, Futurist and Surrealist manifestos. Given her prospectus of a 'century of isms', she concludes that Postmodern manifestos have a 'kind of dryness' that dissipates energy. (Caws 2001: xxii) This is not a distinction I have time to ponder today, but Caws says something that is relevant to the Poetry Society manifesto: 'The present tense suits the manifesto, as does the rapid enumeration of elements in a list or a bullet form.' (Caws 2001: xxv) A committee or multiply signed manifesto may be no less committed but will be the result of negotiated text. The danger is that this creates a 'camel manifesto' in stilted, legalistic diction rather than 'a poem in heightened prose', as Caws defines 'the manifesto at its height'. (Caws 2001: xxvii)

The affair of the Poetry Society began when a group of poets and activists, from about 1970, were elected onto the General Council of the Society, which housed the National Poetry Centre at a crumbling premises in Earls Court, funded by the Arts Council.[1] The 'radicals' (this is Peter Barry's reluctant term) set up a series of readings and lectures on radical poetry at the building, opened up a print shop for poets, and turned *Poetry Review*, a long-running but moribund magazine, over to Eric Mottram, eventually printing the editions themselves in the print room. They also hosted the important *Poetry Information* magazine.

The 'takeover'—textbook entryism—angered both disgruntled members of the General Council and the Arts Council itself and, after a coup by a reactionary 'Reform Group', the Arts Council, headed by Charles Osborne, sought to obtain control of the Poetry Society by commissioning a report that Osborne hoped (or ensured) would guarantee Arts Council scrutiny and a measure of 'control', relatively mild instruments of accountability by today's standards, but at the time, amounting to 'censorship' and 'interference' in the language of the radicals.

The affair ended abruptly. The Witt Report commissioned by Osborne was rejected by the 'radicals' on 26 March 1977; an avalanche of resignations was triggered by chairman Jeff Nuttall. 'Radicals' walked out to operate ineffective boycotts against the Society and to instigate recriminations against those who stayed (for a while, at least) like Lee Harwood, who explained his position in a letter to Mottram: 'As a trade unionist I've never believed in resignation as a useful political weapon—it always seems best to work from inside an organisation...' (Barry 2006: 94)

At the previous meeting of the General Council on 11th September 1976, the chairman, Jeff Nuttall, introduced the draft of the document reprinted in Barry's book as 'The Manifesto of the Poetry Society 1976'. (See Barry 2006: 202–3) Barry comments, with surprise, that it 'is a document of some stature; its crisp and austere rhetoric carries conviction'; it concurs with Caws' general taxonomy for the manifesto, and conforms to her sub-category of the concise present tense bullet-pointed bulletin. (Barry 2006: 82) It is a shame, then, that the manifesto, which was accepted with some difficulty at the meeting, was not issued to the members of the Society as intended; its assertive position-taking in the larger field of poetic production, to adapt Bourdieu's terms, may have made a lasting impression. But the rebels were fiddling, albeit tunefully, while Rome burnt, with only a few months until the fateful walk out. However, the manifesto was 'distributed' by Poet's Conference, an unofficial poets trades union, in November 1977. It is ironical that that this concise manifesto, confidently drafted for a public audience in public language, approved by a committee of professionals, reached few in the larger field of cultural production into which it was both intended incursion and pointed invitation. They were professionals without a public once more, back in the field of restricted production.

The manifesto opens with a rubric defining the Society as 'an association of poets and enthusiasts', which, while appearing non-contentious, exposes one of the debates over the future of the Society: whether it was to be a poets' society, or a poetry society, whether primarily for the promotion of living poets or for the appreciation of poetry (including the poetry of the past). (Barry 2006: 202) Indeed, one of the 12 points has a bearing on this debate, and is the only one that deals exclusively with the institution. Where the society saw its business as combining 'printing, bookshop, performance, and library facilities', point 10 argues that 'precedence be given to printing and publication in order to surmount the present exclusion of the best poetry from commercial publications'. (Barry 2006: 203) This a clear statement of the view of the Association of Little Presses which had been promoting the work of small publishers since 1966, and which bears the imprint of Bob Cobbing, publisher of Writers Forum, and officer of both ALP and the Society.

More importantly for my exploration of public poetics, the manifesto exhorted the Society 'to inform the Nation of the unprecedently large number of poets now working in Britain in the forefront of the creative field' (Barry 2006: 203). The capital expended on the word 'Nation' and the distinct messianic tone suggest delusions of self-importance, but Barry's book demonstrates that such an aim was not unreasonable, given the amount of publicity that the events at Earls Court were generating in the national press, the visibility of, and controversy over, Mottram's editorship of *Poetry Review*, and the potential for 'informing' through its various wings. In short, controversy was not managed to advantage.

The manifesto was not only tabled by Jeff Nuttall; much of the document was drafted by him, particularly the opening four points, which concern themselves generally with 'the creative imagination'. (Barry 2006: 202) Nuttall had done much to chronicle the pre-history of the events at Earls Court. His *Bomb Culture*, written in 1967, is a history of the emergent underground, but with a literary bias that foregrounds the work of Cobbing and the happenings at Better Books, for example, against the background of the political underground. *Bomb Culture*, while being a kind of manifesto itself, contains quotations from nearly 20 manifestos, artistic and political, from early Dada and Surrealist documents through to Alexander Trocchi's 'Invisible Insurrection' and Situationist Bulletins. Many of these prefigure the cooler 1976 declaration that 'language under creative imagination is called poetry and that poetry no longer has any other useful definition' and that 'the creative imagination of each individual is the sole continuing source of new forms, new ideas, and new vocabulary, by which language must be perpetually revitalised'. (Barry 2006: 202) This repeated insistence upon renewal is a classic position of manifestos, particularly those of modernism that 'make it new', and which Nuttall's *Bomb Culture* had seen as precursors to the 1960s underground in any case, and in whose line Nuttall's Poetry Society manifesto draft thereby positions itself.

'British Poetry Revival' poets—who are part of 'a stage of development in which the merit of poetry is most usefully measured by the degree of innovation apparent in its structure' (Barry 2006: 203)—contest what the rubric calls 'the situation of emergency in which British literature finds itself'. (Barry 2006: 202)

In a bullet-point manifesto examples of this oppositional innovation necessarily give way to generalities, such as the conviction that the 'day-to-day function of language to communicate rational information is no longer necessarily predominant when the creative imagination is brought into play'. (Barry 2006: 202) Although this was doubtless worded to contest the civilities of the Movement orthodoxy, it emphasises the dominant role of the poetic function of language (as theorised by Jakobson), various forms of defamiliarisation, and all kinds of linguistic innovation favoured by the 'British Poetry Revival'.

One of Barry's criticisms of events at the Poetry Society was the decision to separate its official journal, *Poetry Review*, edited by Mottram, which contained only poetry, from its twin, *Poetry Information*, edited by Peter Hodgkiss. Many of its articles are the forgotten poetics of the 1970s. British poetry—particularly that of the 'British Poetry Revival'—seemed resistant to poetics as a formal discipline or as an external discourse in any form, except possibly the interview, particularly the long public interviews conducted by Eric Mottram, some of which, like those with Barry MacSweeney and Lee Harwood, were published in *Poetry Information*. Issue 17 also contains Mottram's seminal essay 'Open Field Poetry', which was a wide ranging justification for contemporary free verse and collage poetics, if not the poetics of his own work and others in the British context. I want to use the contents of this magazine to demonstrate how the Poetry Society's manifesto unfolds into a practice of poetics.

One textually specific claim of the manifesto is that it is 'permissible, and often imperative, to suspend the functioning laws of grammar and syntax when the creative imagination is brought into play'. (Barry 2006: 202) Given that this permission would become a touchstone of linguistic innovation—and exemplified in poetry as widely different as Bob Cobbing's and Allen Fisher's—it is not surprising to find it explicitly discussed in the pages of *Poetry Information*, indeed in issue 15, which was published during the same quarter as the manifesto was passed. Jeff Nuttall himself, in a spirited piece of eulogy to, and analysis of, Bill

Griffiths (another poet associated with the Society) notes in Griffiths' work, 'a purposeful use of the sources and the passion inherent in the point of view to dislocate habitual syntax-forms and re-arrange them into dynamic new music.' (Nuttall 1976: 13) More specifically he describes the transformation of content into form: 'The streets, the scraps of talk, the half memories, screeches of reaction, motorways, jails, seascapes, wild skies and cramped squats of Griffiths' image-range are so presented by completely strange syntax that, if they are to be read or recognised at all, they are read as pure form, colour and sound.' (Nuttall 1976: 13) The question of the relation of this defamiliarised discourse to habitual language—the issue at stake in manifesto point one—is raised: 'Syntax and experience are so manipulated as to compel the poem to be read as poetry (as art)—not as a news report (as language in the utilitarian sense),' which is another argument for the dominance of the poetic function in literary language. (Nuttall 1976: 13)

Nuttall quotes a number of 'violently beautiful passages', including the second part of *Cycles* (a publication, in its 1976 edition, that announces that it was printed by Writers Forum and Pirate Press at the NPC). He comments that its 'repeated theme' is 'weather and light and the movement of planets lifting the disgraced senses'. (Nuttall 1976: 15)

> Morning's s'blue
> early, edgy, special
> lay like a gun
> in await
> some sort sun's exploding
> > (Nuttall 1976: 15; Griffiths 1976: *Cycles* 2; np)

It is a loaded explosive aubade, which deliberately avoids grammatical and syntactical resolution (while hovering around its possibility), whose vision narrows to that of its unannounced narrator at stool:

> castellated
> a shitting hole, shat in
> (solitary)
> holy spirit!
> > (Nuttall 1976: 15; Griffiths 1976: *Cycles* 2; np)

The bracketed '(solitary)' is a sudden shift to the lexis of judicial imprisonment, a theme of Griffiths that repeats as much as the weather; 'castellated' suggests the uppermost architecture of a castle with assumed incarcerating dungeon as much as it signifies a species of shithouse Gothic. Later, another parenthetical remark teases at the boundaries of definitive political judgement in an indeterminate syntax: '(but all the crimes against all action:/ all my art, the State, uniformed)'. (Griffiths 1976: *Cycles* 2; np)

I am going to pass over other points of the manifesto—the fructifying interest in foreign poetry, the expansive performative interest in intermedia, for example—to focus more precisely upon the role of politics in the manifesto, since this is its most contentious and the most illuminating aspect.

The manifesto openly asserts political agency for poetry, thus contesting Auden's supposedly quietist 'poetry makes nothing happen'. Point six makes three related claims. One: 'Poetry enjoys a direct social function in the perpetual alteration of the status quo.' (Barry 2006: 202) Barry comments: 'Here it is perhaps the word 'direct' which would make one pause'. (Barry 2006: 82) The perpetual revolution of the word *causes* the perpetual revolution of the world. Secondly, poetry 'is the source of philosophical, moral, aesthetic, and therefore political change'. (Barry 2006: 202) This troubling formulation not only privileges poetry while offering primacy to (successful) political action; it makes philosophy and aesthetics subordinate to the other two in an unlocatable way; it de-values poetry by tying it to its 'direct social function'. Thirdly: 'In order to function as source [poetry] must remain free of existing ideologies and dogma.' (Barry 2006: 202). Barry contends that these combined claims are 'a contradiction', but I think there is a logic of sorts here. (Barry 2006: 82). Poetry as the source—inspiration—of political awareness must remain free of politics in its fixed forms. 'Source' is not just a metaphor of origin; it is a metaphor of flow, unfixedness, like the paradoxical status quo that will be perpetually altered by the effect of poetry, which is imagined as a fructifying, perhaps pure, force. Poetry is language 'perpetually revitalised'.

I would like to explore two contexts for this manifesto point, one via political and aesthetic philosophy near-contemporary with the manifesto, the second through the actual practice of poetry.

What if we were to change the word 'direct' to 'indirect' (or to delete it altogether)? What if we were to think of the unassailable 'source' of all thought, poetry, in terms of art's autonomy from the world, the kind of catalytic detachment for art that Marcuse theorises in his 1977 book *The Aesthetic Dimension*? If we do, I think, we can make some sense of the apparently contradictory formulations of a non-ideological politics. Marcuse observes: 'The movement of the sixties tended toward a sweeping transformation of subjectivity and nature, of sensibility, imagination, and reason.' (Marcuse 1979: 33) Despite the retreat from the public sphere of that movement—whose traces are found in Nuttall's drafting—Marcuse's aesthetics declares: 'Art cannot change the world, but it can contribute to changing the consciousness and drives of the men and women who could change the world.' (Marcuse 1979: 32) While this seems a contradiction of a 'direct'—public—function for art, it makes possible a micro-political aesthetics of liberation: 'The political potential of art lies only in its own aesthetic dimension'; its subversive potential lies in its very autonomy. (Marcuse 1979: xii) As Marcuse summarises: 'In its autonomy art both protests [the prevailing social relations], and at the same time transcends them. Thereby art subverts the dominant consciousness, the ordinary experience' and its ordinary language which the manifesto also questions. (Marcuse 1979: ix) Marcuse sees the 'logic' of art—via its distanciation, some techniques of which are hinted at in the manifesto—as culminating in 'another reason, another sensibility,' which defy prevailing conditions, with its own 'categorical imperative: "things must change"'. (Marcuse 1979: 13) The critical function of the work of art re-establishes the emancipatory dreams of the 1960s in a 1970s formalism—public desire turned private—between which the Poetry Society manifesto hovers in contradiction, both inheriting and prefiguring the stages of Marcuse's own development. Nuttall is drawn to Bill Griffiths for his compensatory ethos: 'In a period numb with disappointment at the 1968 failure he burns out startlingly.' (Nuttall 1976: 17)

Other political impulses are found in the work of the 'British Poetry Revival' itself and in the works of members of the Poetry Society General Council who were present when the draft manifesto was passed. Both represent attempts to devise a public language for poetry and suggest that the wild talk of the manifesto about 'direct' political efficacy for poetry was part of the zeitgeist at Earls Court and beyond. Barry MacSweeney, at one time chair of the Poetry Society, in a public mode of poem he would call later 'a State of the Nation bulletin' (MacSweeney 2003: 138)—note that capital N again—delivers a public address in a clipped shorthand that may owe as much to his journalistic training as it does to the example of Allen Ginsberg's public 'Poems of these States', an excerpt of which provides the epigraph to his 1977–78 poem, 'Black Torch Sunrise'. MacSweeney offers images of potential insurrection, or of '1968 failure':

> Whipped legs
> of left-bank women students
>> blur on the shimmered screen
>> 625 line consciousness
>>>> (MacSweeney 2003: 75)

The public scene is mediated through the latest televisual technology but the language is 'direct'. It is a public discourse that disarmingly answers its own questions: 'Will the Labour Party uphold the jailing of pickets?/ Of course.' (MacSweeney 2003: 74).

Another member of the Council, though less radical than MacSweeney, was a member of that Labour Party, and indeed stood (unsuccessfully) as a candidate in local elections. Lee Harwood's poetry of the time of the manifesto is saturated by civic responsibility. In an article on Bob Cobbing, written in 1974, he too is thinking of the state of the Nation, though he is less inclined to answer his own questions: 'When euphemisms proliferate the further countries sink into chaos.... A country rises and falls—and the indicator is always its use of language, maybe even the cause. How "straight talking" its leaders, educators, press, population are.' (Harwood 1974: 7) And its poets, of course. 'Straight talking' is a term used by Harwood to also describe the 'puritan' pole of his poetry, as against the baroque 'cavalier' fictionalising for which he is perhaps better known, and it is that pole which dominates his work of this period, particularly his 'Notes of a Post Office Clerk', parts of which were first published in *Poetry Review*.

In this open field work he approaches MacSweeney's mode of public address, though in a quieter voice, and even gestures towards a political manifesto, 'now in England 1975 ... a list of simple practical, and just acts,/ moves towards a real "socialism"'. (Harwood 2004: 253) The poem withholds the full manifesto, although it was published with drafts of the poem in a magazine. This apocryphal manifesto promises political, fiscal, wage-policy and constitutional reform, along with a curious mixture of public and private ownership and control. That it was possible to consider issuing what is in effect a public political manifesto *within* a poem is proof of the influence of open field poetics at the time, that 'the field of the poem is ... the poet's life and his times in fusion', as Mottram put it in his *Poetry Information* article. (Mottram 1977: 9) Although perhaps Harwood is not advocating *direct* political efficacy for poetry, neither is he arguing for an indirect effect either. His poem remains committed to a image of catalytic change that extends into the public domain that is consonant with Marcuse's hopes, if not his aesthetics: 'the steps that could change this, that could be taken now, open a few doors and windows, start the change that would produce changes as yet unknown'. (Harwood 1977: 57; Harwood 2004: 253) But in another passage, he hopes for 'a freedom from the exhaustion that takes our energy, our sex, our time from us. Wastes us,' through experiential catalysis: 'The action chemical in that one change transforms the whole into a completely new set of references.' (Harwood 1977: 57)

Open field poetics—straight-talking, publicly addressing, in paratactic page-space, mixing free verse and prose—was a favoured mode of the 1970s, but this poetics must be balanced against another, that of the use of de-regulated, defamiliarised language that is not just paratactic but involves syntactic and grammatical disruption, as Nuttall suggests of the work of Bill Griffiths. It is testimony to the elasticity of the manifesto and the catholicity of the signatories that two approaches are permitted; MacSweeney's *Odes* and his 'State of the Nation' addresses testify also to the ability of one writer to encompass both poetics, and the *Jury Vet* poems that Will Rowe eloquently addresses in his essay in this volume might be thought of as encompassing and combining *both* poetics. Accurate to the times as the manifesto is, its poetics points in two directions.

My feelings about the rich and strange public goings on at Earls Court, mediated through my own experience as well as Peter Barry's book, is that they were a missed opportunity that condemned the poets who followed to years of privatised retardation in the development of a viable poetics for their work, one which turned away from open field poetics towards the manifesto's other, disruptive poetics. On the other hand, the manifesto itself provides one of the few British examples of a public radical poetics. I have followed the bumps and folds, even the tears and mendings, of the fabric of this particular manifesto, to separate out the strands of poetics that have been woven into, but cannot completely be disentangled from, the politics of its unique historical situation. What remains impressive is that, under the pressure of circumstances, this group of writers not known for their debating poetics within their professional circle, using restricted code within the restricted cultural field of the 'British Poetry Revival', should have attempted to go public in this manifest way, in the 'loud genre' of the modernist manifesto, to attempt to 'inform the Nation'.

Robert Sheppard is Professor of Poetry and Poetics at Edge Hill University.

Note
[1] All members of the General Council are listed in Barry's book, and the 'radical' members are briefly accounted for in my 'Poets Behaving Badly', published at http://jacketmagazine.com/31/sheppard-barry.html

Works Cited

Barry, Peter. *Poetry Wars: British Poetry of the 1970s and the Battle of Earls Court*, Cambridge: Salt, 2006.
Bernstein, Basil. 'Social class' language and socialisation, in Corner, J., and Hawthorn, J. eds., *Communication Studies*, London: Routledge, 1980: 59–67.
Caws, Mary Ann. ed. *Manifesto: A Century of Isms*, Lincoln and London: University of Nebraska Press, 2001.

DuPlessis, Rachel Blau. *The Pink Guitar*, New York and London: Routledge, 1990.

Griffiths, Bill. *Cycles*, London: Pirate Press and Writers Forum, 1976.

Harwood, Lee. 'Bob Cobbing', in ed. Mayer, P. 1974, *Bob Cobbing and Writers Forum*, Sunderland: Coelfrith 26, 1974: 7–13.

Harwood, Lee. *Boston–Brighton*, London: Oasis, 1977.

Harwood, Lee. *Collected Poems*, Exeter: Shearsman, 2004.

MacSweeney, Barry. *Wolf Tongue,* Tarset: Bloodaxe, 2003.

Marcuse, Herbert. *The Aesthetic Dimension*, London and Basingstoke: Macmillan, 1979.

Mottram, Eric. 'Open Field Poetry', *Poetry Information* 17, Summer 1977: 3–23.

Nuttall, Jeff. *Bomb Culture*, London: Paladin, 1970.

Nuttall, Jeff. 'Bill Griffiths: An Appreciation', *Poetry Information* 15, Summer 1976: 13–17.

Lyn Hejinian's Poetics of the 'Transpersonal': A Reading of *Writing is an Aid to Memory* and 'The Guard'

KATHY-ANN TAN

In much of Lyn Hejinian's work, conventional structures of language are broken down, interrogated and re-configured in order to provide a wider framework wherein the poems function as communicative gestures. These gestures encompass the public spheres of social and political discourse while reflecting on the more private motivations of the creative impulse. The autobiographical urge in Hejinian's work thus does not align itself with a confessional mode of self-representation; rather, it adopts a 'transpersonal' agency of language that not necessarily excludes the personal, but harnesses it as the starting point of the poet's inquiry into larger ideological and socio-political concerns. Hejinian's poetics of 'transpersonality' also demands her readers' participation as co-creators of the text, jointly interrogating how the interpretive act is itself determined by larger social and cultural forces.

In addressing how meaning arises within the framework of a public language whose late capitalist assumptions have proliferated the way in which readers and writers interact with texts, Hejinian's work calls for a renegotiation of the established orders of language and discourse. Making itself manifest in the form of radically discontinuous syntactic/ logical units that undermine straightforward, linear methods of reading and interpretation, Hejinian's poetics of the 'transpersonal' regards the poem itself as a site of collective consciousness encompassing the spheres of both private and public language. In other words, the poem embodies what Hejinian herself has termed the 'border terrain', which she defines in 'Two Auckland Talks' as a liberatory 'realm of encounter, a realm of transformation, transmutation, the zone in which everything is always in change, a transit zone' (Hejinian 1995). The two questions that this paper poses are therefore, first, what are the implications of a spatial poetics that regards the poem as border terrain, a realm of encounter between public and private language, and second, how is a poetics of the 'transpersonal' significant in terms of pointing the way towards a Postlanguage poetics or aesthetics of literary experimentation?

Hejinian has been associated with the Language school of writing that emerged in the United States in the 1970s as a direct response to the socio-political climate of gradual disillusionment in the aftermath of the Vietnam War, in which political ideology and discourse had become increasingly questionable.[1] Adopting a post-structuralist poetics, Language writing emphasised the existence of multiple, conflicting perspectives via a close examination of the codes and structures of language, seeking to understand how relations of power that inform the everyday are disseminated yet veiled through public discourse. The socio-political context of the emergence of Language writing is also significant, namely, the call for civil rights, the women's movement, the student revolutions in Paris in 1968, and reactions to McCarthyism in the 1950s. The question that these contexts brought to the fore was how a public and private language could be brought together in the writing—that is, how Language poetry could reflect the public opinion and political climate of the period, while avoiding accusations of personal idiosyncrasy or deliberate obscurity. Poet-critic Tina Darragh, for example, expressed the need to carry out 'language 'investigations' [...] done in an interdisciplinary setting' that will 'illuminate the differences between how private language and public language operate in our lives' (Vickery 2000, 235).[2] With regard to this predicament, Lyn Hejinian's cross-generic, 'transpersonal', linguistic investigations are all the more significant because they offer a radical means of conflating traditional autobiographical modes of self-inquiry and critical self-representation with larger socio-political concerns. This mode of what I term the 'transpersonal' is best illustrated in two early works, *Writing is an Aid to Memory* (1987) and 'The Guard' (1984).

Writing is an Aid to Memory offers an alternative mode of composition to the various genres of self-writing (the diary, autobiography, biography, confessional narrative), charting how the construction of the self in the text is closely linked to the shaping and sculpting force of memory. The memories which jointly construct the text's (non-)narrative are perceived, recalled and recorded by a poetic consciousness that is constantly engaged in 'radical introspection', continuously delineating and playfully shifting the boundary between public experience and private recollection, hence re-negotiating the relationship 'between self and other [...] and then transgresses the borders it has established' (Hejinian 2000, 170). For Hejinian, the 'I' always exists as a 'parenthetical plural', one that negotiates and renegotiates her position in the subject-object/ public-private scheme of things. In the forty-two sections of loosely gathered phrases, she creates a fluid text comprising personal memories, details from everyday life, as well as references to the public realms of philosophical and scientific discourse. These seemingly random nodes of information are connected by a narrative voice whose self-reflexivity questions the poem's construction as a whole, and, ultimately, the authority of its narrator. The result is an excess of information, heightened by what Hejinian herself terms, in the preface to the work, a 'restlessness made inevitable by language' (Hejinian 1996, n. pagination). This 'language motivated restlessness' stems perhaps, in the words of critic Peter Nicholls, from 'an intentionality within language which somehow precedes and limits [...] an intentionality which exists in tension with the contingency of our own experience and our desire to disclose it in words' (Nicholls 2000, 250). As Hejinian puts it herself, much of the 'curiosity' and 'anxiety' of the poet comes from the longing to 'join words to the world—to close the gap between ourselves and things—and we suffer from doubt and anxiety as to our incapacity to do so' (Hejinian 2000, 285). This sense of doubt and anxiety is crucial, however, to a poetics of Poststructuralist indeterminacy, where multiple, conflicting perspectives exist in order to keep the text 'open'. Consequently, it is the ensuing creative force resulting from the tension between striving for closure and keeping the poem 'open' that drives the poem forward.

The very 'incapacity' to fuse or close the gap between the public and private modes of discourse is central to the notion of the 'open text' and a poetics of indeterminacy.[3] Section two of *Writing is an Aid to Memory* begins with the following lines:

> diary us a few hoops
>   hap as up-and morrow
>   we lost the familiar stumbling blocks
>   who fills with life just one side of it

and how did this happen like an excerpt
[...]
    how can it be
  composed when brilliantly objective and cast a little
    further
and with such care disintegrates

                         (n.p.)

The diary as a stable structure or frame ('hoop') which holds in happy memories is questioned as the text progresses. The efficacy of writing in the diary form is also questioned ('how can it be/composed when brilliantly objective'?) because its mode functions purely along private and subjective, as opposed to public and objective, lines of inquiry. As the unpunctuated text progresses, the narrator or 'I' figure begins to be less of an autobiographical or confessional first person pronoun, and more of a construct which consciously 'retells' memories, all the while conscious of the latter's 'mimicking', erroneous, inventive, and embellishing modes of operation.[4] The lines 'retell, more retell, and all retell/ I know not where then I remember' and 'I know still that memory only mimics' (both from section two), and 'detour in such detail' (section four) anticipate the following sequence in section seven:

    life is a quantity through language
           substitute inventing music of a series
      of changes very little understood
  binding men for driving through a new internal logic
               (n.p.)

These lines effectively sum up Hejinian's method of composition in the work, offering a fitting commentary on her poetics of the 'transpersonal'. Exploding the literary conventions of autobiography as a life represented accurately and conveyed through/in a private language, Hejinian substitutes the 'music of a[n alternative] series' that is 'little understood' precisely because it is unconventional and governed by 'a new internal logic'—one that, however, 'bind[s] men' together and thus calls for a more public consciousness that engages with political reality and ideology. In line with her poetics of indeterminacy and ambiguity, however, this 'new internal logic', one characterized by the aleatory quality of memory and organized according to a certain musical and linguistic coherence, nevertheless, has its limitations. As Hejinian writes in the preface to the book, 'memory cannot, though the future return, and proffer raw confusions' (Hejinian 1996, n.p.).

Thus, in *Writing is an Aid to Memory*, the diverse memories, details and autobiographical 'facts' are combined and connected by a narrative voice whose self-reflexivity constantly questions the poem's own validity and authenticity. Instead, the work foregrounds its constructedness or status as artefact. The challenge is to achieve what Hejinian describes as a certain 'candor without confession', in a writing that is 'personal and inclusive, but not necessarily self-revelatory' (Hejinian 1986, 137). In other words, she does not encourage her readers to regard *Writing as an Aid to Memory* as a private, confessional piece revealing her personal life and character. One recalls that the work was published in 1978, a time when the avant-garde was explicitly positioning itself against the poetic ideologies of the confessional and Beat poets who had come to prominence in the previous two decades.[5]

Similarly, Hejinian's long poem, 'The Guard', is concerned with inter-rogating how the poem functions as border terrain between the realms of public and private language. It was written at a particular point in American political history, three years after Reagan had been elected as president and the conservative, when Republican right wing was gaining popularity, as well as after Hejinian's first trip to Russia in 1983. In this work, a poetics of the 'transpersonal' is set against the backdrop of social and political reality and the censorship of literary avant-gardism in Russia in the midst of the Cold War, and draws upon Russian Formalist theory, especially Viktor Shklovsky's concept of estrangement. The poem which resulted from the disorientation that Hejinian experienced in Russia marks an attempt to conflate formal and linguistic experimentation within the framework of a socially-located poetics of the 'transpersonal'.

Hejinian's journey to Russia is reflected in the voyage motif which recurs throughout the work, beginning with its source of inspiration, a line from the first canto of Dante's Divine Comedy: 'Midway this

way of life we're bound upon,/ I woke to find myself in a dark wood.'
The guide and guard figure is Virgil, who serves as Dante's companion,
accompanying him on his journey from hell, through purgatory, to
paradise, but also, through the poem itself. This journey can also be
interpreted as a radical poetic quest to move beyond a demarcation of the
public and private realms of language and discourse, which ultimately
leads to a going beyond the very boundaries of the poem itself, or, in
Hejinian's own words, a

> cross[ing of] the very limits of language, and thus to reach an
> unmediated, beatific experience of Paradise—one which, however,
> [...] would be unspeakable; Paradise can only be experienced in
> silence' (Hejinian 2000, 66).

'Paradise', however, is ironically a state of closure, of conclusive finality,
wherein language is silenced. Indeed, there are instances in 'The
Guard' where, it seems, the unspeakable, the moment of silence and
emptiness is inevitable after the poet has discarded the vestments of a
private vocabulary of self-expression. Consider the beginning and end
of section eight of the poem:

>   [...] I
> am indeed no longer a beginner who throws herself
> on such dense inverted picturing—I too have discarded
> and discarded.
> [...]
>   ...the knowledge of 'empty'
> surpasses the capacities of language...
> the swivel, a mound...
> 'I am a construction worker, I work at home'
> with stiff serenity...this
> is the difference between language and 'paradise'
>
>   (34)

The choice of wording in this last section of the poem renders it
ambiguous—the expression 'stiff serenity' is inherently paradoxical,
and in the phrase 'the glamorous anticipation of an answer', any sense
of elation or fulfilment is deflated or undercut by a note of ambiguity,

for what the speaker has 'achieved' is merely the 'anticipation' of an answer, and not an answer itself. The lines 'The knowledge of "empty" / surpasses the capacities of language' also point to the role of language in establishing power structures of knowledge in the public sphere, referring to the theoretical position taken up by the Language group of writers that language constitutes and is constituted by cultural production, hence comprising 'an order of reality in itself and not a mere mediating medium' (Hejinian 2000, 129).

This defamiliarization of language points towards Russian Formalist theory, especially Viktor Shklovsky's concept of estrangement, or to make strange, which is also central to an interpretation of 'The Guard'. The poem illustrates how her poetics of estrangement is extended beyond the boundaries of the text, conflating a foregrounding of the radical artifice of poetic language with a dynamic concept of personhood which perceives the world anew through an objective lens—in Hejinian's own words, 'Sensation of the world and a counter to pessimism' (Hejinian 2002, 105). At the heart of Hejinian's poetics of the 'transpersonal', therefore, lies a triangulation between: first, a dynamic concept of personhood that is based upon a poetics of description and objectification and the dissolution of any sense of essential selfhood, which are central to Russian Formalist notions of estrangement; second, a reconfiguration of the modes of lyric and personal narrative (such as the autobiography and diary forms), framing them within the wider public structures of social and political discourse and ideology; and third, a heightened awareness of the materiality of the text, combined with radical formal and linguistic experimentation that, together, create a new socio-politically charged subjectivity wherein language constitutes and is constituted by cultural production.

In conclusion, two questions remain—what are the implications of Hejinian's spatial poetics that regards the poem as border terrain, a realm of encounter between public and private language, and how is such a poetics of the 'transpersonal' significant in terms of pointing the way towards a Postlanguage poetics or aesthetic of literary experimentation? By way of answering the first question, I would argue that the 'border terrain' of Hejinian's poems is itself one demarcated by fluid boundaries that reflect the poet's urge to move beyond the space of the poem, to push against and cross over the very limits of language. This is ultimately achieved by a poetics of 'transpersonality' which demonstrates that language is constructed by the very power relations and structures that it creates. Such a recognition opens up the possibility for poetic experimentation with new and hybrid forms of writing while critiquing the limits of identity politics and exploring the ways in which cultural boundaries can be shifted and crossed. And this is where it is useful to look at Hejinian's poems as border terrains in a second sense, as the realms of encounter and transit between different methods and modes of formal experimentation, where poetic innovation co-exists with a Postlanguage poetics of the everyday, where language is no longer merely made strange, but used as a tool to analyse the social and political constructions of cultural identity and subjectivity.

Kathy-Ann Tan is a PhD candidate at Eberhard Karls University, Tübingen, Germany.

Notes

[1] In the literary arena, the public nature of Language writing, its collective identity of a group of poets who articulated a project that posited a specific set of political and aesthetic principles, stood in direct contrast to the workshop poem produced across creative writing programs in American universities. Whereas the workshop poem worked within a mode of mimetic representation that heralded the poet as an indisputable authority over the text and posited him/her as a self-determining beholder of the world, Language writing, adopting a Poststructuralist poetics, emphasised the existence of multiple, conflicting perspectives.

[2] Here is Darragh's quote in its longer version: '[I]t strikes me that it hasn't been helpful at all to analyze the failure/collapse of the Left in the late '60s/early '70s in political or economic terms—we don't seem to be learning anything about our mistakes, plus we seem like shells in the face of rising militarism, without the desire to unite with others or challenge individually what's going on. The only hope I have [...] is that language "investigations" (if done in an interdisciplinary setting) will renew our sense of ourselves as social beings by illuminating the differences between

how private language and public language operate in our lives, how they are two distinct processes that, in their simultaneity, obscure each other and blur the way we address our needs.'

[3] In her essay 'The Rejection of Closure', Hejinian defines the 'open text' as one that is 'open to the world and particularly to the reader. It invites participation, rejects the authority of the writer over the reader and thus, by analogy, the authority implicit in other (social, economic, cultural) hierarchies. It speaks for writing that is generative rather than directive. The writer relinquishes total control and challenges authority as a principle and control as a motive. The "open text" often emphasizes or foregrounds process, either the process of the original composition or of subsequent compositions by readers, and thus resists the cultural tendencies that seek to identify and fix material and turn it into a product; that is, it resists reduction and commodification' (Hejinian 2000, 43).

[4] The reader is reminded of the following sequence from section five of 'The Guard': 'The flicker/ and continuing exhibit. Speaks of the "self"/ and improves it from memory./ It's overrealized' (26).

[5] As the speaker says in *A Mask of Motion*, written two years earlier, 'I want you to understand me completely but I don't want to reveal anything about myself lest you misunderstand' (16).

Works Cited

Darragh, Tina. 'Intraview' with Joan Retallack et al. (1987). Reproduced in Ann Vickery. *Leaving Lines of Gender: A Feminist Genealogy of Language Writing*. Middletown CT: Wesleyan UP, 2000.

Hejinian, Lyn. 'The Guard' (1984). Reprinted in *The Cold of Poetry*. Los Angeles: Sun and Moon, 1994.

—. *A Mask of Motion*. Providence, RI: Burning Deck, 1977.

—. *Writing is an Aid to Memory*. Los Angeles: Sun and Moon, 1996; 1987.

—. 'Two Auckland Talks' (1995). Available online at http://www.nzepc. auckland.ac.nz/misc/hejinian1.asp transcribed by Fredrika Van Elburg. 29 May 2007.

—. 'The Rejection of Closure'. *The Language of Inquiry*. Berkeley: University of California Press, 2000.

—. 'Two Stein Talks'. *The Language of Inquiry*. Berkeley: University of California Press, 2000.

—. 'Person and Description'. *The Language of Inquiry*. Berkeley: University of California Press, 2000.

—. 'Afterword' to Viktor Shklovsky's *Third Factory*. Champaign, IL: Dalkey Archive Press, 2002.

Nicholls, Peter. 'Phenomenological Poetics: Reading Lyn Hejinian'. *The Mechanics of the Mirage: Postwar American Poetry*. Eds. Christine Pagnoulle and Michel Delville. Liège: University of Liège, 2000: 241–52.

OULIPO, POETRY AND PUBLIC LANGUAGE

Philip Terry

The Oulipo, *Ouvroir de Littérature Potentielle,* or Workshop of Potential Literature, was set up in 1960 by François le Lionnais and Raymond Queneau with the idea of exploring mathematics and the use of constraints in the production of literary texts. Oulipo's central idea can be put simply: if literature has traditionally been underpinned by a system of rules or formal constraints, whether in the sonnet, the villanelle or the five act tragedy, then the production of *new* constraints is a valid way forward for literature.

From the outset, like postmodernism, Oulipo's work has involved a combination of new departures and backward glances, which le Lionnais describes in 'Lipo: First Manifesto'(28) as 'anoulipism' (the investigation of past writings and already existing constraints) and 'synthoulipism' (the synthesis of new constraints). We can get a good sense of what Oulipo has both resurrected, and often renewed, as well as what it has invented *ab ovo,* in its first 47 years of activity by looking at its work with poetry and poetic form, which has frequently been concerned with poetry and public language.

The relationship, or possible relationships, between poetry and public language can be divided into three fundamental types, which can be represented diagrammatically:

1. Poetry moves into the sphere of public language (occasional verse, epitaphs etc.).

2. Poetry constructs itself out of the discourse of public language, public language becoming a source (Edwin Morgan's *News Poems,* Prynne's *News of Warring Clans,* Lopez's *Equal Signs,* MacSweeney's *Jury Vet*).

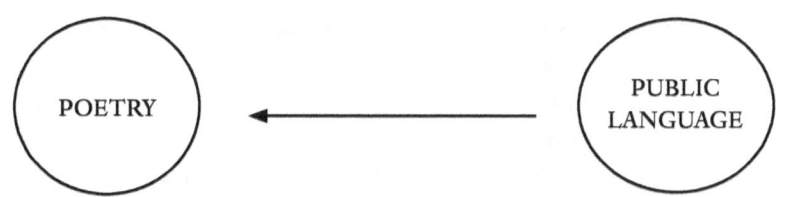

3. Poetry and public language draw together to find a point of mutuality or intersection (the sonnet at certain times, for example in *Love's Labours Lost* where the poem becomes the shared vehicle for the formal and public protestation of desire).

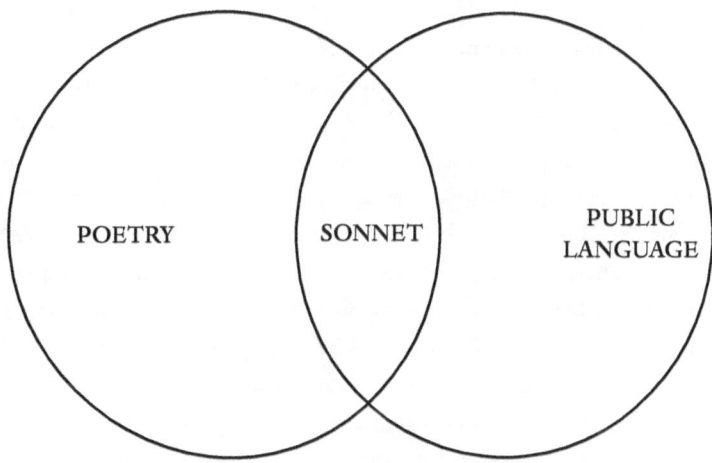

The fact that I find myself turning to theatre to find an example of this third type might suggest that this is an idealised type, rarely actually encountered—and the deferment of the lovers' nuptials at the end of *Love's Labours Lost* might be taken to support this. Moreover, the example also raises an alarming possibility as its obverse or trace, namely that the coming together of poetry and public language might result in the annihilation of both. We might note here how in type 1 writing the poetry is often sacrificed, as the many bad examples of occasional verse prove, and that in type 2 poetry public language is frequently annihilated, as it is subjected to a process of distortion and deconstruction. Certainly, there's a case for saying that this potential annihilation in type 3 poetry, now dual and total, is what happens in *Love's Labours Lost*: the sonnets

are notoriously *bad* sonnets, while the public protestations of future
engagement remain empty, for the Russian princesses will never return
in Shakespeare's promised sequel, *Love's Labours Won*, a play which to
this day remains definitively lost.

These dangers aside, the Oulipo, I want to argue, has done much to
renew all three of these poetry/public language types, and, while this
by no means exhausts their activity, even in verse, we can find numerous
examples of Oulipian poetry for each of them.

Type 1, where poetry moves into the sphere of public language, can
be seen not only in the Oulipo's public art in the Strasbourg Tram project,
where they composed a series of texts for the Strasbourg Tram System,
but in their numerous experiments with occasional verse, which would
include: elegies (such as Perec's 'Élégie de Pierre et de Denise Getzler'),
love poems, and epithalamia, all three often taking the form of lipograms
relating in one way or another to the names of the addressees. So, in
what Oulipo call the 'belle absente' or beautiful outlaw the letters of
the name are conspicuous for their absence (Perec's love poem 'Daphné
fit le visage que j'ombre' is of this type), whereas in the 'beau présent'
or beautiful in-law the poem uses only the letters in the names of the
recipients. Perec's epithalamia are all of this type, composed exclusively
with the letters of the names of the bride and groom. So, his 'Lines read
at Alix-Cléo Blanchette's and Jacques Roubaud's Bridal', for example,
in Harry Mathews' translation, begins, using only the letters of these
names:

> Alix-Cléo is joined to Jacques
> and Jacques is joined to Alix-Cléo
> This is a delicious coincidence
> and so at this hour
> both are allied and united
> as are bird and branch
> Aucasin and Nicolette
> table and chair
> science and doubt
> desert and oasis
> (Mathews and Brotchie, 70)

Type 2, where poetry constructs itself out of the discourse of public language, has also been frequently experimented with and renewed by the Oulipo: Noel Arnaud's Algol poetry (Mathews and Brotchie, 47) is constructed out of the discourse of Algorithmic Oriented Language, a computer language invented in 1960; Jacques Jouet's *The-Great Ape Love Song* consists of poems composed in Great-Ape, a language found in the Tarzan series and codified by Edgar Rice Burroughs (Mathews and Brotchie, 96). Yet perhaps Oulipo's most persistent contribution here is to be found in the minimalist poetry of Michèle Métail, which has consistently taken public language, whether the language of grammatical parts of speech, of French *départements*, or of colloquial French, as its source material. The 'Portrait Robot' or 'Robot Portrait' (Mathews and Brotchie, 73), for example, which is constructed entirely out of 'ready-made' language, takes its cue from artists like Archimboldo and Nicolas

o Habit de Pescheur

Nicolas de Larmessin 'Fisherman's Costume'

de Larmessin, who assembled portraits out of the tools of their subjects' trades.

This type of poem, while no more difficult in English than in French, is fiendishly difficult to translate, as the ready-made phrases of the French lexicon rarely map directly onto English, and I have been unable to find successful illustrations in English, so here is a little piece, after Michèle Métail, composed for the *Poetry and Public Language* conference to illustrate the method in English, 'The Cook':

> Head of garlic
> Eye of potato
> Cauliflower ear
> Parson's nose
> Shoulder of mutton
> Sponge fingers
> Artichoke heart
> Back bacon
> Pine nuts
> Sunday joints
> Leg of lamb
> Shin of beef

Finally Type 3, where poetry and public language draw together to find a point of mutuality or intersection, can be exemplified by a number of Oulipian practices. The sonnet, a key form here, has been renewed by Oulipo in a variety of ways. Firstly, there is Queneau's *A Hundred Thousand Billion Poems*, a sequence of ten 14-line sonnets, inspired by the children's game 'Heads, bodies, legs'. Just as in that game body parts from each section can be interchanged, so any line in any one of these sonnets can replace the corresponding line in any other sonnet, giving 10 to the power 14 sonnets, a hundred thousand billion sonnets in all. The idea of creating new sonnets by randomly recombining lines from already existing sonnets is one we also find in Ted Berrigan's work in *In The Early Morning Rain* (Lopez, 50), where a similar method is used to generate his influential '5 New Sonnets: A Poem', a work which Queneau's anticipates. Another Oulipian attempt to renew the sonnet form is the 'irrational sonnet' of Jacques Bens (Mathews and Brotchie,

163–4), where the sonnet is divided according to the first five digits of the irrational number π, that is, into stanzas of 3, 1, 4, 1 and 5 lines (a form which, in turn, anticipates the structure of Tom Raworth's *Firewall*, a long poem which again uses the number π to determine stanza length).

Such significant 'anticipatory plagiarisms', as Oulipo call them (though here the anticipation is after the event), speak volumes for the largely untapped potential of the Oulipo for the development of poetry in English. And yet, it's the Oulipian form called the 'elementary morality', which represents Oulipo's chief contribution to type 3 poetry, and it's to this form that I'd like to turn in the concluding part of this paper.

Raymond Queneau's last book, *Elementary Morality*, was published in 1974, and it is a book in three parts. Parts II and III consist of prose poems, part I of poems in a form of Queneau's own invention, the 'elementary morality'. This Queneau defines as follows: 'First come 3 series of 3+1 pairs, each pair consisting of a noun and an adjective (or participle), freely including repetitions, rhymes, alliterations, and echoes; next, a kind of interlude of 7 lines, each line 1 to 5 syllables long; last, a conclusion of 3+1 pairs of words (noun and adjective or participle), more or less recapitulating several of the 24 words of the first part.' (Mathews and Brotchie, 142). While this may sound complicated, the form, once seen, is simple and quickly grasped. Here's the first of Queneau's 'elementary morality' poems in my own translation; at first glance it is by no means a perfect example of a type 3 poem, but I would argue that the form has the potentiality to become this type of poem, which, after all, depends at least in part on frequency of use, as with the sonnet:

Dark Isis	Green fruit	Spotted animal
	Clear neologisms	
Red flower	Transparent attitude	Orange-coloured star
	Clear springs	
Brown forest	Russet boar	Bleating flock
	Sparse tree	
	A boat	
	on the water	

soleabrious
follows the current
A crocodile
bites the keel
in vain

Ochre Isis   Crumbly statue   Apricot totem
                    Clear neologisms

The form owes something to Chinese and Japanese verse forms: it is connected to the Chinese *liu-shi,* one of whose earliest practitioners was none other than Li Po, an iconic poet for the Oulipo (as he was for Pound), while the middle interlude bears some resemblance to a double haiku. As Jacques Roubaud has argued, the form's layout and composition also bear a striking resemblance to certain draft poems by Mallarmé, which Queneau may have seen in manuscript (Roubaud 86–7). Queneau first called the form a *lipolepse* (from the Greek for 'leaving out' and 'taking in'), but the Oulipo at once named it the *quennet,* as it had one more line than a sonnet, and seemed to be as easy to grasp and to copy as this most canonical of poetic forms. So far, apart from some poems by members of the Oulipo, it hasn't been widely used, but its flexibility and simplicity make it a supremely democratic form, and it is able to function much like a camera to record people, events, places and landscapes. And it is partly this ease of use, coupled with its flexibility, which makes it a poetry of type 3. In her essay in this volume Susan Nurmi-Schomers discusses the axes of the vertical and the horizontal in Lyn Hejinian's work, axes which she argues are related to the public (as in the vertical public monument) and the private (as in the horizontal page)—her argument is suggestive for an analysis of Queneau's form, for like the Chinese poetry of Li Po, it operates on the page on both vertical and horizontal axes, something which would add further support to the argument that the 'elementary morality' is a poetry of type 3, both public and private at once. Additionally, however, there is nothing to stop this form being used to write a type 2 poem, where public language is the source (as it has been by Paul Fournel of the Oulipo, who has written 'elementary moralities' drawing on the discourse of the novels of Queneau) (Mathews and Brotchie, 65), or even as a type 1 poem, where poetry moves into the sphere of public language—Queneau's inaugural *lipolepse* is arguably of this occasional type, a cryptic elegy for his recently deceased wife (Debon, 1467).

This flexibility of type 3 poems, or poetic structures, is arguably one of their defining features, and we see this in the sonnet too, which has been used to write type 1 poems, such as elegies (Mallarmé's 'The Tomb of Charles Baudelaire', for example), and type 2 poems (such as Lopez's *False Memory*, where public language is both source and object of the poetry). And the 'elementary morality', in Queneau's hands, also resembles the sonnet in the way in which it is capable of sustaining an argument (that most public of discourse forms). Here's an example from Queneau, about renunciation:

Dispersed smoke	Plucked cigars	Abundant butts
	American leaves	
Victorian vertigos	Rough alcohol	Sticky bars
	Noachian echoes	
Half-open valves	Penetrated ducts	Excited posteriors
	Erotic machines	

In the brown night
under the moonlight
a drunk darts about
in the smoke
of silk stockings
of stills
of wooden pipes

Winter awakening	Invigorating snows	Major refusal
	Sudden decision	

I would like to draw this brief survey of Oulipo's contribution to poetry and public language to a close by noting with David Bellos that not even Queneau can invent a new poetic form by an act of the will. As

Bellos writes: 'The quennet may perhaps one day be seen as something as fertile and reusable as the sonnet, but only time and poetic practice over the coming centuries will tell.' And yet, over the last year or two there are tentative signs that the form has started to make inroads into English—Queneau's *Elementary Morality* has at long last been translated in its entirety, and will be appearing from Carcanet in 2007, while the poet Peter Hughes inventively used the form to map a psychogeography of Italy in his sequence *Italia,* published in 2006, a work which begins to reveal the form's fertile and crystalline potential in English, for it is a form which is not only easier, and more full of possibilities, in English than in French, but one which links directly to the very earliest roots of English poetry in the kennings of Anglo-Saxon verse.

Philip Terry is Senior Lecturer in Creative Writing at the University of Essex.

Works Cited

Bellos, David. Unpublished Introduction. Forthcoming in Raymond Queneau, *Elementary Morality.* Trans. Philip Terry. Manchester: Carcanet, 2007.

Debon, Claude, ed., Raymond Queneau *Oeuvres complètes I.* Paris: Gallimard, 1989.

Le Lionnais, François. 'Lipo: First Manifesto'. Trans. Warren F. Motte, Jr. *Oulipo: A Primer of Potential Literature.* Normal: Dalkey Archive, 1998: 26–8.

Lopez, Tony. *Meaning Performance: Essays on Poetry.* Cambridge: Salt, 2006.

Mathews, Harry, and Brotchie, Alasdair, eds. *Oulipo Compendium.* London: Atlas, 2005.

Roubaud, Jacques. 'The Birth of a Form: Elementary Morality'. Trans. Mary Campbell-Sposito. *The Review of Contemporary Fiction* 17.3 (1997): 85–98.

If Poetry is Private Language Aspiring to be Public, How Should One Write?

Scott Thurston

The practice of a language-centred writing in the UK is often seen as being obscure, difficult, evasive—a private language withholding the truth from the audience. This may seem trite, but from the writer's point of view I think something like this does happen—one can feel as if one is writing in private, as part of a coterie, and this influences the kind of work that one produces.

Other strategies in contemporary British poetry, however, promote poetry as a discourse which must be emotionally candid, forthright, lucidly communicating private experience in public. This might also seem trivialising, but then there can be great creative potential in feeling connected to a larger audience and allowing this to influence one's writing.

It's easy to see however that such a binary might break down very quickly. I've found language-centred practices a way of encountering layers of experience in language that other strategies simply don't allow— if this is private language, it is capable of coping with an astonishing breadth of experience. Similarly, there is nothing so hermetic as the 'personal' poem, expressed in the most ready-made structures and images of public language and public poetry—eliding the presence of the poet, neutralising their individual complexity.

And yet I'm drawn to the tension between these admittedly rather artificially constructed alternatives as a way of keeping things interesting—why not partake equally of what appear to be opposing tendencies in contemporary poetry as a way of exploring these different relationships between language and experience, between private and public, between what might be considered hard to communicate and common property?

Part of a license for such an approach comes from the British poet Ira Lightman, but also the work of Bruce Andrews and Barrett Watten as poet-critics who have put forward ways of thinking about poetry in a public context in the broadest possible way.

Bruce Andrews' model of three concentric circles (Andrews, 1986: 48–49) as a dual model for language and society demonstrates what he calls 'a totalizing poetics'—one which seeks to comprehend the entire social whole and then work inwards to expose the ultimate framing of social reality constituted by the outermost circle. This is opposed to a practice which might be simply restricted to an oppositional, public role within the second circle or a private insularity within the first circle. As Andrews elaborates:

> To imagine the limits of language [...] is also to imagine the limits of a whole form of social life—in this case of a predatory social order [...] that desperately needs to be changed. Now, often the horizon goes unrecognised—and unchallenged—so that those limits, and the social world as a whole, are seen as natural, or they're not seen at all. [...] The political dimension of writing isn't just based on the idea of challenging specific problems [...] it's based on the notion of a systemic grasp—not of language described as a fixed system but of language as a kind of agenda or as a system of capabilities and uses. (Andrews, 1986: 53, 60)

Andrews' poetics underwrites his creative trajectory in books such as *I Don't Have Any Paper so Shut Up, or, Social Romanticism* (1992) in which densely patterned rhythms of appropriated public discourses thoroughly deconstruct any straightforward opposition between public and private language.

Barrett Watten could also be said to have a totalising poetics. In his book *Total Syntax* (1985), he argued that Language Poetry had got too caught up in technique and needed to think more methodologically. Watten proposes taking into account 'the activity of the writer as a whole, the extension of the act of writing into the world and eventually into historical self-consciousness' (Watten, 1985: 32). In Watten's more recent poetics, the constructivist moment appears as the realisation of

> an elusive transition in the unfolding work of culture in which social negativity—the experience of rupture, an act of refusal—invokes a phantasmatic future—a horizon of possibility, an imagination of participation. (Watten, 2003: 192)

In the work of Anthony Braxton, Watten sees an alternative to head-on opposition in 'a conscious play among preconstituted structures', reading Braxton's musical practice for its 'emptying out and relativizing of the meaning of musical genres and traditions' (Watten, 2006). Using examples from 'Creative Orchestra Music' (1976) Watten argues that Braxton's avant-gardism is double: constantly playing one cultural code off against another.

However, Watten does not see a dialectic of 'mainstream' and 'innovation' as useful to describe Braxton's procedures. Braxton's most accessible work is seen not as mainstream entryism, but as a 're-presentation of the tradition as a transposition into another register, making it available as an abstracted archive of effects rather than as an homage to continuity' (Watten, 2006).

For Watten, Braxton has two logics. Firstly he 'disrupts the continuity of a given culture and tradition and reappropriates its contents for compositional purposes [...] the postmodern "turn to language" in musical form' and secondly 'imports cultures and tradition whole at a recombinatory level' (Watten, 2006). Watten describes the latter as 'a cultural politics [...] in which the dialectic between mainstream and opposition has been, not turned on its head, but ironized, dissociated, made available for reuse' (Watten, 2006). It is this latter notion, of reuse, that has the greatest creative potential to my mind.

For Watten, Braxton does 'the work of the negative as structural elaboration: distancing, rethinking, repeating, questioning, materializing, contextualizing, constructing—"language music" of direct identificatory possibility across the abysses of culture' (Watten, 2006). In this practice Braxton refuses 'to be pinned down, aesthetically or culturally' instead preferring to 'shift between forms and genres (and modes of statement, including the didactic) in order not to be trapped too easily within the conventions of genre, however other-directed' (Watten, 2006).

Watten's account of Braxton's practice in terms of a cultural logic, and the example of Braxton's own creative trajectory, strike me as an exemplary solution to the problem of continuing to write innovative poetry in Britain. Although the mainstream-innovation opposition is being contested critically, there are few examples of writers who are actively pursuing this cultural logic in their work. I would argue that Ira Lightman's poetry however, thinks things through on the totalizing level of a horizon of possibility in order to play different cultural codes off of one another, reappropriating, recombining, ironizing any easy opposition between competing stylistic trends in poetry and refusing to be pinned down.

Born in 1967, Lightman completed a PhD in Critical and Creative Writing at the University of East Anglia in 1996 and has produced a substantial body of writing which includes poetry, visual poems, translations, reviews, articles, academic papers and song-writing. Although his work has been associated with the innovative and experimental scene in the UK for some time he has often operated in an oblique, even slightly marginal relationship to it. In recent years Lightman has reinvented himself as a 'conceptual poet' and has participated in a number of public art projects. This has given him access to coverage in national media with recent interviews on Radio Three's *The Verb* and Radio Four's *Midweek*—rare contexts for writers of an innovative background in the UK.

Lightman's poetics in *Disabuse* argue how his use of specific techniques, such as rhyme in his songs, gain their effects not by

> using the form alone but in the overall history of the particular writer's particular use of that form given stated positions about their own use of form or about other people's use of form, within the area where they live. (Lightman, 1996: 193)

—a position which feels close to Watten's notion of method, and a totalising poetics.

Lightman's writing demonstrates a cultural logic of appropriation, importation and chameleon-like adaptation. A text published by Reality Street rewrites the rules of the Cageian mesostic by using it to reorder one of Lightman's own texts to create a vertical word series, rather than as Cage, using vertical words to catch words from chosen source texts (Lightman, 1998). Lightman has also written in a conventional 'mainstream' idiom in, for example the unpublished poem 'The Keeper of the Cross' written for a writer in residency post at Norwich market in 2000. The series of poster poems published as *Alter Space Times* make a multi-dimensional use of the page space whilst his recent Powerpoint poems play with low-fi technology and are time-based works (Lightman, 1999, 2006).

Lightman's *Trancelated* (2004) is amongst his most radical and challenging writing. Primarily a work of translation, it is disruptive and provocative in both its freedom and its violent yoking together of texts in double columns which allow them to be read horizontally, merging one into the other, as well as vertically. An appropriative attitude is implied by the fact that the source texts are not referenced, other than by authors' names.

Despite this project's radical credentials what interests me is how it has become one of Lightman's most publically successful texts to date. Published on the web by Ubu Editions, Lightman performed extracts on the *The Verb*, and also during his *Midweek* interview, when the presenter performed with him. If one's awareness of one's audience shapes one's creative work, Lightman's surprising difficulty in publishing this experimental writing with a UK avant-garde press, contrasts greatly with its success in the mass public media. This is certainly the road less travelled for the innovative writer and reveals a creative opportunity overriding any narrow commitment to this or that audience.

One text in *Trancelated* gives us two parallel translations of 'La Musique' by Baudelaire. Lightman describes his performance on *The Verb* as reading the left hand column in a Terry-Thomas voice whilst thinking about Stockhausen and the right hand column in an Edith Evans voice whilst thinking about Beethoven. Some critics have related Baudelaire's poem to Wagner and Beethoven.

In the left column version, Baudelaire's ship metaphor is transformed into an airplane—perhaps paving the way for the stereotypical upper class accent Lightman performs it in (Terry-Thomas playing RAF airman)—whilst the right column remains closer to the nautical imagery. The left version is slightly lighter in tone—'life as a life-raft | when plainsailing' versus the right's 'beleaguered hull'; 'unlaughed' versus 'unmerciful'; 'trod in fleck | of air field's on deck' versus 'melancholy, silver backed', but it is not easy to trace an overt opposition between the versions

(Lightman, 2004: 32). Lightman indeed plays up the disjuncture across the columns by using two voices, whilst for the reader there is at least the possibility of exploring new continuities throughout such as 'one bucks the bronco of turbulence || to ride the foregathered waves' or 'as if in a beleaguered hull || when plain-sailing, when typhoon and choppiness || with a fair wind, then a gale and convulsion || of times unlaughed || huge and unmerciful || can rock' (Lightman, 2004: 32).

What is important here is how Lightman appropriates a classic Late Romantic text and delivers a delightfully arch and tricksy pair of translations. The sombre task of the translator seems undermined to facilitate maximum disruption—to the extent of playing off alternative versions with one another to no clear argumentative end. Lightman answers back to Baudelaire, ironically undoing the rite of passage of the Romantic individual, but also answers back to himself, or to multiple versions of his self as translator. This process seems to be about the power of language to evoke difference itself, not to recuperate this to easy aesthetic or intellectual ends, but to generate as much creative energy as possible. One can recuperate fragments of meaning from these translations—although it is not always easy to recognise the original—but one is certainly more caught up in the defamiliarising effects of hearing another language distorting and pulling at the English, put through a mixing desk of anachronistic pop culture references for good measure. Lightman's work here, as elsewhere, seems to take difference as its starting point and its main goal.

Lightman's is a poetic practice which draws energy from the animating tension between what I have identified as the so-called private language of innovative writing and the more public modes of mainstream writing and address. Whilst many of Lightman's poems are clearly preoccupied with technical experimentation, they seem capable of opening out to a larger audience in unpredictable ways. By disavowing any straightforward alliance with one branch of contemporary poetics or another, Lightman is actively making a new audience for his work based on a large scale total concept of where his activity lies within language and society. He uses this awareness to produce work which is irreverent, appropriative and elusive yet assertive, provocative and communicative.

Scott Thurston is Lecturer in English and Creative Writing at the University of Salford.

Works Cited

Andrews, B. 1986. 'Total Equals What: Poetics and Praxis' in *Poetics Journal*: Marginality: Public and Private Language, issue 6, 1986, 48–61.

Lightman, I. 1996. *Disabuse*. Unpublished doctoral thesis, University of East Anglia.

Lightman, I. 1998. Untitled poem in *Vital Movement*. London: Reality Street Editions, 59–72.

Lightman, I. 1999. *Alter Space Times*. Norwich: privately published. Viewable at: http://www.soton.ac.uk/~bepc/poets/Lightman.htm

Lightman, I. 2004. *Trancelated*, from *Coinsides*. New York: Ubu Editions, http://www.ubu.com/ubu/lightman_trance/html
See also www.archiveofthenow.com for recordings of poems from *Trancelated* and www.iralightman.com for a link to a recording of the *Midweek* performance.

Lightman, I. 2006. Powerpoint poem. Viewable at: www.iralightman.com

Watten, B. 1985. *Total Syntax*. Carbondale and Edwardsville: Southern Illinois UP.

Watten, B. 2003. *The Constructivist Moment: From Material Text to Cultural Poetics*. Middletown, CT: Wesleyan UP.

Watten, B. 2006. 'Transposing the Limits of Open Form: Language Writing & Anthony Braxton': http://www.english.wayne.edu/fac_pages/ewatten/posts/post26.html

The Expanded Object of the Poetic Field;
Or, What is a Poet/Critic?

Barrett Watten

If it be granted that the "subject matter" of poetry is in a broad sense the moral realm, human actions as good or bad, with all their associated feelings, all the thought and imagination that goes with happiness and suffering ... then the rhetorical structure of the concrete universal, the complexity and unity of the poem, is also its sophistication or richness or depth, and hence its value.
— W. K. Wimsatt, 'The Concrete Universal'[1] (82)

Objectism is the getting rid of the lyrical interference of the individual as ego, of the "subject" and his soul, that peculiar presumption by which western man has interposed himself between what he is as a creature of nature (with certain instructions to carry out) and those other creations of nature which we may, with no derogation, call objects. For a man is himself an object, whatever he may take to be his advantages.
— Charles Olson, 'Projective Verse'[2]

This essay, as many I have written, performs a kind of 'thought experiment' in poetics. Its goal is to show how, in a series of discrete stages, the poem as 'object' in my work expands in terms of form, genre, and media. The poem as object thus expanded in its construction is a public act, toward wider horizons of meaning. I base this account of my work on a larger periodizing claim: that cultural production (art, literature, media) in the postmodern period (from the end of the Second World War but especially from the 1970s on) underwent a series of structural changes that led to expanded modes of address. The postmodern is the necessary break from the autonomy of the modernist work, and I thus contrast my position with recent efforts in UK criticism to link current forms of experimental writing with high modernism, even as the term 'modernism' has varying histories at its different sites.[3] The obdurate materiality of experimental writing can no longer be simply a question of hermeticism or restricted meanings: what was intended all along, my thought experiment suggests, was a breaking of the bounds of autonomous art toward larger political and cultural goals, including the transformation of the postmodern subject, seen as refunctioned through the act of writing. Poetics is subjectivation: this is an even more fundamental claim than the historicist one. New forms of art find their imperative in undoing, renegotiating, expanding, and mediating the experiential, postmodern subject. This relation between the historical ground of production and subjectivation of the poetic (or aesthetic or cultural) object is also a reflexive one, but not in the earlier modernist form of reflexivity that finds its stable mode of production in the autonomous object.[4]

I am connecting as well the critical agency of the poem as object in its expanded form with a new account of the possibility of the 'poet/critic.' In an earlier essay, I tried to delineate a field of possibility for new genres of art based on the productivity of writing in poetics;[5] I want here to bring expanded fields of meaning into the form of the work itself, to show how the intentional and reflexive act of the poet/critic is entailed in formal construction. For the poet/critic both kinds of writing are primary; neither aesthetic work nor poetic discourse is supplementary to the other. Poetry and poetics thus form a dyad in which questions of a greater comprehension and agency are expanded toward new meanings. Art as a form of pleasure and knowledge includes art as critical reflexivity and social agency. In taking up the formation of the poet/critic through the expanded field of the object, I am advocating a method whose horizon is socially comprehensive, both in and as aesthetic possibility. If the separate vocations of poet and critic are constrained by limitations on their reception, the poet/critic necessarily is a mediation of those limits in the act of transforming them. By short-circuiting the priority of either poet or critic, the poet/critic refuses autonomous pleasure or normative valorization as limits on his or her agency. I want to approach this possibility, not through discourses of legitimation or their limits, but through mediations of the object that make a dual form of authorship possible.

Refunctioning the Object

If I were to write a *Biographia Literaria* where life begins only on entry into the field of the poem, I would begin by charting a faultline between two contrasting imperatives of the poem as 'object' in modernist and postmodern poetics—unfolded in terms of its means of production, kinds of representation, and manner of use. In the two epigraphs above, such a faultline exists between the poem seen as a normative mediation between presumed universals and subsumed particulars, with Wimsatt, and the poem as an agonistic, unfolding, open field of entities that are simultaneously objective and subjective, for Olson. These were the competing paradigms of American poetry when I entered it, visible in the evident gap between Donald Hall, Robert Pack, and Louis Simpson's anthology *New Poets of England and America* (1957) and Donald Allen's *The New American Poetry* (1960). The poem as object in Hall, Pack, and Simpson's collection of thematically overdetermined, technically redundant, and emotionally policed versification had all the authority of institutional discipline: it was the poem as taught in universities, reproduced as a normative procedure. Oppositely, the poetry in Allen's anthology made no practical distinction between object and subject, opening the poem to fields of meaning making that were not determined by such normative protocols and could not be guaranteed. Even so, the aims of this poetry, in the construction of that anthology, were representable as unified in a manner that could found a wider field of meaning—a moment of social reflexivity and discursive construction in a poetics that refused 'object status.' Nothing less than a social movement with countercultural aims led to that possibility.

It is the reflexive relation between the poem as object and poetics as a field of meaning that I want to investigate in my genealogy of the poet/critic. One may recall that the poem as concrete universal—the regulative norm of the poem as object that reproduces an interpellative scene, the scene of literary instruction as moral education—emerged with the figure of the modernist poet/critic, from Eliot to the Fugitives and many minor figures.[6] The poet/critic authorizes that the poem as concrete universal has value, in two senses: it is a species of the genus *literature*, thus universal, and it is specifically interpretable, derived from and applied to specific human situations. The poet/critic brings both halves of the universal/particular dyad together in [his] authorizing agency, in two senses: as author of the specific work and as conveyor of its general meaning. The poet/critic is thus in a split and/or antagonistic role toward the shared object, the poem: what the poet insists on as the necessary value of individual uniqueness, the critic valorizes. All this gets us only so far as the 'sclerotic Hegelianism' I have complained of in conventional accounts of the avant-garde, until one sees the 'object' in a psychoanalytic sense.[7] Here, the discrepant demands of individuation intersect with their legitimation: an abstract but efficient thumbnail for the Oedipal triangle, with the poem as object gendered feminine in relation to the transgressive/punitive dyad of the male subject position.

Some of this struggle is visible in the classical origins of the 'concrete universal' after Goethe (a more direct lineage than the combination of second-hand Hegelianism and English romanticism that informs the New Critics). For Goethe, the concrete universal solves the problem of 'inner form' in poetry so that it is not just a matter of subjective inspiration: 'The poet should seize the particular [das Besondere], and he will, if it is something wholesome [etwas Gesundes], make it general [ein Allgemeines darstellen].'[8] Goethe's distinction between symbol and allegory depends on the substance of the concretization of this wholesome particularity such that it is 'a living momentary revelation of the inscrutable' (a formulation that precedes the current Baudelairean touchstone of the 'transitory and eternal' and thus clarifies the early use of 'symbolism' for what we now know as 'modernism').[9] It is the productivity of this concretized subjectivity, such that 'the idea remains always active and unapproachable in the image, and will remain inexpressible even though expressed in all languages,' that suggests the poem has become an object in the psychoanalytic sense, with the poet daring to know and present a direct relation to this living body (*Darstellung*) and the critic regulating its access and use.[10] If one route out of this dynamic, unstable crux of subject and object has been a regulative formal ideal, another, via the Kristevan account of the avant-garde, sees the poem's body as irreducibly textual and material, and not subject to the containment of a formal ideal (thus, in a shorthand that depends on vast corroborating detail, the 'turn to language').[11]

Having lost its connection to the 'body' cathected into the concrete universal, Wimsatt's orthopedic adjustment of the poem's content and form as touchstone of value reveals either its Oedipal origins (if the 'body' of the poem is living, gendered, or sexual) or parthenogenesis (as ideal effusion of intellectual history) as illicit consort/offspring of the poet/critic. Not wishing to strain analogies by exactness, I want simply to characterize the New Critical poem as either incestuous union or monstrous birth—in either case, a difficult moral example. The New Critical formal ideal is in any case hardly regulative; rather, it installs an unstable object as the center of attraction in the scene of instruction: Slavoj Žižek's 'antagonistic kernel' as hard core of desire in English 101.[12] Something of the convulsive rejection of 'close reading' that occurred from the 1960s on, and which led directly to the turn to theory of the 1970s, may be seen to begin here: with the transgressive excess not organized in an 'object' but legitimized by 'authority' that was left over from the regulative norm of the lyric poem as inculcated in teaching. Semeiosis, *différance*, and subjectivation appeared forthwith to channel this excess, into either the play of signification or discursive regulation. In bracketing that literary history, I want to return to the primal scene of the modern lyric for its phantasmatic potential, in which the poem is a miscreant or prohibited object and the critic the fraudulent double of the poet. Imagine the psychic fantasies condensed in the object that would soon come undone with the reaction to 'close reading' in circumstances no longer subject to its institutional rule. This is precisely what occurred in the 1970s, with the theoretical and historicist rejection of autonomous form. Theory and history took over the disposition of illegitimate excess, the claim of the Lacanian/Žižekian 'obscene father' to reproduce himself in poetic form.

If I am, in this thought experiment, a poet/critic, albeit in an expanded, nontraditional sense, I am free to argue both through discourse and by example. I want to juxtapose, then, the paragraphs of framing narrative I have roughed out with an argument via example in the form of a hybrid lyric I wrote about 1978 and published in *1–10* (1980):

> Conviction fills the body
> The presence of dead souls
> flute-like at the base of the ear.

> A particle enters the soundings
>   suddenly open, a door
>   separating bright from careless
> patterning, forcing a language
> memory designs from sleep.
>   The body is more primitive
>   attached to the ground.
> A frame lights up horizons
> to lead forward, larger than life.[13]

The shortest of the five poems in *1–10* (alternating with five prose poems and framed by lyric introduction and coda), the poem presents the effective history of its construction as meditation on lyric form. Its language was sampled and adapted, for the most part, from Lee Harwood's stellar translation of Tristan Tzara, issued by Trigram Press in 1975 (an act of literary borrowing or outright theft I have always avowed and never regretted).[14] Materials for the poem were thus obtained by illicit means, and organized in the form of the work by arbitrary ones. I was thinking, for reasons I cannot now recall, of four stanzas of thirteen lines each, for a total of fifty-two lines, as in a standard deck of cards (but it appears I wrote, in fact, four stanzas of twelve lines each, for forty-eight lines). Intention, like the logic of a dream, is subject here to condensation and displacement, and I am left only with the work's surface language to reattach to its deeper elements, such that they exist. The stanzas are imagined to present the form of an argument by example, of the kind that seemed to connect non sequiturs in the dream but whose connections disappear forever. The poem was intended to be a dream of poetry explaining itself through its own emergence as form, as only the poem it is—we begin to see a hint of an Oedipal moment. Something of oedipality's inability to explain its own desire, yet its guilty insistence that it can do so, is conveyed by the interrupted chain of inference in the syntax of the poem. A particularly metalinguistic crux shows how this logic of parallel production works:

> Two eyes blinking through a door.
> The missing head must be seen whole
>   where one word leads

> clouds to accident of end.
> The machine never tires.
> Edges of stations start to come in. (Lines 31–36)

The imperative to visualize an impossible scene of castration or decapitation—to see the head as both missing and whole—leads to a logic by which any one word can engender the overall argument. 'Clouds' then are both occasions in the world and the words themselves; their coincidence as a mere accident (of the sexual or fatal kind) is goal-oriented. History might be arbitrary and produced automatically by an 'evil genius' or automaton; high postmodern subjectivity, with its desiring machines and pastiche, is soon to arrive. Automatism, however, provides a possibility for meaning, as search engines or station scans locate at least a channel of transmission. Thematically, what is worked up through the poem's broken language as 'edges of stations start to come in' (a reference to Cocteau's Orpheus turning the dials of his car radio, the moment immediately prior to lyric transmission of the 'outside' that so inspired Jack Spicer) thus departs from oxymoronic anxiety in 'the missing head must be seen whole' to produce the next stanza's anxiously triumphalist assertion: 'The head of a king's son / multiplies at crossroads.' Oedipality branches out in multiplication and excess as it destabilizes the poem's concrete universal. Avant-garde non sequiturs like Yves Klein's burned sponges, Marcel Duchamp's missing head seen through the crack in '1. Given the waterfall,' and Tzara's 'night for the blind' are refunctioned in the poetic form of communication. The avant-garde poet can explain the moment of his birth in a form of particularity available anywhere—'the best descendent / were bred / in shallow waste'—a presentation of contingent particulars that would be a provisional solution to the crux of desire and descent as a moment of legitimation.[15]

It is important to note that what I just performed here is illicit—I read my own poem. There is no shortage of people who have commented, often very negatively, about the impropriety of doing this. The chair of my department, for instance, was reportedly undone by the appearance on page 267 of *The Constructivist Moment* of a 'head of a king's son'—my own, drawn about age 5, about the time when my father was stationed on a destroyer and in Japan during the Korean War. My own private *anamorphosis* is the crux of my chapter on negativity; it is so motivated as a moment of ellipsis as to risk self-canceling. The difficulty it presents as a violation of standard academic protocol should be obvious.[16] The concrete universal invoked by my drawing is a figure of the purely private, which I use to criticize the containment of poetic form and to create a transgressive scene of reading. Poet and critic converge in the practice of an illicit object, which in the example of 'Radio' produces out of thin air the condition of possibility of statement it authorizes (as itself, as a transgressive act), a horizon of meaning read out of the object as primal scene. 'Wo es war, soll Ich werden' (Where *it* was, so *I* will be): 'Radio' is an essay on the reproduction of the psychic economy of the lyric, through its displacement in the radical particulars of the avant-garde, which I re-present as an object under construction. There are three entailments of this scene of instruction: first, there is a necessarily unstable relationship between particular and universal in the lyric poem, due to a psychic economy that cannot produce content and confirm meaning simultaneously without violent transgression. Second, such instability of the lyric is not a site for any form of 'unity' but functions as a scene of its reproduction in another (a.k.a. the reader) and is thus social. Third, the dissociation of the language of the poem from its formal reproduction (of the objects organized by the poem, in Olson's sense, against the poem itself as object) opens the autonomy of form to the historical contexts that the poem *as* form cannot contain and regulate. Theory and historicism enter as dissociation of the object, taking their revenge on the psychic economy of originary exclusion that motivated their deployment.

It is a bit embarrassing to cite the ancient strictures of the New Critics and their institutional offspring, particularly as the genealogy of modernism and formal autonomy has been so reconfigured in the last two decades as to render them mere curiosities. For the concrete universal of mid-century modernism, one can substitute the disjunct poetics of William Carlos Williams's *Spring & All* (1923) as the primal scene of the poet/critic. It is well to recall that, for readers of Williams before the 1970s, the available versions of the lyric cycle cut the prose of the original and provided each poem an individual title, an act of Oedipal disavowal if there ever was one. It was only with the 1970 Frontier Press pirate edition and the subsequent appearance of New Directions' edition of *Imaginations* that the prose was restored.[17] This move to undo the opposition between poetry and prose was, it may be noted, a period concern in the 1970s (evident in Robert Creeley's *Pieces*, *In London*, and *A Day Book* and Allen Ginsberg's *Indian Journals*, but also in the Language school's frequent elision of the poetry/prose divide as 'writing').[18] Williams makes a clear distinction of value between poetry as 'the contraction which is felt,' the formal order in which new meaning is made, and prose, which represents states of mind and contexts of all kinds that may give rise to the poem but that do not condense in it. The postmodern moment, it follows, would be to undermine the hierarchy of this distinction—to see the poem as equally prosaic and filled with the contingent and excessive, and the development of poetics as a necessity for making poetry. Williams may be said to anticipate this later moment in his decision to publish the prose, and to explore it on its own terms in *Kora in Hell* and *The Descent of Winter*, which appear alongside the other experimental works in the posthumously edited *Imaginations*. A modernist genealogy of the poet/critic may well begin right here—not with the formal gridlock and moral rearmament of the concrete universal but with its dissociation. Williams's insight is that form and context are indissociable only when brought together and codetermined critically; the form of *Spring & All* re-presents the context(s) that constitute its own legitimacy.

The transformation of the concrete universal into a hybrid object places poetic form squarely within larger cultural logics, beginning with the mutual relation between social rationality and poetic form. In with his experimental texts, Williams correlates the difficulty of poetic form with social aporia ('No one / to witness / and adjust, no one to drive the car'), offering the poem as object as first approximation of a legitimate ground ('So much depends upon' its object status). Later, the 'machine made of words' connecting poetry to 'the work of Henry Kaiser and of Timoshenko' in the introduction to *The Wedge* (1944) would interpret these experimental logics as artifacts of rational totality, which Williams would go on to investigate more fully in *Paterson*.[19] This struggle between total form and social rationality, contingent particulars and systemic safety valves became a hopeful figure for radical democracy, anticipating the oppositional, open poetics of the 1950s. Unfortunately, the 'concrete universal' became the institutionally preferred mode of social reproduction; taught in English departments in the 1950s and 60s, it is still reproduced everywhere even today in creative writing programs that teach creative writers how to teach creative writing. Such utter circularity of object and value was one of the primary motives for the turn to 'poetics' in the Language school—to begin with, to take under our own responsibility such self-constituting authorizations of value. But the 'concrete universal' as a social form continues to have a reproductive potential: because it was identified with particular cultural values (Eliot's conservative Christianity, for example, and all the baggage of 'God and man' reinforced by that tradition), it allowed for a formal register of difference from other cultural traditions. In the era of its dominion, the New Critical lyric excluded these traditions with a vengeance: women writers from Gertrude Stein to Edna St. Vincent Millay; the Whitman/queer lineage, apart from Hart Crane, through the Popular Front; the Harlem Renaissance; and the avant-garde. However, there is a cunning of institutional reason in this installation of the norm: it seemed possible thus to change the cultural model simply by changing the object, setting up the anthology wars that were a major scene of literary revisionism in the 1970s and 1980s.

Two routes to the social reproduction of poetry are thus implied: one through the object itself—change the object, change the paradigm— and the other through the subject, with the language-centred self-reflexivity of the avant-garde. A critic like Charles Altieri importantly identifies such self-reflexiveness with the object itself, but this still yields circular results: only poets available to the aesthetic traditions of German idealism or English romanticism provide proper models for the identity between form and self-reflexivity.[20] The second route, which I explore, sees reflexivity as not containable within poetic form, and reads the formal construction of the work in relation to external, social logics. Here, Williams showed the way in his dissociation of the poetry/prose dyad. For Williams, the two components of poetry are nonidentical—the poem is not just the condensation of exemplary form but bleeds into the world out of which it is produced; poetic prose as material held outside of form-making activity is its condition of possibility. On analogy to this dissociation of form, the value-conferring critic portion of the poet/ critic dyad does not merely stand apart from the object-making poet; both set the terms for social reproduction. This is what Wordsworth did in his famous preface, in which a poetry of the 'real language of men' in a state of passional excitement is upgraded to a standard of cultural value. For the modernists, unlike the romantics, the act of making is comprehended, reproduced, and valued for its fundamental dissociation. To be on both sides of the dyad is thus an impossibility, yet it is that impossibility which is compelling. Something is left incomplete in the subject, something is left over in the object—this is the condition of the modernist poet/critic. The unfolding dyad preserves a remainder that refuses impossible Oedipalization as it brackets the parthenogenetic formalism of the New Critics. Williams left the door open for his heirs and assigns (not all of them men, after Alice Notley and Bernadette Mayer's claim of descent in *Doctor Williams's Heiresses*) to find new means of poetic reproduction that are at once subjective and social.[21]

In a hybrid, experimental text published in $L=A=N=G=U=A=G=E$, I rethought the form of the 'object status' of the poet after receiving an interpellative call in a postcard from Tom Raworth. My series of meditations on the poetic 'object' began with:

> 14 Cosin Court, Cambridge
> March 29/ '79
>
> Dear Barry,
>   Would you, if you have the time: for a booklet I'm doing: send me the name of, or a brief description of, or a photograph* or drawing* of, the first
> > O B J E C T
> > > To enter your mind now!?
>
> > > Love, Tom

---

*black, white, postcard size.

which I answered with my own subvocalized/written responses to its initial provocation:

> The first OBJECT to come to mind was the KEY RING next to your CARD. Immediate steps taken to erase this response were impossible while all around white noise not connected to OBJECT continued as before. Waiting for the 'appropriate' response while hovering over the CARD, there came BLUE ROCK. BLUE from a BLUE flyer in hand under the CARD and ROCK from Clark Coolidge's 'A ROCK is the inside of space' in his book OWN FACE, read this afternoon. A THUMBTACK posted the BLUE flyer, I remember it as a plastic push-pin. The BLUE flyer showed an exploded OBJECT being either constructed or taken apart.[22]

The object here (which would have been a concrete universal but for Williams's prose in *Spring & All*) appears by virtue of a social logic of interpellation: 'Hey, you!,' calls out Raworth in his postcard, and my response—not exactly Althusser's—is, 'It's my poem!' The poem itself is a hybrid construction of various kinds of objects—the poetry of Clark Coolidge, read in *Own Face*; the *objets dards* seen in a conceptual exhibition in Catalonia; the archaic museum pieces in Les Eyzies; the 'wicker haze' in the worker's head as he theoretically approaches the scene of construction, after Marx's *Grundrisse*; the 'contraction which was felt' in the condensation of a fictive object, the 'blue rock'; and finally the excluded object which turned out to be the mother of them all, a piece of red volcanic rock that had hailed me in an open field in the Sierra Nevada foothills, and which I was finally able to connect to the piece (and to first meeting Ted Pearson at The Grand Piano reading series, it turns out).[23] The ensemble of relations here is, in my account, a poem—remote from Tom Raworth's form of textuality, but I hoped acceptable to his project.

Later, in a hybrid (critical/creative) chapter in *The Constructivist Moment*, I attempted to extend the refunctioning of the poem as object to a social logic, through the mode of production of the 'assembly line' itself. In refusing the autonomous horizon of 'literariness' that is at times identified as 'language' in the Language school of poetry,

'The Bride of the Assembly Line' interprets Gertrude Stein's abstract principle of 'composition as explanation' as social production through her admiration of automobiles and Henry Ford. Stein's Fordism, of course, was suggested by and demanded an account of the larger mode of production I live in, the ensemble of productive relations in Detroit, as a site of form-making activity that is indissociable from its historical context. In what way is a poem as object comparable to 'the automobile' as product of the rationalized, automatic assembly line? What authorizes the poet/critic to make this analogy?

> *Cars burst into the light.* The missing X of [the poem immediately above this paragraph in the essay] is the product rolling off the assembly line, the Bride of all those Bachelor Machines that have been so hard at work in their <u>auto</u>-matism. Visiting the River Rouge assembly line of the Mustang Division of the Ford Motor Company, I was awestruck to witness one of modernism's primal scenes: the automatic sex Marcel Duchamp could only dissociate in *The Bride Stripped Bare by Her Bachelors, Even,* brought to fruition every ninety seconds as a new car rolls off the line. Here the Bride is being built up as she is stripped bare by robotic bachelors in sequential steps along the way, component parts being supplied by feeder lines from the sides and rived onto chassis or body forms by angular metal arms that shower the floor with loud sparks and violet auras. Dollies of shining tanks roll by to be bolted into place—the illuminating gas to be siphoned through blossoming barometers, the nine malic molds to be brought to the assembly point by gliding sleds, oculist witnesses adjusting coruscating planes of flow, given the waterfall speed of the windmill in the form of a toboggan but more or of a corkscrew, and the splash at A is everywhere an uncorking. So when the Bride finally appears, all dressed up with everywhere to go, it is a miraculous reversal of the destructive impulses that went to work on her ... in a carefully plotted sequence. The Bride is a shiny new car, with seat belts and gorgeous multicolored paint job, which an inspector then leaps into and drives to her first parking lot.[24]

This description, with its structural overlay of Duchamp's *Bride* and Ford's assembly line, tries to imitate, in a mode of sequenced production, an expanded poetics of the assembly line. It is followed by a more sober account of the development of the assembly line itself as a model of social reflexivity, in which economies of scale, markets for products, and manufacturing innovations develop in a continuous form of social feedback. A poetics of social production as condensed in an 'object' that presents itself as identical to its larger mode of production is presented in turn by a sequence of my long poem *Under Erasure:*

> *The industry,*
> > *a component designed*
> *To produce cars at the same rate ...*
>
> *As destinations with exit signs*
> *I invariably select,*
> > *to demonstrate [...]*
>
> *What words can mean,*
> > *if each frame*
> *Of its blank as a vanishing point ...*
>
> *Approximates self-consciousness*
> *In clouds,*
> > *our pseudo-objectivity ...*
>
>
> *Wants elsewhere to be,*
> > *I will go*
> *And be happy with their results ...*[25]

In *Under Erasure*, I tried to write social subjectivation in the form of the poetic object, triangulated in a deliberately mechanical hybrid of reflection, signification, and structure. The automatism of the resulting analogy between avant-garde form and modern production stands, exactly, in the place of the 'value-conferring' activity of earlier forms of criticism; the making of the poem, in this sense, is being analogized, or even allegorized, by the poet. I am interested in the kind of feedback structures this implies, very different from those of the romantic lyric or the concrete universal. My goal, of course, was not to insist that poets recast poetry in terms of humanly degrading repetitive work, even as I wanted to locate the measure of the 'human' in wider frames of industrial production. Rather, it was to look for ways in which specific cultural logics—in this case, that of the suspension of authorship within the highly rationalized and anonymous auto-teleology of the assembly line as a figure for social meaning—could suggest new ways of writing and reading experimental poetry. It was also to suggest that there is no autonomous zone for poetry outside these larger cultural logics; the 'bride' that appears at the end of the assembly might be either a brand new car or a poem. The 'object' can only be socially constructed.

I will continue my genealogy of hybrid objects in which the poet/ critic dyad is being refunctioned with two examples from recent work. The first is my section of the third volume of our 'experiment in collective autobiography,' *The Grand Piano*, which intersperses thirteen stanzas from my poem 'Non-Events,' another of the five poetic texts in *1–10*, between every four paragraphs of the fifty-paragraph essay.[26] While this autobiographical prose is to some extent an act of memory, it is also an attempt at explanation and even critique, through its organization of parallel incidents taken largely from the period in question, of the poetry I was writing then. Rather than Zukofsky's 'the words are my life'—a slogan I was becoming increasingly critical of at the time and find even less useful now—words and life are unlinked and recombined in the hybrid form. In this section, I wanted to show how logics of class identification led to the aesthetics of language-centered poetry, and how the 'non-events' (wasted, discontinuous, absurd) of my young adulthood might be explained (if not redeemed) by the poetry I was writing then:

> Different landscapes balance matters
> with the force of clear ideas.
> A blueprint for flood channels
> empties music of its sound. Notice a trap
> made for oneself. Out of the constant
> bright wounds circumscribe the work.
> You becomes another constant, unresolved
> war of nerves on a separate planet.

I was lusting for the stability of structure, in which the foreknowledge is absolute. Death and the young man. I would pour my energies into it forthwith. Bill Berkson phrased this perfectly, in his poem "Negative" with its logic of push/pull. For him, the stasis of energy meeting its equal resistance was a technical note to an effect of art, while for me it was a description of a social process by which one is brought into one's fate. The outcome is fixed as the structure from which one emerged but in which one can only act. "You are left wondering if just/holding [the door] wouldn't involve involve exactly the/same level of force." Hans Hoffmann as pure dialectician. Philip Guston as class cartoonist. [...]

That all energy and form would return to the mode of production out of which they emerge: this was the problem of culture for the newly educated Marxist. However decisive the poem might be, its agonistic excess placed at the crux of a decision that might have fateful consequences—it had been anticipated. "The foreknowledge is absolute." Absorption returns us to structure—never, certainly, to our rewards. The idea of art acquiring symbolic capital—prestige, the surety of the canon—was unthinkable at the time. Art was an addition to a fully rationalized world and thus subject to immediate reintegration. Art could appear or disappear at will, as it did. I thought this insight was progressive, and I intended to act on it.[27]

My claim in the prose section of this work is that class relations are a 'cultural logic' in ways that filter down to a baseline of the aesthetic. In poetry, I was attempting to write 'language as such,' but this was analogous if not identical to the idea of material culture I was also attempting to live. But it is from the *disc*onnection of this analogy—the unlikeness of its terms, that which is not subordinated or contained by the form, the way that the materiality of language is never subsumable, and the slash between poet/critic that inevitably results—that the work's aesthetics were formed. The poem is a material condensation of the social logics that created it; the poem is a differential creation of an inaccessible world that argues only by approximation. If there were anything that joins the two, it is the 'anti-poetic' as material and as experience, which provides a site for self-reflection on all the entailments of the act of 'making' I could imagine in both registers.

My final example of the hybrid object is a current work-in-progress (which I read at my conference performance in Dartington)—a 'correlation' between Book 1 of Williams's *Paterson*, sampled by aleatorical means, and a parallel text of 'knowledge sentences' (representations of complex states of affairs) that I wrote in an attempt to *say in other words* what Williams's poem *says*. My thesis is that *Paterson* does not simply trade in the aesthetic but is a nuanced meditation on constitutive social logics distributed among the kinds of writing Williams deploys in the poem; it is an essay on social comprehension and its (im)possibility, with the famous Falls as the register of our modern compulsion toward sublime disconnection. My project, in other words, was to criticize *Paterson* as a poetic act of reconstruction of what I see is a central enabling condition of poetic production: that we can't understand a word we are saying to each other, and that we suffer this condition without acknowledging it. This disconnection leads directly to the turn to language of language-centered poetry, but for me that isn't enough. I want to dig through to this formative impasse, which is where we fail to comprehend the stuplimity of our current 'state of disconnection.'[28]

XXI

A quart of potatoes, half a dozen oranges,
a bunch of beets and some soup greens.
Look, I have a new set of teeth. Why you
look ten years younger   .

[...] They are the divisions and imbalances
of his whole concept, made weak by pity,
flouting desire; they are—No ideas but
in the facts   .   . [2.12]

In democratic form, content seeks its own level by
the force of its displacement from the absent norm
which it is in the process of creating. Absence then
defines the facticity of the content creating norms.
The positive is the impossible but dumbly insisted
upon in a series that ratifies itself as only possible.
These things that you have brought forward to us,

they are the materials of poetry? The poetry is just
these things, and the poetry is a displacement that
only is enacted where such things could never be.

XXII

Twice a month Paterson receives
communications from the Pope and Jacques Barzun
(Isocrates). His works
have been done into French
and Portuguese. [1.10]

Coming in and going out—centrifugal, centripetal—
information locates the common center that unites
sender and receiver in the throughput of dispersal.
This is a knowledge sentence that attempts to say
what a complex form of activity really is and does.
Thus it takes the form of a complex, but differently.[29]

What I often find lacking, I will say, in much poetry of the present—
not that it is not worthwhile in other terms, no—is a connection to the
conditions of its own production. If that sounds like a prescription for
what counts as aesthetic experience, again I'm sorry. By 'conditions' I
mean motivating factors, not surface effects that can never locate them,
that dissolve in the bitstreams of channel switching or the identity
profiling of data pools. The act of 'erasure' only gets us so far; I want to
see the larger logic or motivation that makes such acts of abstraction and
recombination necessary and productive, on other terms than simply
as a placeholder for producers of like objects seen as a 'community'
(maybe 'community' itself is one such logic; in which case let's hope for
an engaged one). But even more I am struck with the pervasive inability
to read or comprehend the information one is given. We need high-level
interpretants, and poetry can produce them.

The poet/critic is a construction site, a site of intervention.
Paralleling Nietzsche's genealogy of the forms of historical discourse,
the poet/critic refuses both monumentality and the accretion of objects
(discourse in a static, normative sense) and engages the effective horizons
of the critical act.[30] Moving from the rejected concrete universal, with

its moral project of regulating the value of complexity, to an open and productive engagement with complex logics that subtend the making of the object, the poet/critic refunctions the mode of production of meaning and value that once went under the name of *literature* but which has, of necessity, taken new forms. There is no particular genre now to which his or her activity is restricted; the poetic is a made relation motivated by the conditions of its possibility and the necessity of its occurrence in a larger cultural field. The poet thus becomes the maker of an object that enacts and criticizes the conditions of its own possibility, while the critic becomes the site of discursive knowledge that explains and expands the resulting reflexivity of the object. It should go without saying that both sides of this dyad refuse to externalize institutional structures, in which the poem is a disciplinary object or the critic the disciplinary subject, as they displace the interpellative call of the autonomous poem toward a social imperative that is, after Althusser, delivered at many sites of meaning. Even more, we can look for a logic in which dyadic structure of this opposition itself is recast, even as a mere positivity of their identity would risk losing the force of the negative 'slash' of nonidentity between the two opposed functions.

I began by claiming that gender and sexuality were key aspects of the concrete universal—in Goethe's notion of a living and embodied spirit contained by the form—that necessitated its refunctioning in other terms. While my critique has been mainly to recover the social logics of the poet/critic dyad, gender and sexuality appear at key points. Of course, seeing the poem as object in a psychodynamic sense is gendered by definition, even as one possibility of gender would be to see the 'critical' element of poetic making as something like an act of parthenogenesis, the birth of Athena out of the head of Zeus. In moving from the 'sclerotic Hegelianism' of the concrete universal to an open spatio-temporal field of objects in the postmodern, parthenogenesis often appears as the first move toward a better account of the object in terms of desire. Such an early postmodern challenge to the dualism of subject/object is readable in Charles Olson's spatial allegory of 'The Moebius Strip,' which refuses the object status of the poem in its complexity:

Upon a Moebius strip
materials and the weights of pain
their harmony

A man within himself upon an empty ground.
His head lay heavy on a huge right hand
itself a leopard on
his left and angled shoulder.
His back a stave, his side a hole into the bosom of a sphere.

His head passed down a sky (as suns the circle of a year).
His other shoulder, open side and thigh maintained,
by law of conservation of
the graveness of his center,
their clockwise fall.
Then he knew, so came to apogee
and earned and wore himself as amulet.[31]

The birth of beauty in the poetic act stems from the parthenogenesis of self, seen as the primal androgyne of the aesthetic, straight out of the head of the poet. Yet a moment of doubling necessarily results in this refusal of Oedipalization, whose logic is kept outside. Olson suggests, in his medial position between the overthrown concrete universal and the displaced logics of the postmodern, that sexuality and reproduction—as cultural orders—are the necessities that aesthetic form failed to respond to in the modern (in modernist form). *Spring & All*, for Williams, was the moment of its frustrated but split comprehension (recall the original edition with its ovum and sperm paralleling the split between poetry and prose). If we are on the way to another relation of the poet/critic dyad, it may be in the reproductive potential of the dyad itself—and what is meant by reproduction as social rather than individually embodied. New possibilities of gender and their resulting psychic investments, which refuse the Oedipal containment of autonomous form and its constraints on meaning, will motivate, in all senses, the exploration of this little divide. More needs to be said to develop a transition—which I hope at least to have suggested—from an Oedipal 'default mode' of the concrete universal as a mode of social reproduction, to an exploded, hybrid object in terms of new psychic formations of gender and sexuality. In my genealogy of the poet/critic, to refunction the poetic object changes the relation between form-making and value-conferring aspects of the poem, opening the work as site for poetic agency and social meaning to much wider frames of activity.

Barrett Watten is Professor of Literature and Cultural Studies at Wayne State University in Detroit, Michigan.

Notes

1 W. K. Wimsatt, *The Verbal Icon: Studies in the Meaning of Poetry* (Lexington: University of Kentucky Press, 1954), 82.
2 Charles Olson, 'Projective Verse' (1950), in *Selected Writings*, ed. Robert Creeley (New York: New Directions, 1966), 24–25.
3 Cf. the implicit claim that what Americans might call the 'postmodern' is really just a continuation of modernist aesthetics in criticism such as Anthony Mellors, *Late Modernist Poetics: From Pound to Prynne* (Manchester: Manchester UP, 2004). I am interested (and slightly concerned) about the degree to which this notion of the continuity of modernism can be assumed in UK experimental verse practice.
4 For a benchmark account of the reflexivity of modernist poem, organized around the crucial dictum of mid-century modernism that 'It must be abstract!,' see Charles Altieri, *Painterly Abstraction in Modernist American Poetry: The Contemporaneity of Modernism* (Cambridge: Cambridge UP, 1989).
5 Barrett Watten, 'Poetics in the Expanded Field: Textual, Visual, Digital ...', in Adelaide Morris and Thomas Swiss, *New Media Poetics: Contexts, Technotexts, and Theories* (Cambridge, MA: MIT Press, 2006).
6 Herman Rapaport has usefully termed the moment of interpellation a 'scene of instruction' in the Symbolic dimension; see his discussion of the British reception of Althusser and 'subject positions' in *The Theory Mess: Deconstruction in Eclipse* (New York: Columbia UP, 2001), 67–88. On Athusserian interpellation, see Judith Butler, *The Psychic Life of Power: Theories in Subjection* (Stanford, CA: Stanford UP, 1997, 106–31).
7 I discuss the Hegelian aporia of the avant-garde, and suggest ways beyond it, in Barrett Watten, 'The Secret History of the Equal Sign: $L=A=N=G=U=A=G=E$ Between Discourse and Text,' in *The Constructivist Moment: From Material Text to Cultural Poetics* (Middletown, CT: Wesleyan UP, 2003), 45–54.

8 Quoted in René Wellek, *A History of Modern Criticism*, vol. 1, *The Later Eighteenth Century* (New Haven: Yale UP, 1955): 209, 325n. Thanks to Susan Nurmi-Schomers for her comments at the conference.

9 Quoted in ibid, 211, 325n. On the use of 'symbolism' for 'modernism,' see Edmund Wilson, *Axel's Castle: A Study in the Imaginative Literature of 1870–1930* (1931; New York: Norton, 1959).

10 Goethe, quoted in Wellek, *History*, 211, 325n.

11 Watten, 'Secret History of the Equal Sign.'

12 For a Žižekian reading of the New Critical poem, see my chapter on Laura Riding in Barrett Watten, *Horizon Shift: Progress and Negativity in American Modernism* (PhD diss., University of California, Berkeley, 1995), and an MLA presentation adapted from it, 'The Sublime Object of Close Reading,' Washington, DC, 1996.

13 Barrett Watten, 'Radio,' in *Frame: 1971–1990* (Los Angeles: Sun & Moon, 1997), 54–55; this is the first stanza of four.

14 Tristan Tzara, *Selected Poems*, trans. Lee Harwood (London: Trigram, 1975).

15 'Ode to Bourbaki,' the first poem in my first book-length collection, *Opera–Works*, reprinted in *Frame*, 279.

16 I have also heard someone ask whether one is allowed to use the pronoun 'I' in critical writing, and whether it is permissible cite one's own work. Once and for all, it must be said: I know the risks I am taking when I do this; it is part of a larger analysis; it is meant to work in certain ways connected to the structure of desire; I am sorry if you don't like it.

17 William Carlos Williams, *Spring & All* (Buffalo, NY: Frontier Press, 1970); in *Imaginations*, ed. Webster Schott (New York: New Directions, 1970). As with the 1970s pirating of Ezra Pound's radio speeches, but for very different reasons, the illicit edition seems to have had an immediate effect of canonical revision.

18 Ron Silliman's section of part 4 of *The Grand Piano: An Experiment in Collective Autobiography, San Francisco, 1975–1980* (Detroit: Mode A/This Press, 2007), points as well to the crucial importance of Williams's prose/poetry hybrids in the development of the Language school. I entirely agree, and with Ron would like to promote Williams as the denied/neglected alternative to Pound/Stevens dyad in American modernism.

19 William Carlos Williams, introduction to *The Wedge*, in *The Collected Poems*, ed. Christopher MacGowen, vol. 2, *1939–1962* (New York: New Directions, 1988), 53.

20 See Altieri, *Painterly Abstraction in Modernist American Poetry.*

21 Alice Notley, *Dr. Williams' Heiresses* (Berkeley, CA: Tuumba, 1980).

22 Barrett Watten, 'Object Status,' in Bruce Andrews and Charles Bernstein, eds., *The L=A=N=G=U=A=G=E Book* (Carbondale, IL: Southern Illinois UP, 1984), 110–14. I have remediated and interpreted the work in 'Recovering 'Forty Poems' and 'Object Status,' at http://www.english.wayne.edu/fac_pages/ewatten/posts/post28.html

23 The series of objects developed in this piece are all available on my website.

24 From Barrett Watten, 'The Bride of the Assembly Line,' in *Constructivist Moment*, 139–40.

25 Barrett Watten, from *Under Erasure*, in *Progress/Under Erasure* (1991; reprint ed., Los Angeles: Green Integer, 2004), 260–62.

26 Barrett Watten, 'Non-Events,' in *Frame*, 13–21.

27 Barrett Watten, 'Non-Events,' in *Grand Piano* 3:78–103; 82–83.

28 I use the term 'stuplimity' in the sense developed by Sianne Ngai, *Ugly Feelings* (Cambridge, MA: Harvard UP, 2005), 248–97. 'State of disconnection' riffs on Giorgio Agamben's concept of the 'state of exception'; in *State of Exception*, trans. Kevin Attell (Chicago: University of Chicago Press, 2005). The implication is that the current public discourse situation we are in of 'disconnection is 'exceptional' both in the suspension of basic human rights and for the unique and pervasive distortion of social communication that has resulted from their refusal.

29 From 'Correlation of *Paterson*, book 1,' MS; a section will appear in the journal *Antenna* (Karlsruhe, Germany) in 2007, and the opening sections are available on my website at http://www.english.wayne. edu/fac_pages/ewatten

30 Friedrich Nietzsche, *On the Advantage and Disadvantage of History for Life*, trans. Peter Preuss (Indianapolis: Hackett, 1980).

31 Charles Olson, 'The Moebius Strip,' in *Selected Writings*, 162–63.

Anthony Caleshu is the author of the collection of poems, *The Siege of the Body and a Brief Respite* (Salt, 2004). He has published criticism on the American poets John Berryman and James Tate, and his poetry and fiction have appeared in various journals and anthologies such as *Poetry Review*, *The Dublin Review*, *New Irish Poets*, and *The Forward Book of Poetry*. He is the Editor of the new journal, *Short Fiction*, and is Lecturer in English and Creative Writing at University of Plymouth.

Tony Lopez is Professor in Poetry at the University of Plymouth, and is the author of more than 20 books of poetry, fiction and criticism. His most recent poetry collections are *Covers* (Salt, 2007) and *False Memory* (Salt, 2003). He has received awards from The Wingate Foundation, The Society of Authors, and the Arts and Humanities Research Council. His poetry is featured in many anthologies including *Twentieth-Century British and Irish Poetry* (Oxford), *Vanishing Points* (Salt), *Other* (Wesleyan) and *Conductors of Chaos* (Picador). His critical writings are collected in *Meaning Performance: Essays on Poetry* (Salt, 2006) and *The Poetry of W.S. Graham* (Edinburgh, 1989), the first study of that influential Scottish modernist poet. He is well known as a poetry performer and has given readings throughout the UK, Europe and North America.

www.ingramcontent.com/pod-product-compliance
Lightning Source LLC
Chambersburg PA
CBHW030409030726
47497CB00002B/540